The Courage to Love

Surviving and Thriving in your Relationship

About the author

Dr Colm O'Connor is a clinical psychologist and family therapist with over twenty years' experience working as Clinical Director of a large couples counselling agency in Cork. Author of *The Courage to Be Happy* and co-founder of the Cork Domestic Violence Project and the Association for Agency-based Counselling in Ireland, he has lectured widely on marriage and couples therapy for many years.

The Courage to Love

Surviving and Thriving in your Relationship

Colm O'Connor

Gill & Macmillan

Gill & Macmillan
Hume Avenue, Park West, Dublin 12
with associated companies throughout the world
www.gillmacmillanbooks.ie

© Colm O'Connor 2013
978 07171 5105 9

Typography design by Make Communication
Print origination by Síofra Murphy
Printed in Sweden by ScandBook AB

This book is typeset in Minion and Neue Helvetica.

The paper used in this book comes from the wood pulp of
managed forests. For every tree felled, at least one tree is
planted, thereby renewing natural resources.

A CIP catalogue record for this book is available from the
British Library.

The following quotations are taken from *Patrick Kavanagh:
Selected Poems*, edited by Antoinette Quinn, Penguin, 1996:
p. 44, 'On Raglan Road'; p. 176, 'In Memory of My Mother';
p. 199, 'Canal Bank Walk'.

For Mom

Contents

Preface

THOUGHT EXPERIMENT:
ANALOGY FOR YOUR RELATIONSHIP

Consider this analogy for your intimate relationship: as you set off on your journey across the sea of life, you had a single boat. At some point, you decided to have a partner and you began to sail together in one boat. In this analogy, the boat represents your relationship. The ocean and the weather represent the forces of life. The horizon represents your ultimate destiny.

You are not sure who created this ocean or what lies in wait on the horizon. Yet the two of you persist. You cross the ocean together, looking for happiness and meaning. As you sail, you are exposed to extremes of weather and the many moods of the ocean. You are swept towards the horizon by invisible ocean currents and winds. Even though your destination is predetermined, you have the ability to steer your boat to avoid obstacles; and you can use the prevailing winds to your advantage.

There are certain unavoidable conditions that go with this journey:

- There is nothing you can do to control the ocean or the weather.
- You must try to survive and thrive as long as you can.
- You must work together to steer the boat and stay afloat.
- Many things can impede you, such as stormy weather and rough seas.
- Ocean currents can sweep you in different directions.
- At some point later in the journey one of you will be taken by the ocean or a storm.
- One of you will eventually be left alone in the boat.
- The journey is worthwhile and, despite its many challenges, can be deeply enriching.

There are many other boats sailing nearby. Let's observe the couples in some of them.

- Some spend the entire time fruitlessly trying to get back to the shore.
- Some huddle close together and keep each other warm and comfortable.
- Some nag each other and bicker over every small error.
- Some sit contentedly with their feet out over the edge of the boat.
- Some blame each other for every shower of rain.
- Some sit in silence and take in the beautiful scenery.
- Some drink to excess and fight endlessly with each other.
- Some tell each other stories to pass the time.
- Some become violent and abusive.
- Some study the stars at night in order to learn more about their journey.
- Some drift aimlessly.
- Some take turns in steering the boat so that they both get a chance to rest.
- Some are very unhappy and become depressed.
- Some live in terror that their boat will spring a leak; they spend all their time fretting and worrying.
- Some already have a small leak in their boat; but they sing as they bail out the water together.

As you consider these couples, ask yourself what way do you sail the sea of life?

You can also ask many interesting questions about the unhappy couples. Why are they constantly fighting? Why are they abusive towards each other? Why do they get so defensive? What is at stake that could cause such distress? In what way do their life conditions contribute to their irritability? What is the solution to their conflict? What might need to happen for them to understand why they are unhappy? What do they need to learn in order for them to work together as they cross the sea of life?

The ways that you answer these questions will depend on the point of view that you take.

MICROSCOPIC VIEW VERSUS MACROSCOPIC VIEW

When you try to understand a relationship, there are two very different vantage points from which you can view things. You can zoom right in and put the couple under the microscope in order to find the causes of their behaviours and feelings.

You can also zoom out and take a wide-angled view—as if from a distance. This way, you see much more than just the couple in their boat. You see the small boat on the ocean, under the weather conditions, being swept along by invisible currents and winds. From this wide-angled vantage point, the conclusions you come to are radically different from those you come to when you have only a narrow view of things.

Unfortunately, when we look for solutions to problems in relationships, we tend to take the narrow, close-up view. We tend to conclude, for example, that the solution to a so-called 'problem relationship' lies in changing our partner or our boat.

We seldom look from above and see how the life conditions within which our relationship exists create our most essential problems. Because we cannot control the ocean, the weather or the winds, we try to control that which is closest to us—our sailing partner. Sadly, we often take out our frustrations on them and punish them for our overall predicament.

USING THIS BOOK

This book does not take a close-up view of relationships. It suggests that many of the solutions to the predicaments of love can only be found when we take this wide-angled view. The book does not ask you to go beneath the cabin of your relationship to find the cause of your distress, such as flaws in your partner or yourself. Instead, it invites you to understand your relationship problems in terms of your overall predicament. It asks you to see yourself in the full-round of life. It asks you to look all around you: up into the sky, down into the ocean, back towards the shore and forward towards the horizon. Doing this will enable you to see your everyday distress in a revealing new light.

In examining the predicaments and solutions to intimate love, this book seeks to startle you with the reality of your human condition. You will see how your emotional life stems from how well you co-operate with this condition. From there, the book seeks to stir your imagination and compassion in ways that inspire you to find solutions to your life by doing less and being more.

It doesn't matter how damaged you think your relationship is. If both of you can suspend your conflict and come up on deck under the night sky, you will be able to watch the stars, feel the heaving ocean, remember things you had forgotten and see things you thought you might never see.

When you think of intimate relationships, it is right to wonder: 'Why do some partners abuse each other violently, while other partners love each other tenderly?' The answer to this question can only be understood in the context of how they handle the wonderful ordeal of life. There is little onboard any couple's boat that can explain love, compassion and joy—or indeed hate, violence and sorrow. These things can only be understood in the full arc of life. They must be viewed all the way from the shore to the horizon.

*

In 1998 I conducted some research that asked: 'What is really at stake for couples who are in conflict?' In seeking to answer that question, I examined hundreds of cases of couples in distress. I spent many hours leafing through case studies; looking at videotapes; and challenging myself to look closely at the data. I spent hours locked in my study trying to decipher some ancient hieroglyphic. In examining each couple, I kept asking myself the basic questions: 'What is the real issue here?' and 'What is really at stake?' I eventually found the answers I had been looking for. This book will reveal these insights to you as they have evolved and crystallised over the years.

I have held a privileged position in listening to couples for twenty-five years. I have been placed at a sentry point in dealing with the emotional lives of couples; and I have a sense of responsibility to 'report back' something of what I have found.

I hope that you will find this book to be both wise and practical; and I hope that it helps you to understand your relationship in a way that promotes self-challenge and self-compassion. While I have learned from many scholars, I have learned (and continue to learn) the most from the real couples I work with. The unique qualities, integrity and suffering of each couple ensure that I learn from them how their worlds work.

For many years, I have read books giving advice on relationships. Many of these have been scholarly works presenting the findings of researchers in the field of relationships, none more so than the pioneering work of John Gottman, Sue Johnson, and the foundational work of Neil S. Jacobson and Alan S. Gurman. I have read these works with great enthusiasm. However, I have always felt that there was some missing ingredient in the literature. For a while I could not figure out what it was. Now I have. This book reveals what the missing ingredient is. I hope to add something to our understanding of love and to pull back the blinds on the secret life of intimate relationships.

I piggyback on the work of many other writers who have given me ideas and thoughts to blend with my own intuition and experience. More than most, I must acknowledge the seminal work of anthropologist Ernest Becker. Those familiar with his writings will see his influence throughout this book. Becker's commentaries on life and death provide a compelling counterpoint to the myth of success and 'getting what you want in life'. I think this is more at home with the Irish psyche, which can blend grief with joy.

Popular instructions on how to have successful relationships are often ineffective at creating lasting change. When you read something in a book, you can be impressed by the advice and you can even commit to trying it out; but once the book is put aside, you tend to forget what it was that interested you in the first place. Therefore, I won't patronise you by giving glib advice. Instead, I hope to inspire you to *feel* something. I hope to engage you at a level where you *experience* yourself differently. I hope to shine some light into some darkened places. In doing so, I hope to make you feel better about who you are. I hope to help you relax into yourself in ways that ease your anxiety, self-doubt and guilt. While helpful hints are great at the right time, real change comes about when we *experience* something new. When we see ourselves from a different point of view, things can change by themselves.

This book will not try to tell you how to have the successful marriage or relationship. Rather, it will encourage you to do as Dan Wile suggests: to 'inhabit the one you have' in a new way. As David Schnarch has said, it's not about *finding* the right person, it's about *being* the right person.

Finally, throughout the book, I will interchange the words 'spouse' and 'partner' to refer to the beloved. I will also use the word 'marriage' to refer not only to the institution, but more generally to the committed emotional and intimate bond between lovers.

Let's walk together.

Acknowledgments

My heartfelt thanks and appreciation are due to a number of people who have assisted me so willingly in getting this book across the line:

My supervision group, who have for years provided a safe and enlightening place where so many of these ideas found purchase—thank you one and all.

My friends and colleagues, whose keen eyes edited early drafts of this book. I am particularly indebted to Johanna, Breda, Don, Fionnuala, Jean and Theresa.

Eoin O'Flynn, whose generous spirit and thoughtful affirmations were such a blessing to me at the outset of this quest.

Emma Farrell and D Rennison Kunz, whose perceptive feedback and kindly patience helped midwife this creation into the world.

Gerry, for your many valued encouragements towards this end.

Jean, for your support and love and for believing in me when I so often did not.

My children, who are the gateway to my spiritual life. Bless you all.

Part I

Vulnerable Love:
Relationship Predicaments

Chapter 1
Vulnerable Love

We must not try to understand life, but to be equal to it.

So great is the expectation on love to provide the solution to life's unavoidable predicament, that our esteem rises and falls depending on the degree to which we feel loved by our partners. Those who are in loving relationships can become smug and self-satisfied in the proof of their status; in denial of the tragic, accidental and unfortunate, which can happen in any home. And those who feel unloved can experience real damage to their sense of self-worth and human effectiveness.

Divorced people, especially parents, can feel tattooed as an example of social failure. They can feel as if they have failed one of the main tests in life. What seems easy to some has become traumatic for them. The same social (or self-inflicted) judgment can be experienced by people who are single and by couples who are childless.

A lot of family distress or breakdown arises not from personal failure but from the accidental, unfortunate and random events of life that leave some people burdened with a great weight, while others are untouched by its cruelty. We must be so careful not to judge others or designate 'failure' to those who have been struck by the lightning bolt of fate. Nobody is immune to falling into the ditches of life that lie ahead.

So what are we to do? To the degree that we value integrity and courage, we become softer with ourselves and with others. Our spouse's purpose is not to provide us with a sense of control, significance or acceptance. Their role is to be true to themselves in all their awkward imperfection.

Love always has to be vulnerable. In its vulnerability is the recognition that it cannot give you everything you need. Your partner will, because of their unique humanity, let you down. Love therefore needs the grace and humility of soft hands. Love must have a lightness of heart.

Family life and love are tragic. It is in your home that you experience grief, trauma, hurt and emotional suffering; just as you experience love, security, care and joy. However, to see the tragic as negative is to miss the point. The tragic events in everyday life are symptoms of life itself and make love necessary, meaningful and responsive. And I do not just mean desperate catastrophe but the little tragic moments concealed in everyday fights, conflicts, hurts, betrayals and losses.

In fact, it is the tragic strain in all of life that gives love its passion. The tragedy in every family home is that love brings joy *and* suffering, delight *and* hurt. The family home redeems and enslaves people. Within the home, where love comes to rest, abuse and degradation also incubate.

By the second half of life, people have known suffering and tragedy. Love begins to take on a more mature meaning. In many ways, true romance is found in life's later stages when life's structure has been revealed. Tragedy is, unfortunately, what gives love its meaning, richness and dignity. The suffering of life makes possible compassion, mercy, empathy and care. It is hard for me to write this next sentence, but it is true … Suffering gives everything value; it is what makes love possible.

Acknowledging the tragic in life and love is taboo. We will not find tragedy properly addressed in research or academic psychology. It is distasteful to those of us who want to provide solutions and solve problems in life. We like to write books that promise relief or escape from life's tragic motif. So we find it in soap operas, literature, newspapers—even in the tabloids, where the tragic in life becomes a source of entertainment. Here we can see vividly the problems of life and love. We can see them in ways that are far more convincing than many academic publications could ever be.

How we live with tragedy and human vulnerability is ultimately a spiritual issue.

THE MICROSCOPE APPROACH VERSUS THE MACROSCOPE APPROACH

Most scientists who try to figure out why something is the way it is will put it under a metaphorical microscope. Social scientists examining relationships will examine them under the microscope and look closely at the many ingredients that go into making a successful or unsuccessful relationship. This approach holds that, if you look ever so closely at the small parts of something, you will figure out why the big part is the way it is. The 'microscope approach' takes things apart to find answers hidden within. However, this provides only a certain kind of data.

There is another approach where you look at things in the context within which they are set. This could be called the 'macroscope approach'. Instead of examining something very closely, you pull back and look at it in the context of its environment and life conditions. Darwin understood why a small animal was the way it was, not by taking it apart but by looking at the conditions in which it lived. Newton did not discover why an apple fell to the ground by cutting it open, he did so by studying the behaviour of the planets and discovering gravity! Einstein anticipated atomic energy, not by breaking up the atom but by developing his theory of cosmic relativity.

These brilliant people understood small things by first understanding the larger context within which these things existed. You do not understand why a fish is designed the way it is unless you know about the sea. If you cut open a human body, you will not find love or a human thought. Simply put, we understand human behaviour not only by looking more closely at it but also by looking more expansively at the conditions within which it is set. When you take a wide-angled view, you see many things that are quite impossible to see under the microscope. In fact, when it comes to your own personal problems, you often make a breakthrough not when you look more closely at your problems but when you look more expansively at yourself.

When we put couple relationships under the microscope, we can miss seeing the larger issues that make such things as affection, desire, defensiveness or violence come about in the first place. It is vital that we can see ourselves from a distance as well as up close. We need to understand our personal problems not just at a personal level but, more important, at the level of the human condition. To solve your problems, you may need to stop looking at your partner under the microscope of your analysis. You may need to view them under the sky beneath which you both exist.

When you broaden your perspective, life takes on a different meaning. Local problems fade when you remember your cosmic place. This is something that you suddenly remember when, for example, someone you love becomes seriously ill. You suddenly see yourself and life in a much broader context than the microscope of your daily complaints. You learn about the meaning of love.

We do not find the answer to love by examining, like a mechanic, the laid out parts of a disassembled relationship. Therefore, this book places human intimacy in the full-round of human experience and, in doing so, it exposes the meaning and purpose of love. It uncovers the energy and fuel that drive it; and it exposes what is really at stake for couples in conflict or distress. In truth, this book longs to be a poem: it tries to reveal what lies just below the surface of everyday relationships.

*

If we turn our face away from both the terror and desire that drive love, then we ignore the essential forces that can result in both affection and abuse. This book suggests that, while the use of techniques and problem-solving skills are essential to couples in learning how to deal with conflict, we must also appreciate the bigger picture and the intensity of the forces that create distress and conflict in the first place. Sometimes the application of a skill is like showing up at an earthquake with a dustpan and brush. Yes it works, but does it make a difference? The solutions offered to couples by popular psychology or advice columns can often seem minimalist (if not patronising) unless there is an understanding of the terror, despair or loss of desire that is being felt by those in the situation.

The person who uses the skill or tries to apply the technique does not necessarily *feel* anything. For example, training in anger management skills is often the recommended treatment for someone who has brutally assaulted and raped his wife. It is as if the underlying problem is a skill-deficit rather than a character or virtue deficit.

When we dumb down our expectations, we provide ourselves with an anaesthetic by avoiding love's terrors and an antiseptic by focusing on its technique. Many of the research findings on what makes marriages work are invaluable, but they can only be effectively implemented with the more important ingredient of genuine human desire. And desire arises not from thoughts but from the passion for life itself; a passion that, as we shall find, is at source a bodily experience of human vulnerability.

Hopefully you will find that this book directs your attention away from your specific problems towards the reasons your problems exist in the *first* place, and then towards the energy source for your solutions. When we take a macroscopic perspective and can truly understand what is at stake for people in intimate relationships, we can make sense of their passion, violence, tenderness, and sometimes ugliness.

If we use scientific findings to suggest that marriage is a painting-by-numbers skill-set, we diminish entirely the ordeal that is family love. The 'top ten list' of things to do to improve your marriage is doomed to fail because the problems in the relationship are not caused by not knowing what to do, but by not wanting to do them in the first place. Problems for couples are not caused by a lack of knowledge or skill, but more by a lack of will or desire. If desire and will can be generated, then skill development becomes easy. Sometimes the practice of a skill improves desire; but, if the erosion of desire itself is not corrected, the effect of the skill wears off. Relationships do not fail for technical reasons: they fail for emotional reasons. These emotional reasons point to characteristics of the human condition.

In downgrading marriage to the development of skills or the acquisition of knowledge, we ignore the source of love itself. And what is the source of love? Why is it that we love at all? Very simply, it is our enduring response to the unavoidable isolation and vulnerability of life itself. If we understand the sources from which love springs, we will be able to accept and understand it rather than trying to manipulate it. Love is our solution to the problem that life presents us. *How do we find a secure base in a world where we have been shipwrecked without knowing either our origin or destiny?*

The reason we need to love in the first place is one that heightens anxiety. The reasons that you become attached to someone, fall in love with them and become entangled with them are ones that you often prefer to avoid. In fact, they are taboo. But if you can look at these reasons and discover *why* it is that you love at all, you find something quite extraordinary: courageously appreciating the vulnerability of life helps you to love well.

Taking a skills-focused view of love or sex, for example, provides us with much relief. Sex has been reduced by pornography to acts and acting, to performance and role playing. It is deprived of its human passion and inescapable vulnerability. Sex is inherently guilt- and shame-inducing not because it is wrong but because it reminds us of how *vulnerable* we really are. We are shamed by what we have been pretending to be—righteous and invulnerable adults.

We want our domestic life and relationships to be based on rational agreements—where everybody buys in to the ground rules. You find yourself saying, 'If everyone could just be more reasonable and rational about everything, we would be all right.' Appealing as this may be, it is an impossible attempt to find some relief from the intensity, tenderness, vulnerability, drama and anger that is at the heart of love. No matter how hard we try (and it is right that we do) we can never make love a rational operation—*because life never was.* Though we dream that it can be, married life is no shelter from the terror of life itself. In fact, both love and violence are different ways that different people cope with this vulnerable life.

The family home longs to be a safe haven. But it can never be less than a place where emotions bleed, wounds are inflicted, compassion repairs and love endures. Don't expect perfection. If, in terms of emotion, your home is a bit like an accident and emergency unit, maybe that is not so bad. If it is, then hang in there. You're not alone.

By anaesthetising feeling in order to communicate better, by using science to hide sensitivity, we tend to diminish love. The trivialisation of both sex and intimacy is very much part of modern life. When the tasks of intimate connection with another person are separated from passionate vulnerability, we cut off this connection at its source.

Vulnerable life is the cause of love.

The Thought Experiment Revisited

I presented the Thought Experiment in the Preface in order to offer an analogy of our human predicament. If we consider the microscope and macroscope approaches here, the microscope approach would zoom in on the couple: it would have only the couple and the boat in its view. This approach would probably recommend that the couple learn how to row properly, how to patch up leaks, how to thread the sails or how to sit in the boat. It would recommend that the couple also learn good communication techniques to inhibit fighting.

A macroscopic approach would zoom out from the boat. It would see the couple in the context of their situation: the conditions under which they exist; the nature of the ocean and weather; and the couple's overall destiny or purpose. It would see love, passion and desire as the emotional expression of a mortal being. It would probably recommend that the couple study ocean currents, weather patterns and sea-sickness. It would recommend that they learn how to read the stars. And it would ask them to consider how being in this situation has affected their relationship and emotions.

This book will take the macroscopic approach, too. It will show that the problems in relationships are often a form of sea-sickness; that anger and frustration between partners is an inevitable consequence of their condition; that their need for each other arises out of their unspoken awareness of their destiny; that their anger towards each other arises out of their vulnerability; and that righteousness is a feeble, counter-phobic attempt to experience certainty and power in such a vulnerable life.

This book will show how violence is a reflex of one person's desire to be powerful and controlling in their own boat because they cannot cope with being vulnerable and helpless on the ocean. It will show how passengers are prone to making victims of themselves or their partners, if they do not remain aware of their place and condition. But more than that, this book will show that the way we nurture and inspire love is through disciplined imagination. Skills, techniques and on-board problem solving are essential to survival, of course. But the heart of love (desire, passion, tenderness, hope, empathy and compassion) arises from being able to see oneself as if from above. It comes from being able to fully inhabit the conditions of life; and to always have one's origins and destiny as the frame that gives love its meaning and purpose.

For these reasons, I suggest that love—between spouses and lovers or between parents and children—is necessarily *heroic*. I hope to show how life requires the courage to love, the courage to be essentially vulnerable in a passionate and beautiful life.

The reason your partner becomes a source of frustration and disappointment for you is because they are unable to undo your predicament. Your emotional reaction to a perceived injustice is, as I will show, a direct derivative of your inability to overcome the conditions of your life. Your drive to ensure that you are not wronged is your way to feel right in a situation in which you really are not.

The boat analogy illustrates that everyday problems are caused by universal concerns. Our struggles with everyday life are influenced by how we deal with the consequences of our own mortality in a mysterious and magical world. The forces of violence and romantic love emerge from this because of our vulnerability and our need to blame the other passenger for the storms. Romantic love can degrade into emotional abuse. Love can fall easily into despair. A joy-filled family home can deteriorate into anger and negativity.

Partners argue and fight not because of their poor navigational techniques or because of the quality of the boat or their comforts. No, they fight because of the conditions they find themselves in and the anxiety, uncertainty and helplessness this evokes. They blame each other for their situation and fate. In failing to look beyond themselves, they find the fault for negative events *between* themselves.

Just as passengers on the boat attempt all sorts of solutions to their dilemma, we too look for solutions to the problems of existence in the confines of our little life. We invariably draw our partner into this project. It is a project that is quasi-religious because, in the absence of knowing, we have to create our maps, half-truths and rituals. We seem to do this for better—towards a compassionate and tender love; or for worse—towards a hostile and abrasive conflict. We are capable of both. It often seems that love is a glorious act of survival in a vulnerable world.

THE MEANING OF RELATIONSHIPS

The most important entities in our personal worlds are other people, particularly those to whom we have been intimately attached: parents, partners, children and siblings. As social animals, we require transactions with others to satisfy our needs and fulfil our potential. Even when we are most alone, our minds conjure up images and scenes that keep our imagination centred on our relationships with others. Who we are is best revealed in the patterns of these intimate relationships. The uniqueness of the self is moulded from the clay of our interactions with significant others throughout life. The template of the self is a template of how to relate to others.

Everything in popular culture seems to emphasise and confirm the pursuit of love-experiences as a way to find significance and status in life. Love songs, movies, magazine articles and popular fiction reveal that society points us towards intimate sexual relationships as the context within which life's fulfilment and heroic purpose can be found. Just listen to any popular music to see how deified romantic love and sexuality has become. A quality of divinity, salvation, relief, meaning and wonder is attributed to romantic love. As we shall see, to the degree that this happens, the tragic consequences of such idolatry are also evident.

Most people will spend some portion of their day reflecting on or worrying about an intimate relationship, be it with a spouse, partner, child, family member or friend. It is through relationships that we survive, define ourselves and find meaning in life. It is also through relationships that we experience the suffering of life: grief, helplessness, pain and guilt. Relationships are both our problems *and* solutions in life.

The bond of love does not always feel like love because it evokes so many other emotions. It can feel like a prison or a trap as much as it can feel like a relief or an escape. Love does not always feel good.

In this book, I will look at intimate relationships and how they can become such an ordeal for so many people. When I talk about love, I am also including its darker elements that deteriorate into violence and abuse. Love is a passionate attachment that includes rejection, abandonment and abuse as much as it includes their opposites: acceptance, safety and affection. Love can even morph into evil when the need to be in control of another person overrides the need to emancipate them.

Affection and rejection are two sides of the same coin. Songs are all about love as being an extraordinary romantic escape and I have no wish to enhance that illusion. This is part of the experience of love but it is a small part. Love is nature's way of drawing you into its larger project of contributing to the survival of the species. Nature needs you to bond.

*

As if God will give me spare days to count my blessings …
We must cheerfully take whatever comes our way.
This is love.

WHAT IS AT STAKE

> *Had I the heavens' embroidered cloths,*
> *Enwrought with golden and silver light,*
> *The blue and the dim and the dark cloths*
> *Of night and light and the half-light,*
> *I would spread the cloths under your feet:*
> *But I, being poor, have only my dreams;*
> *I have spread my dreams under your feet;*
> *Tread softly because you tread on my dreams.*

This is how Yeats described the haunting wonder and sensitivity that attends love. Relationships stir up the most powerful and disturbing emotions we can experience. It is those closest to you who evoke the deepest feelings of your life. The impetus for this book came from a simple question I asked: 'What is really at stake for you when you are trying to win an argument with your partner?'

What is at stake that makes relationships cause such distress? Some of what is at stake is explained by psychology. Attachment theory, for example, explains why small babies (and later, adults) respond with distress when their needs for secure bonding are not met. Psychoanalytic theories explain how people project their inner problems out onto the other person and try to sort them out there.

However, such theories do not go far enough in exploring why relationships become so vital to us. In being psychological, these theories stop short of venturing into the existential, philosophical or even theological. Psychology does not like to cross that sea. Psychology and psychiatry look in one direction for understanding. They see humanity within the range of their own perspective and research. However, to understand why we love (or fail to love) we must look at existence itself, at the predicament of life itself. We must include not only what we know but also what we do not understand, what is perplexing, awe-inspiring and miraculous about being human. We must see ourselves within the 360 degrees of life that surrounds us, rather than the narrow arc of what we *know* to be true.

One of the wonderful things you will notice is how the most learned of people do not go to academic research findings to cope with and enjoy life. The findings of modern psychology contribute only a tiny fraction to our overall wellbeing in life. When it comes to figuring out how to live, we draw on so many sources other than research and science. We use music, good company, exercise, sport, nature, recreation, hobbies, comedy, religion, art, learning and even a little bit of alcohol to enjoy life. Finding enjoyment in such things can be a source of courage and hope; and can amount to so much more than knowledge and information alone. We find inspiration in a wonderful piece of music, in visiting our favourite place, in prayerful mediation, in sport or in having a few pints with a good friend. In doing this, we are not looking to understand life: we want to be in harmony with life. We are not searching for the meaning of life: we are searching for the experience of being fully alive.

This is all as it should be, because life pulsates and breathes to rhythms and sensitivities that have nothing whatsoever to do with mental analysis. We are driven by forces that have nothing to do with our thoughts. We are drawn by a gravitational pull away from reason.

Like a small boat on an open sea, each of us drifts with the currents and winds. Our course is not determined by the angle of our rudder. Unless we know these tides, currents and winds, unless we are guided by the stars, we are lost.

A lot of popular psychology suggests that the best way to survive life is to learn about your boat and the skills and techniques of good boatmanship. That's all very well and necessary but I also want you to look upwards at the sky and the stars that shelter you; to look beneath you to the deep ocean that holds you afloat; and to consider the current of life that guides your little boat. It is here that you will find answers that cannot be found in the 'How to Operate Your Boat' manual. At some point, you will need to rest your oars and lean back into the folded sail and let the ocean, wind, currents and swells do the work! All the frantic rowing in the world will make not a tad of difference if you cannot accept the wind.

When you look expansively at life, you begin to understand the source of your anxiety, the necessity of love and the meaning of abandonment.

The Symbolic Nature of Rejection
If I ask you why you argue with your spouse, it is actually a very important question about your place in the world. If I ask you how is it that you feel so offended by something your partner did or did not do, it is actually a question about what is at stake that leaves you

so vulnerable to such offence. How is it that you get so emotionally upset about so many little things? Why does your partner 'get to you' so much? We shall begin to answer these questions here.

It is likely that your answers to these questions are similar to mine. You will give a psychological or literal answer to the question. 'I argue with my husband because I need to defend myself', 'I argue with my wife because it is important that she listens to me', etc. These answers do not, however, expose what is at stake or explain *why* you feel such distress at times. To do so, we must begin to understand what it means to the human person to feel rejected.

Rejection has quite remarkable effects on a person. I bet that you can, right now as you read this, recall instantly the people who have rejected you in life, be it in big or small ways. Personal rejection is, at times, received like a sledgehammer to your body. Even in its more subtle forms, it feels like a dagger in your back. It hurts terribly and can leave you with many injuries. However, in almost every situation, the reaction is disproportionate to the objective rejection. I will explain why later. For now, just get a feel for how rejection and all its forms evoke primitive and powerful emotions in you that have nothing to do with the objective danger of the situation. The source of these feelings is one that is more physical than reasoned.

At the other end of the scale, passionate and romantic love is not guided by reason. Romantic declarations of love are as 'unreasonable' as aggressive declarations of anger. They come from the same source: our acute sensitivity to this precarious life.

The life-or-death quality to marital conflict reveals that there is much more at issue in everyday life than proving a point, being listened to or being understood. For example, you will be aware of the outrage that can be evoked when you feel you are the victim of some injustice at home or at work. Your sense of moral outrage is often powerful: 'How *dare* they do that?' The interesting thing to note here is that your *morality* is necessary because of your *mortality* and your associated urge to protect it.

The passionate, terrified urgency of humanity is to be seen everywhere. When we turn away from our existential or religious anxieties, we turn away from the actual necessity of love. By 'love' I do not mean its soft, emotional sentiment but its cellular, physical and muscular necessity. Love is a passionate reflex of death. We love precisely because of death. Things are beautiful because of their transience—because they come to pass. Romantic passion is the urge to live in the face of death.

The sorrow and joy of life exist because of mortality. We are burdened with anticipatory grief knowing the loss that awaits us. We are awash with the sorrow of humanity. We exist because of the toil of generations that have gone before us who have suffered mightily in sustaining the life that created us. Through war, famine, plagues, poverty and tragedy, those who have gone before have passed on the baton of life to us.

We also pulsate with the joy and love of creation. We are driven with a force that *wants more life.* Almost despite ourselves, our bodies carry us forward. So, in the midst of a mysterious and majestic universe, close to the sweet beauty of life, we find the passionate ability to love. Herein is our redemption.

Yet we deny and resist love. We turn our face away from the abject vulnerability it implies. We have made *status* and *control* our personal gods. We believe that these gods will protect us from decay and frailty. However, these beliefs distract us from our impulse to love and our compassion for others.

In finding the courage to inhabit our fading, failing and transient self, we release the impulse to love. We find the possibility of imaginative love. We find the necessity of forgiveness and gratitude. When we are aware of these things, we make love with a passionate tenderness. It is born out of knowing that the one we embrace is an image of the divine. The one we embrace is part of ourselves; and they are trying as hard as they can in a world that is beyond them. Every act of tender love is laced with the passion of anticipated sorrows. Every act of angry rejection is laced with the denial of vulnerable love.

> *Because of this,*
> *when in the night*
> *I hear the lonely sound of rain,*
> *I find I love you all the more.*

DEATH (SORRY ...)

> *The beauty of the world hath made me sad,*
> *This beauty that will pass;*
>
> Pádraig Pearse

You will hate the mention of death, of course; hence my opening apology. You probably do not even like the look of the word on the page; it may make you nauseous. There is a very strong social and psychological taboo surrounding it. 'Don't be so morbid' is the response of most people when you talk about death in literal terms. The taboo is stronger even than the taboos around discussions of sex or financial status. Notice the reactions of family members if you venture to say, 'I dreamed last night that I was going to die.' Do that as an experiment and see what happens: people will usually respond negatively to that statement. It is a taboo worth exploring, because the effects of our denial are not always positive.

You will need courage to turn your face towards that which defines you, towards that which gives love its meaning, purpose and passion.

We repress and deny the fact that love is a consequence of our human vulnerability; a human vulnerability that is our emotional experience of the proximity of death to all of life. We are physically vulnerable at all times because we are mortal and because illness, accident and death threaten us constantly. As a consequence, we are emotionally vulnerable; we are forever anxious and afraid. Our anxious vulnerability defines us.

It is because of our mortal condition that we need and seek out love. We look for a secure base in a world that is often not secure. Why would we need a secure base? Whether we admit it or not, part of us is always afraid. We fear suffering, death's messenger. The suffering of distress, anguish, pain and hurt are the emotional equivalents of physical illnesses. Emotional pain is the sign and symptom of vulnerability to inevitable death.

Emotional attachment to another person opens us to the negative and positive in life. Marriage and family relationships create grief and hope, sorrow and joy, frustration and contentment. In these ways, attachment to another person in a loving relationship triggers the desire for life and the fear of death.

There is also the presence of mortal vulnerability in our commitment to another person. *Will this be the death of me? Will this relationship destroy me? Will I die in here?* Therefore, the thing that is so hard to bear is how joy itself is joyful because it momentarily relieves the anxiety of mortality. Joy is therefore a transcendent experience.

Every family celebration, ritual and birthday is, if you allow the truth to surface, a celebration precisely because of the passing transience of life. Subconsciously, you know that the thread that holds you together will break at some point. That is why you drink and sing into the early hours. You forget the circumstances of life and revel in the 'eternal now' that you do not want to end. Think for a moment about the importance of marking someone's birthday. The reason it is important is almost impossible to admit, for to do so is to destroy the bliss of the temporary illusion. Yet the loveliness of the candles and the meaning of blowing them out, of making a wish for your future, all reveal the truth that I find hard even to write here. Every birthday is a celebration precisely because there was a time that you did not exist. Because of our unmentionable death, we are obliged to celebrate our birth. It is such an exquisite joy that it seems strange to blow out the candles; but we must. In doing so, we symbolically salute mortality. And when we make a wish, it is an admission that we do not control our destiny.

It will gradually be revealed throughout this book that, while we avoid naming how our vulnerable mortality defines so much of our life, we acknowledge it in countless symbolic ways every single day: a greeting, a kiss, a consolation, a kindness. They are all profoundly symbolic gestures towards the heavens and the earth. But we dare not name this acknowledgment, because to do so partly betrays the necessary illusions of life. We tend to leave these things to the musicians and artists, who can colour it melodically. However, in this book, we shall part the curtains. We shall bring into awareness that which you may think is morbid, but which is actually blissful and sublime.

*

Love is more than just a reminder of our mortality; it exists *because* of it. Love is your response to mortality; it is your solution to it; and it is necessary and essential because of it. Without death, there is no love; there is no reason for it. Without the passion of wounded vulnerability, estrangement or emotional homelessness, there is no impulse to reach out and connect. There is no evolutionary imperative to sustain life. Love, in one way, is the physical experience of evolution itself. It is where the great movement of life itself seeps into consciousness through desire, the wanting to connect, the wanting to endure. All of human history gets funnelled down to the still point of your next small gesture, your next expression of loving kindness or angry rejection.

*

Love and attachment derive their intense power from the anxiety of our human condition, an anxiety that is our unconscious awareness of our precarious life. The cycle of birth–growth–decay–death is the background music to every day and every moment of our lives. If our anxious mortality makes love and desire necessary, our love of living makes love worthwhile.

It is not by coincidence that when we experience grief and bereavement in life, our love for those we care about is heightened. When we lose someone we love, like a parent, friend or spouse, it is only then that we really begin to know what love is about. When we are awakened from the trance of everyday stress, through death or tragedy, we remember what life is about. Equally, when joy or beauty waken us from that same trance, we remember who we are.

The song of the poets, artists and musicians, the song of your own dancing heart, is much more important than the reduced findings of microscopic research about how to get what you want or how love can be learned as a skill. But it is no wonder that we try to reduce love and marriage to a skill and legal obligation. In doing so, we detach ourselves from a love that is courageous enough to *look beyond*. This is a love that is passionate, vulnerable, wounded and broken for the *individual*, but ultimately victorious for *humanity*.

Is it possible to be married to someone without fear being a part of it? No. To think you can have love without fear is to want to escape the anxiety that is an inseparable part of love. You feel the fear of being abandoned; the fear of revealing yourself; the fear of grief and loss; the fear of being out of control; the fear associated with knowing that your lover is the one person in your life who has the power to diminish, if not destroy, you. Without this fear, love loses its meaning. Therefore, the guarded, walled-off, self-protective person is incapable of love. The person who thinks they have banished their ever-present fear by maximising their control over others may find some kind of temporary relief; but this is always at the cost of love itself. Therefore, I believe that every intimate statement a lover makes to their partner could be accompanied by a silent closing phrase: 'because I am afraid'. We all are. It is our human condition. And it makes love necessary and passionate.

I am hopeful you will appreciate that when you look at intimate relationships from the perspective of life's existential and spiritual tasks, you get a different *feel* for the origins of your problems and distress. All human distress is a consequence of our unavoidable, heroic struggle with the conditions of life. When we appreciate this, we can see that the nature of our interpersonal problems is shaped by this struggle. You begin to see that you and your temporary opponent are, in fact, one. You think you fight against him or her, but you fight with life. You dare not admit it because it exposes you.

Our interpersonal problems are determined by the terms and conditions that existence has dealt us; and how we cope with these terms and conditions. Most psychological problems can be understood as the symptoms that are caused by our efforts to override these terms and conditions. In refusing to sign up to the terms and conditions of life itself, we are really looking for a *feeling* of immortality. That is what we spend so much of our day doing: trying to achieve a kind of success or significance; trying to arrive at a point of real, unchanging happiness. But it slips through our fingers like sand.

Everyone's life problems are really symbolic enactments of this essential struggle with life. As we shall see, your everyday criticisms of your partner are really symbolic ways that you elevate yourself and diminish your partner. And the reason it is *necessary* that you elevate yourself and diminish your partner is your craving for significance or power. And the reason you need to have these little experiences of superiority and significance is because *deep down you doubt your significance at all.* And the reason that you doubt yourself, the reason your hold on your status *seems* so precarious, is because *it is.* So you need to establish and exaggerate your status.

In small, everyday ways you want to *feel* superior to something or someone. You also abhor feeling diminished (for the same reason) and you rise up in protest. 'How *dare* that driver pull out in front of me without indicating first?!' What does it matter? It matters if your hold on your status is so precarious.

This 'condition of life' lens is a way we can see how things really are. When we see things this way, we develop sensitivity through which the meaning of things is revealed.

Meditation

You can dream and fall in love and yet grow ill and die for the most trivial of reasons. You can see your parents waste away, your child killed, your brother consumed by cancer, and acts of terrorism obliterate the innocent. Floods, tsunamis, earthquakes, hurricanes, famines and droughts can all obliterate the striving of millions. This can happen in an instant, with careless and cruel disregard for any man, woman or child. The relentless indifference of death does not spare you. When you allow yourself to dwell on your condition, on the fate that awaits you and all of those you love, it can be the most chilling and unforgiving of realities. The decay and death that awaits every one of us is unforgiving. It is almost unbearable for the loving parent to consider the suffering in life that awaits their child, the parent preferring it were laid upon *them* instead.

My friend grieves over the gravestone of her beloved daughter. A widower wanders the empty house remembering his wife. I sit at the edge of the ocean awash with anticipated grief. Yet as I do, each wave rolls with an exquisite beauty, the sun dances on the sparkling sea before me, great clouds rise up into the heavens, and gulls soar on the updraft from the cliffs behind me. All this beauty that will come to pass. It is sometimes unbearably beautiful and unbearably sorrowful. It is this sensitivity that must remain awake in a relationship: without it, we engage in flight.

In superstitious ways, we keep the fact of life's inherently tragic motif at arm's length. At a subconscious level, you are in tune with your vulnerability to illness, accident, injury or death. You are aware on a daily basis how tragedy has struck the families of either you or your partner. You see how a sudden death, car accident, terminal illness or relationship break-up can randomly strike anyone. You see on a daily basis the poverty, famine and catastrophe visited on vulnerable people. You wonder how we can continue to function with a sense of power and control in a life in which we have little of either, in the midst of a fate in which we have none.

We do so with courage. Passionate love has meaning. Kindly love has purpose. This is why a simple, unanticipated kindness can bring tears to your eyes.

THE GREAT MYSTERY OF LIFE

When you have arrived
you understand that
all things in your life are one.

The great mystery of life is something we tend to ignore. It is too much to try to comprehend. So we concentrate on the smaller things we can take apart and understand. However, this book does not aim to reduce the problems of family life into smaller elements; it seeks to expand the problems of living out onto the large canvas of existence. When we see ourselves expansively, we can understand why we manage everyday problems the way we do.

To understand why relationships are so intense, and why so much seems to be at stake, we need to see them located on the large stage on which we play out the drama of life. To understand love, we must understand our deepest passions and fears as they relate to the earth on which we stand and to the sky under which we live. This explains so much of our irrational and emotional behaviour. It is because of uncomplicated mortality that we have passion and desire.

It is important to emphasise that psychological distress is no less painful than physical injury. Psychological distress evokes the same fear of death that is evoked by physical injury or illness. Emotional conflicts in marriage or family life can feel like (and sometimes actually become) battles for survival. Relationship issues are not usually life-and-death scenarios, but psychological conflicts can unleash homicidal and suicidal forces. This is because the anxieties about life get funnelled and reduced down into a family conflict. However, our psychological explanations for such conflict often reduce the primitive and biblical drama of family life down to naïve, logical explanations. The security of an intimate relationship promises us some shelter from the storms of life. Romantic love is infused with this dizzy promise and potential. In this way, an intimate relationship can be both a refuge from life and a vehicle through which we experience it fully. However, if this promise to provide shelter is not delivered, intense emotions are released. I see this in my practice every day.

*

In this book, we will look at some of the essential conditions of a relationship: the 'facts of love', so to speak. We start at this point because we cannot divorce the challenges of intimate relationships from the challenge of life itself.

Many of the conditions of a relationship are ones that you try to reject. However, the acceptance of life's conditions allows you to take the first steps towards joy and meaning. I shall describe some of the shadows that give life an extra dimension out of which emerges the singular light that is love.

In the models of couples therapy, there is no reference to the following facts: that we are dying; that we are powerless to affect fate; that love and desire are a reflex of this; that courage is necessary to survive; and that we exist within an irresolvable mystery. It seems more pragmatic to tilt our heads away from the implications of such large issues, to concentrate on the smaller ones that we feel better able to handle. The choice between looking towards and looking away from the unknown is ultimately a philosophical and spiritual question. Often, we prefer to concentrate on the things we seem to understand, rather than on the things we don't. I suggest that this turns out to be a grave error.

A relationship becomes difficult when someone uses it to try to escape from the ordeal of life. If they reject some of the basic conditions of life, they are forever at war with themselves and their partner. They want life on their terms. This guarantees a conflict between who their partner is and who they want them to be. This, of course, is the source of most marital difficulties.

Chapter 2
The Symptoms of Vulnerable Love

... June is short
And we must joy in it and dance and sing.
And from her bounty draw her rosy worth.
Ay! soon the swallows will be flying south,
The wind wheel north to gather in the snow,
Even the roses spilt on youth's red mouth
Will soon blow down the road all roses go.

Francis Ledwidge

'June' by Francis Ledwidge beautifully encourages us to live for the moment because we all go the same way and blow down the road that all roses go. Ledwidge describes better than I can the facts of vulnerable life: that you have been blessed with life and that you must choose how you inhabit it.

Throughout this chapter, I will describe the simple but compelling consequences of life and its conditions. These experiences are critical to love and to what we will uncover later. I will describe how these physical and emotional experiences are converted into symbolic everyday activity. I will illustrate how we seek to overcome and eliminate these symptoms of life. I will show how we are at war with ourselves and our nature. And I will reveal how love is made possible by how we resolve and inhabit these passionate conflicts and realities.

Let me lay down some essential truths that will guide our ship towards the meaning of love. All of these states are a consequence of life. They are the ground floor from which our love, courage, passion and hope ascend. The unavoidable symptoms of vulnerable love are:

- Woundedness
- Vulnerability

- Anxiety
- Insignificance
- Helplessness
- Inadequacy
- Guilt

*

WOUNDEDNESS

The unsettling truth is that we are mortally wounded. We experience the injury of life. We hurt. The wound of life is that the time you have with those you love is brief. The noble truths of Buddhism remind us of this when they state that life is the process of birth, growth, decay and death. All life is enlivened by this passion. The passion and suffering of love itself is an extension of the passion of temporary life. Anything else we have to say about how we relate to another person is shadowed entirely by this fact. Though it lies outside our everyday awareness (because it is too big to grasp at times), everything we do is done because of this wound, this terminal injury.

In our awareness of our proximity to death, we touch our most essential humanity. Death gifts you with the fragility of life. It quickens your senses to the transient impermanence of all that is beautiful. It awakens you to that which is essential. It forces you to separate it from what is wasteful. It prompts you to live an intimate and honest life. It demands that you savour life's preciousness. It makes you a pilgrim. The remarkable thing about our woundedness is that it is the place from which love springs. How you relate to your lover is determined by how you deal with the wound that both of you carry. The simple joy of having a baby is just so because of these things.

Death is not a physical state. It is an emotional process within which you experience the passion of living, the grief of loss and the joy of birth. All of life's basic emotions exist because of this mortal wound. It is through sorrow and grief that death makes itself known to the human heart. It is through love and joy that we overcome it.

In 'Mirror in February', Thomas Kinsella writes about his acute awareness of how he will have to face the indignity of decay. On looking at a nearby orchard, where the trees have been 'Hacked clean for better bearing', he thinks about the mutilation his own body will have to endure through being human. However, he summons courage as best he can; and he chooses to live his life with grace and dignity:

… In slow distaste
I fold my towel with what grace I can,
Not young and not renewable, but man.

The everyday character of intimate relationships is shaped by the fact that, though we are mortally wounded, we have to put it aside. We have to 'fold the towel' as best we can. We must embrace the inherent sorrow of life if we are to love with passion and integrity. It is through sorrow that mortality makes itself known to the human heart. It is through sorrow that our bodies feel the heartache of death. The body converts the coldness of death into the grief of sorrow.

Grief begins in the quiet, unseen places in your heart. Away from the rushing world and the hustle and bustle of your everyday worries and uncertainties, there is a place within you that is wrapped in the garment of sorrow. A quiet sensitivity to everything where:

Even in the mind of the mindless one arises grief
When the sparrow rises up from the morning grass.

Saigyo

You busy yourself with all the 'important' things to worry and fret about. Yet, when you stop, when the urgency of your life is taken from you, you can sit in the long grasses at the bend of the river and your tears can flow with all the sorrow of the world. I know that, in the quiet of the evening, when you remember the name of love, when the memories flow through you, you have a name that is 'sorrow'. You know about death in ways that you have never spoken. Its movement within you is wordless. It is the still, sad music of your soul.

The wound of life can be a state of absolute spiritual poverty in which, having nothing, you possess all:

A world of grief and pain
Oh God, but flowers bloom, even then.

Issa

The transience of life makes the most ordinary things quite beautiful. A haunting beauty touches you through those you love and those you have lost. It is in your wound that you are touched by compassion. In these places, your heart awakens. You walk along the quiet shore, as you listen to its song. The song is the sound of the waves, the colour of the sky and the scent of salt air. You know, with reluctant acceptance, that all these things come to pass.

Death makes us aware of the fragility of life, the impermanence of beauty and the passing river that is love. Transient life awakens the hunger in our hearts for a home, a kiss and a loving embrace. Every greeting and every goodbye is our simple, unconscious acknowledgment of our wounded life. The Gaelic greeting is 'Dia dhuit', which means 'God be with you'. It is a simple, everyday acknowledgment of the need for something or someone larger than ourselves to hold us and to bless us with good fortune in an unpredictable world.

This acknowledgment of need is wordless. We dare not speak this truth, but our body feels it in vague and indescribable ways. The tear in the eye on parting, the delight of the embrace on arrival, the wave of the small child on the doorstep… All of these things affect us because our heart knows our wound and our every breath is life gasping to hold onto itself. It is at times too much for the mind to bear.

> *You wave to your child*
> *as she heads off to school*
> *and, for some reason,*
> *the physical distance between you*
> *unsettles your leave-taking,*
> *as if reminding you*
> *that you cannot protect her*
> *from the suffering in life*
> *that awaits her.*
>
> *Tears come to your eyes,*
> *as your heart gets tugged,*
> *fish-hooked with the grief*
> *of anticipated sorrows.*

Meditation

Identify experiences in your life that caused you to live more fully and soulfully; experiences that called you to live more passionately with the essentials of life. Make a mental note of these things as they come spontaneously to your mind.

Those experiences that cause us to live more fully are often experiences that we would not wish on anyone. They include the death of a loved one; the trauma of a broken relationship; the survival of a serious illness; or the loss of a job.

For so many of us, it is the experiences of death, loss or trauma that trigger some form of personal transformation. This is deeply revealing because it is our wounded humanity that awakens us to that which is essential. The experience of pain can cause us to live a more intimate and emotionally honest life. It can prompt us to savour life's preciousness.

In the film *Shadowlands*, the characters of C.S. Lewis and his wife Joy try to make sense of her terminal cancer. At one point, they remark: 'The pain now is part of the happiness then. That's the deal.' Here, we see that love and death are inextricably entwined. But in our everyday lives, few of us see that woundedness is the companion of love's passion. It is such a mixed blessing.

All spirituality seeks to address and come to terms with suffering. It tries to help with our unavoidable pain. It recognises the wound of life. Suffering is simply our creaturely experience of death and dying. This is the central, unpalatable truth that remains unavoidable.

> *Though we sing and dance,*
> *laugh and cry,*
> *bear beautiful children,*
> *build and create many wonderful things,*
> *make love and see great beauty,*
> *we nonetheless are slipping through the hourglass.*
> *From one perspective,*
> *this is tragic.*
> *From another,*
> *death makes everything possible*
> *and makes everything what it is:*
> *beautiful.*

VULNERABILITY

Though you may not identify with your mortal woundedness, you experience it constantly through your unavoidable vulnerability. Vulnerability is the emotional experience of your mortal wound. Vulnerability is an experience of how precarious your foothold on life and love really is. Your vulnerability is that everyday sensation and feeling that you are never entirely secure, safe or in control of life.

Your vulnerability is your everyday experience of being afraid, uncertain or inadequate. It is also experienced in your humility, softness and tenderness. It comes from knowing that you are dependent on and in need of others to survive and be safe. It comes from an understanding that you are never truly self-sufficient. Your vulnerability in life is a feeling of always being somewhat 'at risk'. You are never really in control, no matter how hard you try. Therefore, you are at your most human when you are comfortable with the fact of your vulnerability. When you do this, you can then reach out to another person with authenticity and humility. The humility of vulnerability knows that you are not a god in your own life. You are dependent on others, on life and on the gifts of the universe.

From this vulnerability arises love. It is in the physical experience of one's vulnerability that one reaches out to others for safety or connection. It was through your physical dependence on your caregivers when you were a child that you survived at all. Dependency and its associated vulnerability are what make you human. The precarious vulnerability of love lies in the fact that your lover is the one with the power to expose you to the intensity of *emotional* death.

Of course, most couples don't worry about death. If you were to make a list of your top ten marital concerns, it is unlikely that you would put mortality above your financial, occupational, sexual or parenting problems. When you wake up at night, it is rarely because you are worrying about your mortal wound. Or so you think ... Bear with me and we shall take a deeper look at this.

Though you may not think about your mortal condition, you continually experience it as your inescapable human vulnerability. Vulnerability is the emotional experience of the precariousness of the certainty and security you have in your relationship. You experience this vulnerability on a persistent basis, yet you seek to minimise and deny it. You know that fate can strike at any time. In relationships, this suffering (with a small 's') is experienced in such things as rejection, hurt, disappointment, frustration, betrayal or anxiety. So, even though you do not think about your mortal woundedness, you are constantly *feeling* vulnerable because of it.

We all react to the emotional evocations of our woundedness, the tentacles that wind their way into the chambers of our hearts. These can be: the cold shoulder of a lover; the harsh, rejecting word that makes us feel unsafe; the dark shadow of long-term illness; the grief of relationship breakdown; the helplessness to relieve a lover's suffering; and the powerlessness to change things. When a partner rejects us, puts us down or makes us feel small, it awakens our vulnerability. What we try to protect is not our self-esteem but the threat to life itself—our very *lives*. Make no mistake: even though we never talk about it, death talks to us constantly, dressed up in the vocabulary of the everyday.

The precarious vulnerability of love lies in the fact that your lover is the only one in your life who can break you with grief, awaken your rage or prove your ultimate impotence. On an everyday basis, we are reminded of this in form and symbol. Your partner forgets you, dismisses you, leaves you, brings suffering and pain to you and (often inadvertently) pulls back the comforts of your life. Death is not an event that waits at some checkpoint. Rather, it is your companion on the path of your everyday married life. It does not pose as the morbid Grim Reaper but as the tender companion that is human vulnerability. When you are open to this truth, you open yourself to the first possibility of love.

The image of death as the Grim Reaper is a dreadful, cartoonish image that suggests that death is a final act. I prefer an image like the hourglass, which shows that *there is only dying*. And after dying, there is the nothingness of sleep. So we must not fear death. We must just *experience our own dying* which is, in truth, what living is! Death is not the Grim Reaper but rather the Guardian Angel—the gentle touch of life that is our vulnerability and woundedness, the grace that gives us life.

*

ANXIETY

As a consequence of your natural state of woundedness and vulnerability, you are always anxious. Anxiety is a constant presence in your life. At times, it takes up the foreground of your daily life; at other times, it slips into the background. Anxiety is a necessary and unavoidable symptom of being a human animal. It keeps you alive and alert. It is a warning system that has allowed all species of life to survive and evolve over millions of years.

Anxiety has been your intimate companion all of your life. You are afraid of so many things. Even as you sit reading this, you have a thousand worries, anxieties, fears and phobias standing at your shoulder—everything from the trivial and insignificant to the substantial and life-altering. You worry about big things and little things. You worry about the health and wellbeing of your children; and you worry whether or not you will make a meeting on time. You worry about your weight, finances, status and relationships. You worry what people think. You worry more or less about these things every day; but anxiety is a constant.

At its most basic level, anxiety is a consequence of your fear of death and your will to survive. Without it, you would be entirely indifferent to safety and you would not last long. Anxiety makes you vigilant and careful. It makes you protect and mind your children. Your physical anxiety is so constant that you hardly even notice it, unless you are startled by something and you get a 'fright'. This is usually a harmless revelation of just how hyper-alert we really are.

Anxiety is also experienced in relationships in countless ways. You are not just concerned with physical safety but also with psychological safety. You will tend to react with some intensity when your emotional safety feels threatened. You may notice that you sometimes have a disproportionate fear of saying or doing the wrong thing. You will also feel anxious that your partner may react to you negatively and thus make you feel unsafe and exposed. Like all of us, you will feel afraid that you will either lose control or lose approval; that you will be rejected or undermined. You will also be familiar with status anxiety: the anxiety you feel about ensuring that other people's opinions of you are positive. Because our self-esteem can be desperately dependent on other people's views of us, we can spend a lifetime anxiously seeking to maintain a positive self-image.

These are all examples of how anxiety is ever-present in our lives. We invest a huge amount of nervous energy in trying to predict what might go wrong in order to prevent it. This is normal; it is in our nature.

Anxiety in a Relationship

The night time is the worst. It's when you feel exposed, when all the little terrors kept caged and cloaked during the day are allowed their time to roam and rattle through the corridors of your mind.

By day, you are a competent person—strong and well regarded. There is hardly an issue you cannot handle; hardly an emotion you cannot tame. You stand comfortably in your competence. However, at night you become a child. You are frightened of the creaking floorboards of your thoughts. The footsteps of uncertainty seem to come ever closer. You worry about your children, spouse and endless 'to do' list. It is as if death itself were waiting down the street to catch you for your inevitable errors. You feel the disapproval of the world. You feel the judgment for things gone wrong. You expect the guilty verdicts to be handed down for your sloppiness, neglect and failure.

The anxieties are everywhere: the fear of saying the wrong thing; hurting the other; betraying the self; evoking anger and rejection; experiencing isolation; feeling vulnerable; and being hurt and violated. Even in the most loving of relationships, this terror exists. It is only the courageous lover that can tell his beloved:

> *I am afraid of you. I am afraid of you because of what you have come to mean to me. I am afraid of losing you, surrendering to you, being hurt by you, hurting you, being rejected by you, rejecting you. I am afraid of your disapproval and anger. I am simply afraid. The risk of love has exposed me to your power and to my dread and isolation. And yet, my desire, faith, love and courage believe in you. Despite my fear, I try to trust you. I try to be open, vulnerable and strong. I try to know my fear and trust my courage.*

This is what every couple has to admit if they are to move forward towards a love that fosters freedom, dignity and courage. If a couple is to admit to love, then there is no escape. The passion of love is a companion to the passion of anxious vulnerability: a beating heart; a trembling body in the face of death; a passionate desire in the face of life. Love and anxious vulnerability are entwined: the one you love has the power to expose you to the absolute terror of life. Your beloved exposes and welcomes your vulnerability. Your awareness of this touches the anxiety inherent in every love relationship. It is this unavoidable anxiety that makes love a risky enterprise and a blissful relief.

Hardly a loving couple sit before me who are not also deeply afraid of each other. While they proclaim strong positions, certainties and convictions about who they are and what they want in their relationship, the *fear* is unmistakeable. It is as visible as a trembling hand. It is both a terror and a passion: the terror of isolation and the passion for connection. People are rarely aware of their anxiety and fear; they tend to convert it into hurt and anger. It is easy to be angry at the other; it is easy to feel hurt by the other. It is difficult to grasp the anxious fear that lies beneath. Couples never admit to this but the huge efforts in defending and attacking each other reveal it dramatically. 'I am terrified of you' is a truth that is rarely spoken.

Anxiety as Existential, rather than Objective

When you worry about your children, relationship, security, money, work or health, the energy source that drives these worries is your actual physical body. It is hard to get a full grasp of this fact because, in your mind, your worries are deserving of anxious attention and they are entirely psychological and logical. But this is not always so. Experiences of psychological worry and distress emanate from your physical vulnerability in a precarious life you do not control.

Humanity has, over millions of years of evolution, fallen from being an animal entirely innocent and unaware of its own existence to being a human acutely conscious of their status in the world. Through the fall from innocence to awareness, we have developed the symptoms of *depressive anxiety*. Unlike animals, we are aware of our own nature and destiny. This has underpinned our lives with a proneness to depressive anxiety. Depression and anxiety are not just illnesses or neuroses: they are symptoms of the human condition.

If we had remained as animals, our lives would not be depressively anxious. We would have no fears, worries, guilt or desires to be different from who and what we are. We would inhabit ourselves without worry. Instead, we long to be little gods. We try to be the master of our own little universe, an effort that fails. So we are caught in the tension between being either a happy slave to life or being an unhappy god. Every morning when you sit at your breakfast table or lean against your kitchen counter with a cup of coffee, you are faced with this choice. 'How will I approach this day?' you ask yourself. 'Do I make life happen or do I let life happen?'

As I have mentioned, though your anxiety appears to be about external things (such as family, work or health), it is really your inherited fear. This is the pulsating anxiety of life itself.

An animal feels anxiety but does not label it as good or bad. A gazelle flees in terror from a cheetah. The gazelle experiences pure terror but it never thinks: 'This is terrible!' Nor does it ever wish to be another animal free of this threat. The gazelle does not escape into the undergrowth and say: 'I wish to God I was born a lion. Life sure is cruel ...' No. The gazelle fully accepts its own terror and life without judgment.

However, all humans are burdened with self-awareness. You experience your nature and then try to overcome it. You want rid of being yourself and, in doing so, you create a new anxiety worse than the first. You try so terribly hard to be other than you are. It is both your blessing and your curse.

Meditation

See if you can bring your anxiety into your awareness. Think about how your everyday fears (of rejection, disapproval or being ignored) affect how you are and how you behave. Maybe you really need approval and you get anxious if it is not forthcoming. Maybe you do a lot of things because you need this recognition and that anxiety drives you to accomplish so much. Maybe you experience a certain amount of disrespect or a lack of recognition—and your fear of your partner affects you. Maybe you have a good relationship but guilt, self-doubt or feelings of inadequacy make you relate in ways that are not good for you.

You have probably never spoken about the electrical current of anxiety that influences you always. It may be vague and hard to get hold of. Maybe you recognise your irritation, anger and disappointment, but you do not realise that underneath them all is the ground of anxious life.

Love needs you to admit to the fear that is just part of life. Think about it. Draw an abstract picture in your mind of what it might look like.

INSIGNIFICANCE

Your life, and the lives of those you love, is vital to you. It is all that matters and it is the centre of your world. At the same time, you are occasionally haunted by the realisation that, in the great scheme of things, your little life is not that important. You often laugh at your condition when you realise that your life is as brief and unremarkable as that of a leaf in any forest. Against the majesty of the world and its apparent indifference to individual life, you cannot but feel insignificant and small. You realise your insignificance when you get a feel for the vast movement of evolution, when you look up at the stars at night or when you realise that you are one of billions of people struggling to survive on this planet, all facing the same unremarkable destiny.

You feel insignificant also in the face of fate, tragedy or misfortune. When some accident takes the life of someone known to you, when a serious illness attacks the body of someone you love or when some tragedy befalls your own family, you are shocked out of your complacency. You are reminded that you are neither immune nor special and that the accidental in life can strike you and those close to you at any time. In this awareness, you know you are not as important as you thought you were; and, if it is not too late, you are prompted into gratitude for your accidental life.

It is most likely that within 120 years, every person alive on the planet at this moment will have died. Every child and family member, every famous person, will be dead and gone. Every person living in China now will be gone by then. Every current citizen of the US will be just a memory. Your marriage, relationship and family will be gone. The things you are worried about, the offences you have experienced and the insults that trouble you will have dissolved into the ether. While your life has meaning for you, in the context of the great movement of evolution, it is insignificant. Your life is brief and it can, at times, feel as unremarkable as that of a single autumn leaf buried on the floor of a forest.

The most powerful thing that emerges for us out of this subconscious awareness is a compulsive need to *prove this wrong* and to deny these facts. (You might have felt a conscious urge to do this after reading the previous paragraph!) You try to prove your significance against the background of this ever-present and upsetting insignificance. How depressing is that? You are insignificant because you are powerless to alter the very conditions of your life. In a sense, your life has happened to you and will be taken from you without ever considering your feelings or views. It could be said that you will be a victim of death and there is nothing that you or all of human creation can (or has ever been able to) do about it. (Though, as we shall explore later, it could equally be said that you are blessed and chosen by life.)

Every cell in your body wants to reject the reality that you have emerged from the soup of evolution and are destined to rejoin it. 'How can this be? I have a name, people I love, status, success, meaning and belonging. Surely there is more to it than that?' It all seems like a bad joke, really: that you have this potentially wonderful life that is destined to just fade away to nothing. Therefore, you use things in life to try to overcome this truth. You use your relationship and your partner to prove to yourself that you are significant, powerful and worthy. You use your partner as a shield against some of the harsh truths about your life.

When you experience the enormous majesty of creation, the stunning universe and the aesthetic wonder of the tiniest of natural creations (such as a single leaf), you inevitably feel small and somewhat insignificant. Against the wonder of the world, its relentless unfolding and its indifference to individual life, you cannot but feel insignificant and small. 'Lord, I am not worthy to receive you,' says the Catholic prayer.

So how do we find and secure significance in a universe that seems to belittle us? Sometimes, we can overcome insignificance by being noticed for some personal quality; or by having status in the eyes of our partner, family or friends. We need confirmation that we are special in some way. We have an urge to believe that what we do in life has value and meaning.

A common way to overcome insignificance is to try to make yourself more significant than you are by pumping yourself up to feel bigger than you are, or by leaning on something larger than yourself. This might play out in a relationship: you can either make your partner surrender to you or else you surrender to them.

Marriage is, without doubt, one of the primary enterprises through which one seeks this significance. This happens in both healthy and unhealthy ways. In your marriage, you may have a real desire to please your partner, to surrender to this other, to surrender with courage to the fate of the marriage. This can feel right and good and, in doing so, you can find a deep sense of belonging. You can be at peace with that. However, you can sense here the danger of handing oneself over *too much*. There is a danger that you find a feeling of significance in life through negation of yourself and surrender to the will of the other person.

You have a drive to join with your beloved, to merge and lose yourself in a relationship or to overcome insignificance by exaggerating your significance. When you merge, it is because you long for some other to lean on, to submit to and to give you some relief from the burden of having to justify yourself. This comes from the fatigue of always having to hold yourself up when life itself seems to want to knock you down. Therefore, being carried along by someone other than yourself can make you feel safe and give you that extra energy. It can allow you to draw on more than just your own meagre resources.

Marriage is perfect for this. You need this support and refuelling from your partner. And then, of course, you can rage against them when they cannot do this or when their own energy sources run low.

The truth of our woundedness is hard to bear, so we inevitably seek to counter it with proof of our significance. And there is no better place to look for this than in your partner. Here, after all, is someone who might ratify and prove your sense of significance and power. In a vague and wordless way, they can distract you from your mortality and make you feel immortal. Sometimes a partner serves to prove the status of your life by improving, being perfect and complying with your expectations. Sometimes a partner loves you because of all of this.

Meditation

Notice the things that offend you in your marriage or relationship. Notice the things that you get defensive about with your spouse. What are the issues that make you overreact or become angry or stubborn? It may be: being told what to do; being ignored; not being listened to; or being criticised. Or it may be more specific and related to your role and how well you parent, mind the house or do your job. It may be judgment on how hard you work, how devoted you are or how considerate you are to others.

Whatever the issue, just be aware of your sore or sensitive points. Consider the possibility that these are the ways that you try for some experience of significance, importance or competence in life. Consider how you need these things because maybe you doubt yourself in other areas of life. Either way, notice how your defensiveness really has less to do with the issue and a lot more to do with your sense of significance in life.

Maybe if you spoke about this with your spouse, they could get a better feel for what is at stake for you when they criticise, neglect or fail to notice how profound a meaning this role or activity has for you in life. Perhaps these are the ways that you find significance in life because life itself does not necessarily provide it for you. Behind your eyes and behind the scenes of your everyday life, you know that the hourglass is shifting and you desire so much to have your place in this world.

Symbolic Life

Your symbolic life refers to the symbols through which you measure your self-esteem, self-significance and self-importance. Your symbols of self-value include things such as: your financial security; your inner contentment; your belief that you are right; the happiness of those close to you, etc. Therefore, an experience that threatens these symbols is often felt to be as threatening as something that threatens your physical life. These could be experiences of being controlled, blamed, attacked, ignored or excluded. You fear all kinds of symbolic abandonment and rejection. Therefore, you get upset when your partner threatens your symbolic life.

You also fear everything that threatens the symbols of your victory over wounded vulnerability and mortality. These threats can include humiliation, disapproval, small failures, disagreements, minor rejections, dismissals and verbal attacks. All of these things expose you to your small deaths, your terrifying awareness of your vulnerability. All of these rejections are your momentary shock of mortality. Every humiliation or rejection shatters the security you have temporarily found. Security seems to banish vulnerability and helplessness to the edges. So when your partner rejects you, puts you down or dismisses your opinion, what is at stake is not your *opinion* but your established sense of *status* and *significance*, and your illusions about your power and control.

HELPLESSNESS

We are powerless and helpless, yet we strive to deny it.

Mortal life is experienced derivatively in our helplessness and powerlessness. We do not control life. Our fate is sealed—at least in

terms of our ultimate destiny. This is why feelings of helplessness
are so discomforting and distressing: they awake in our hearts and
bodies this dormant awareness. The strange thing about all of us is
how we strive so hard to control a life over which we have limited
control. It is therefore no coincidence that virtually all of the clients I
work with identify helplessness as *the* most distressing of feelings. It
is that feeling of being powerless or impotent to do anything about
that which is upsetting you. In fact, we seek *help* precisely because we
are *helpless*.

We live in an age of helplessness—in a state of feeling that nothing
that we say or do really matters. In marriage, it becomes a form of
depression wherein desire is drained away. Depression is the emotional
consequence of helplessness.

It is no coincidence that Alcoholics Anonymous and similar
twelve-step programmes have this as their first step: *Admit that you are
powerless*. This is based on a fundamental spiritual truth about life. All
spirituality demands surrender: a surrender of the desire for control
and power. However, to counter innate helplessness, we try to control
our lives. In many ways, this is necessary but there is a tipping point
beyond which controlling one's life becomes a neurotic compulsion
that *creates* more helplessness than it relieves.

Your realisation that people do not co-operate fully with your
daily efforts to control is something I am sure you identify with. Your
children do not listen to you. Your spouse often ignores you. And work
colleagues seem to shrug their shoulders at your efforts to get things
done. Despite the unavoidable human condition of powerlessness, we
frantically fight against it.

The trouble is that love cannot be controlled nor coerced. Either
it comes willingly—or not at all. The *illusion* of control and power is
essential to us but, as life passes, we realise how ineffective it is. The
regrets of life seem always to have to do with efforts invested in trying
to secure control or status in a life that simply cannot provide it in the
way we expect.

We need to recognise our limited control over the essentials of life
and our compensatory and addictive control of the non-essentials.
We are in constant danger of interpreting our control over the non-
essentials of life as *power* over life. We are powerless to get more love,
significance, status or safety from life than it has already provided. We
are all given these things in equal amount at the moment of birth.

We are powerless seeking to be powerful. We are helpless seeking to be in control. We are vulnerable seeking invulnerability. We are inadequate seeking competence. We are peasants seeking to be a kings. We are tragic seeking to be heroic. We are insignificant seeking to be important. We are cowards seeking to be courageous. All our efforts are towards those ends.

At the heart of many human problems is our difficulty in coming to terms with our inherent powerlessness over our fate. Mothers know this in their hearts. You worry about your children; you do your best for them; you try to teach them about life; you lie awake at night worrying about them; and you feel a deep ache in your heart when you realise how vulnerable and unsafe they are. This pain emerges from the fact that you are ultimately powerless to control the life and fate that awaits your children. This is a spiritual truth that must be understood at the deepest level if, as a mother, you are to find peace. It means giving of your best but respecting the fact that you are powerless to determine your children's lives. This requires serenity and the ability to know when to 'let go'.

You inhabit a life that is not your own. Your children do this also. In time, they too will die. The ability to embrace these truths is the essence of deep spirituality and the path to inner peace. To truly respect that your children are separate from you and are only temporarily in your care is your challenge and opportunity. Healthy psychological living means being able to admit that you are powerless over many things and then being able to inhabit that reality with a lightness of heart and a confidence of body.

Tragically, achieving power and control becomes, for some, the only way to deal with life. When that happens, the consequences for those close to them can be distressing and, at their worst, disastrous.

With regard to each of these life symptoms, they are not the whole truth. I am emphasising them, however, because they are the direct symptoms of mortality and, as such, are those experiences that we seek to avoid. As we shall see, how we accept and come to terms with our vulnerable condition becomes the gate through which we find a harmony and exuberance in life.

Meditation

Be aware of how your compulsion to control people or situations in your life can cause more stress for you than the problem itself. Think of an ongoing problem you have. Now think about the degree to which your efforts to control or guarantee a certain outcome may be inhibiting your ability to deal with this situation.

Think about what you need to let go of. Think about how you are trying to make everyone happy when that may not be within your control. Think about how hard you try to achieve a certain outcome when it may not be within your gift to make it happen.

Let go. Let go the compulsion to keep other people happy, to choreograph a happy outcome, to be vigilant about everyone else. Consider your own integrity and how you may need to give expression to your helplessness. Consider that you may need to make demands of others to take responsibility for themselves. Think about looking after yourself and doing what relieves you of the responsibility to solve everything.

INADEQUACY

Every person feels inadequate. It is inevitable, because each person is placed in a life where they have to discover and learn how to live. You are born into a life where you do not have a rule book, you cannot predict the future and you have only limited control over your immediate destiny. Life is bigger than you; and you have to respond if you are to survive. Inadequacy is inevitable. How you handle it reveals your humanity and courage.

Think of any negative personal trait you have and doubtless you will have spent a lot of energy trying to change it. You can be so hard on yourself. You reject yourself in many ways, unhappy as you are with so many things. At the same time, in moments of self-compassion, you will accept yourself as you are, even with all of your imperfections. We all want to be better than we are and, at the same time, accepting of how we are. We all struggle with this tension.

If you are a parent, you know that this tension is experienced by your children. You encourage your children by telling them they are good enough. You are so aware of how self-critical even a small child will be if they are not able to do what they want to do. For children, learning any skill displays that tension between what they *can* do and what they *want* to be able to do. Feeling inadequate seems to be part of the deal.

It's as if you are forever straining against your own limitations. You are always striving to be better than you are. You are often left with the discomfort that, without such effort, you will sink back into the mud. You strive to be a good partner, to achieve something. There is so much striving to be better, to recover and to improve. It all requires effort—an effort that is against a self that always threatens to pull you down. Our everyday speech reveals these simple truths: 'It's an uphill battle', 'I am putting the shoulder to the wheel', 'It's a struggle, but I am getting there'. This is a universal conflict and our universal condition.

The conflict lies in the fact that while you are stuck with yourself, you are always striving to be better. You are forever straining to pull your roots out of a soil that inhibits you. Because you walk, you want to run. Because you run, you want to fly. You are always wanting: wanting to learn, love, accumulate and procreate. You want to find security and love. You want to create. You are always wanting to be more than your body allows you to be. This is both the blessing and tragedy of your life.

You strive for confidence, self-esteem and happiness. You want to feel good and right about yourself. You want to be confident but you have no clear idea how exactly you might achieve this. There is not a person on earth who is not striving to feel truly good about themselves. Yet no one can do it perfectly. Disappointment with oneself is inevitable at least some of the time. We all swing between accepting and rejecting ourselves. We want to expand out with confident self-esteem; and we want to relax back into the grace of self-compassion.

Bookshelves are filled with unfulfilled promises of eternal happiness. So are pubs, corporate buildings, small businesses, churches and family homes. Nature's trick on us is to give us this inner sensitivity about the way things ought to be; but also to put us in a condition where we cannot ever quite achieve it.

You are two years old. You are in the church. You stand at your father's feet, looking at all the faces, colours and people. In sensing the lack of danger, you take some steps away and then look back at your father, smiling about your distance. He gestures at you to come back. You do. But you liked the feeling of exploration; and the next time you wander you go further down the aisle. You stand twenty feet away, looking back and looking forward. Even at two years old, you sense the excitement of being away and the comfort of knowing where your father is.

Now you go a little further, around the corner. Forgetting yourself, you are drawn to a coloured umbrella six feet away. You move tentatively towards it. Now out of sight of your father, you step closer. In the presence of simple colour, you have forgotten yourself. You go to pick up the umbrella and some stranger's hand prevents you from taking it away. You are startled; you step back and turn to find your father's face for reassurance. But he is not there.

You are suddenly lost! Panic surges through your tiny body. You move quickly towards where you came from but you cannot see your father. You cannot find his smile, his face. Tears well up in your little eyes as you turn the corner back towards the rear of the church. A small terror has invaded you; and people smile, remembering the innocent fear of being so little.

But your father finds you... His hand reaches out to you and the terror begins to flow away as he lifts you up into his arms. The tears are still there, the urge to cry. You look back towards the umbrella and the strange hand and all the unfamiliar faces. You point back towards the dark forest into which you stumbled. Your father understands and strokes your head. He smiles. You are back again. You stepped out into the world, feeling more adequate than you really were. You feel now you never want to go too far. But the colours of the world are vivid in your anxious heart...

And the next time you walk down this same aisle is twenty years later. You walk in the same direction again: towards the sun. You and your father walk side by side, arm in arm. At the top of the church, you turn to him. You see that the tears are now his. But there is no need for them; because now you know your own way home.

GUILT

At one of my recent workshops, I asked a group of about 150 people for a show of hands of how many suffered from guilt in their lives. Nearly everyone raised their hands! Simply by being human, we automatically experience some guilt and self-doubt. It is not that everyone is inadequate or doing things badly, but that everyone doubts themselves. You doubt yourself for all the reasons we have addressed so far. You ask: 'Why am I not better than I am?' You think that you *should* be better and, therefore, you feel bad at times. Guilt is universal.

Philosophers have suggested that because we are moral people, guilt is always present. Guilt is experienced as a feeling of having failed oneself or the other. It is a feeling of having done something wrong or taken the easy option. It is a fear that we have been cowardly or that we are not good enough. There is a morality associated with every decision you have to make, even small ones. You have this moral compass working all the time, measuring whether what you do takes you in the direction of what is good or what is bad. You judge yourself, feel inadequate and then reject yourself for your inadequacy!

In relationships, we often feel guilt if we feel we have wronged our partner—or if we do not get the kind of recognition we need. Guilt can be caused by over-responsibility for others, under-responsibility for oneself and the self-condemnation that ensues. Over- and under-responsibility can be fuelled by guilt. The *consequences* can then create even more guilt, resulting in a cycle of never feeling good enough—and feeling bad about that. When this happens, your guilt becomes chronic. When it becomes chronic, it can drive you towards complete self-rejection. This occurs when, on a daily basis, you condemn yourself for *everything*. This is deeply unsettling. Many of us are very familiar with this feeling of never-ending guilt. You can tolerate your guilt about specific things but it is very hard to tolerate the guilt that comes from being oneself. This is guilt about *who you are* because you imagine that you are never good enough. Your guilt can condemn you to despair about your destiny and competence.

Guilt illustrates that you are responsible for your own life and relationship; and that *you* have to answer for how you live your *own* life. The person to whom you are answerable is, of course, yourself. The pain of self-judgment is more distressing to the human person than the pain of stress and adversity. The internal monologue of self-judgment continues because we are moral beings, not self-serving ones.

When it comes to deep-seated guilt, you discover that another person cannot relieve you of it. To the degree that you need another person to find you 'not guilty' in life, you commit the very crime from which you seek relief. That is the crime of deferring your responsibility for yourself onto another. Every day you have a choice to make between a disposition of self-affirmation or one of self-rejection. The anxiety of guilt lies in the background as you feel that your relationship deteriorates because of your failure to carry the burden of your own responsibility.

The religious and superstitious qualities of guilt are interesting. While some guilt is rational and reasonable, most of the guilt we suffer from represents a form of magical thinking that we have failed others or ourselves. Many people suffer from a form of vague, free-floating guilt that has them feeling that they are constantly inadequate in how they work, parent, love or live. The thinking that you have failed or are failing is magical because it is somewhat removed from reality. It is built on a hangover from your childhood and from the secret conclusions you came to about yourself. These conclusions were based on subjective feelings, unreasonable expectations and your attempts to make sense of that which was beyond you. As an adult, you seem unable to shrug it off; it clings to you like a wet coat.

Meditation

Guilt is resolved by self-affirmation and self-acceptance. The relief from guilt can only come through your attitude to yourself. The antidote to guilt is a kind of moral self-affirmation, a courageous disposition that comes from your ability to affirm yourself from within. This happens when you can inhabit the full vulnerability and inadequacy of your humanity; when you can draw it into yourself; and you can declare, through your life and existence, that you are good. You know that you are good enough and, with humility, you know that you do not have to prove or justify yourself.

In every act of moral self-affirmation, you contribute to the fulfillment of your destiny. This is the extraordinary possibility that is accessible to every person, even a person who is confined to the smallest of prison cells. In every disposition, act or thought of moral self-affirmation, you are actually contributing to a destiny of freedom and acceptance. However, with chronic guilt, you can go against your own being. Guilt can be overpowering and it can mean that you lose both your destiny and your identity.

It takes courage to deal with guilt and to transform it. It takes courage to be responsible for yourself. Instead of judging and doubting your choices, and being anxious about whether you have done the right thing, you believe that you have always done the right thing, that you have always made the best choices possible. Instead of finding yourself guilty in the courtroom of your own mind, you issue a verdict of non-guilt. The jury of your own mind affirms your self, your existence and your humanity. You stand over your choices with pride. You claim your inherent morality and your potential. Your accusations of guilt get thrown out of court. The judge and the jury applaud your courage and they set you free. Do not be guilty for being human.

The problem with relationships is that they are ordinary. You are living with an average person with all the natural limitations. Within this limited relationship, you may seek some approval. You hope that the relationship will give you this. However, if this need for approval is too much, then you seek an *extraordinary* accreditation in the confines of an *ordinary* relationship. The controlling and abusive spouse needs approval as much as the needy spouse. The former needs to be approved by his partner's submission; the latter needs approval by submitting. Either way, it is an impossible task. So many people get trapped in a quiet despair, gradually letting go their sense of possibility, freedom and hope. While others—maybe with less ambition or maybe with less baggage—can find in their home a place of serenity, joy and fulfilment.

Chapter 3
The Consequences of Vulnerable Love

... my reason must allow
That I had wooed not as I should a creature made
of clay—
When the angel woos the clay he'd lose his wings
at the dawn of day.

Patrick Kavanagh

The consequences of vulnerable love are:

- Love and loss are inseparable.
- Love demands heroism.
- We are irresistibly religious.
- Life is symbolic.
- Life is magical and superstitious.

LOVE AND LOSS ARE INSEPARABLE

We went up with you into the attic to do some of that necessary 'clearing out'. Sitting among the dusty books and boxes, we were unsettled by the feeling that arises in discarding small items from one's past. Little things like medals, photographs, toys, old coats and gifts; the things that seem to capture small moments of history. Awkwardly, we considered the status of these mementos. We wondered what we would want to leave behind for those we love.

> *As we sat on the roof beams, you laughed, welled up with tears and shared the stories behind a hundred small 'forgettables'. We looked through boxes and boxes of things: your old school photographs; the clothes you wore as a child; the baby things belonging to your own children; the small toys; the old dresses; and the Christmas ornaments. That visit to the attic was a beautiful tribute to life. It was an honouring of death. It was a sanctification of love. It was sorrowful and wonderful. And it was made possible by the strange ghost of mortality, the brittle beauty of our transient lives. Sorrowful, beautiful, blissful, frightening, sacred, holy… life.*

*

I began to read Joseph Campbell's *The Power of Myth* on the early train to Dublin one morning. At around 5 a.m., I was exhilarated to come across the following passage:

> *The secret cause of all suffering is mortality itself, which is the prime condition of life. It cannot be denied if life is to be affirmed.*

I was thrilled—because the very reason I had bought the book was to see if Campbell would have anything to say about the relationship between mortality, love and suffering. And, of course, he did.

The vitality of love is a consequence of our unconscious awareness of death. Love and death cannot be separated. We love because we die. The acceptance of dying is the ultimate affirmation of living. And when we extend this to the life of relationships, we can conclude that the grateful acceptance of our partner's inadequacies is the affirmation of their life. In other words, to accept someone's inadequacies is to accept their mortality, their humanity. It is also to accept that it is not within our gift to eliminate these inadequacies and imperfections. For the same reason then, the grateful acceptance of our powerlessness and lack of control is, paradoxically, the ultimate affirmation and gratitude for our singular life.

When we abolish all that reminds us of death and our inherent vulnerability, we exile the possibilities of love. To erase vulnerability is to erase our humanity and to dehumanise the other. When this is taken to extremes in either domestic or social life, we attack and degrade others while becoming arrogant and tyrannical. Our flight from our vulnerability and frail mortality are our first steps towards righteousness in our world. As we shall see, the first seeds of human evil take root because they begin with the rejection of what it means to be human. We must find ways to incorporate and welcome the symptoms of vulnerable love. Failing to do so creates the climate within which the impulse to control, exert power and diminish the other emerges.

I am defining 'love' here in general terms, as the longing in our heart for more; the longing for more intimacy, belonging and life. It is the reaching out to other life with empathy and compassion. It can be invigorated by the passion of romance or sanctified by the devotion and care of a love that has aged with the years. I do not mean a sentimental love that stands on weak legs. I mean a love of intense passion or virtuous devotion. It is a love not just of another; it is *a love of a way of being* and a love of a life of virtue and passion. It is a love that is a reflex of sorrow, of the fragile beauty of our precarious existence expressed uniquely in the body of the beloved. It begins with the acceptance of the symptoms laid out in Chapter 2: woundedness, vulnerability, anxiety, insignificance, helplessness, inadequacy and guilt.

When our intimate relationships serve to deny our mortally vulnerable and wounded life, we construct mechanisms to maximise our sense of power and control. Violence and abuse are the extreme consequence of this; blaming and rejection are the more average variants. But just as flight from one's mortality and apparent insignificance creates the climate for control, abuse, violence and evil, so too the embracing of one's mortality and all its derivatives creates the potential and impulse for human love.

The courageous life braids the two strands of life and death together into an integrated whole. A vital and full life combines both death and life—and all of their associated emotions, reflexes and impulses. The full life weaves both strands together into a whole: sorrow is braided with joy; helplessness is braided with hope; anxiety is braided with acceptance.

One of the functions of art, poetry, drama, music and literature is to keep this wound open for us. Art enables us to get close to the piercingly beautiful fragility of life, against the background of a daily life that avoids this. Works of art bring a heroic sense of dignity and character to this heart-breaking, absurd, majestic, miraculously created, sorrowful reality we all seek to be worthy of. As the old prayer beseeches: 'God, grant that I may be worthy of my suffering.'

This, in fact, is why we go to the movies. To expose ourselves to emotions and situations that remind us of something else within us that is other than our ordinary life. Whether it is through drama, comedy, action, horror or suspense, you want to be disturbed from the complacency of your life. You want to be reminded in an emotional way that there is something else within you; and that there is something outside of you that can give you a better experience of being alive.

The desire to open up to another person, to share the mystery and fear of life is the human quality of love. Love is the burning point of life. And because much of *life* is passionate suffering as well as delightful participation, so too is *love*. The deeper one's love, the greater the grief that love bears. Love itself is the ache of being truly alive.

*

Our subconscious awareness of mortality, tragedy, vulnerability, powerlessness, inadequacy and guilt is also central to the concerns of couples. This might not seem to be the case because in your relationships you appear to be worried and upset about everything *but* these things. However, the things you seem to get angry and upset about are just the symptoms. The dance of intimacy is not just about offering a reassuring love; it is about coping with emotional defencelessness. Mortality makes love necessary.

You might find yourself saying: 'No, that's not really the case. Death is at the back, not the front, of my concerns in life!' This happens because we cannot get our head around death at all. It is such an enormous, ever-present reality that we are unable to see it. We are like the baby fish that asks the mother fish: 'What is the sea?' We ask: 'What is death?' It becomes almost impossible to see the sea in which we swim. It becomes impossible for us to appreciate *how this permeates every single action we take in our everyday lives.*

One of the great benefits of the practice of prayerful meditation is that we awaken ourselves to the vitality of our physical existence. We notice: the pulse in our veins; the rise and fall of our lungs and breath; the will and the life force that actually keep us alive; the life that loves and lives us.

The sheer mystery, miracle and wonder of this delightful, precarious life are too much to bear when laced with the uncertainty that we equally deal with. We need the courage to stay close to this reality, not to shrink away from it. We have a spirit that can lift with a light-hearted joy and a soul that can move us towards a courageous sorrow.

I am convinced of the necessity of this exploration to fill out and expand many of our approaches to intimacy, marital therapy, domestic violence and all of life's dilemmas. Stay with me and help me. Knowing that you too are interested in the quest will sustain me.

LOVE DEMANDS HEROISM

Are you a coward or a hero? This may seem like a childish question but within it lays the essential challenge of life and relationships. Religion, philosophy, literature, art and psychology all tell you one thing: life demands a heroic response from you. It demands courage.

Your call to heroism is evident in everyday life. Look at how you have had to strive, overcome, succeed and master life. Though you may feel you are a failure because of broken relationships, unfulfilled dreams and unending self-doubt, the truth is that even in the midst of these struggles you have been trying your best. Though almost defeated at times, you have persisted. You have tried. And herein is your heroism. It does not lie in your success but in your *efforts*. Every day you exert some effort to be equal to your life. Such heroic defiance is a courage that embraces all of life. If we are without courage and we do not face death, we *fight against life* and against other people. We battle against vulnerability and powerlessness.

What is a hero? When you look at movies or read great literature, what characteristic defines a true hero? The characteristic of the hero in great mythology and drama is a person who faces their own death with courage. This is the ultimate trait of the hero: an ability to accept one's fate with courage while holding onto oneself. Think about every hero you've seen in an inspiring movie and you will see that this is the defining characteristic. They remain true to themselves while accepting their fate.

Now, while heroes in everyday life may not face their literal death, they do face into its derivatives: loss, helplessness, tragedy and vulnerability. Therefore, in everyday life, the true hero is the person who faces their own vulnerability with courage and integrity. True heroism is measured by how you face your failures and defeats more than your successes. It involves how you surrender an argument, make an apology and step back from righteousness to humility—or from cowardice to integrity. It is how you rise to the occasion of life.

Your life is heroic because the things that you have to deal with are often overwhelming, while the resources you have at your disposal are paltry by comparison. However, while you are bound by the frailty of your mind and body, you are also blessed with imagination, freedom and the ability to live a symbolic life.

Heroism in Intimacy

Because life asks for a heroic response I can now add that intimate relationships demand a heroic response from you. The intimate relationship (be it between: a parent and child; lovers; friends; or siblings) is the vessel within which all of life's greatest spiritual struggles are played out and potentially resolved. The heroic in intimate life is the effort to resolve life's most profound challenges at the level of family relationships. Your intimate life demands this heroic response.

Why does intimate love demand a heroic response? Because life asks you to live with helplessness and vulnerability and to inhabit a life over which you do not have ultimate control. You go where it takes you.

In daily life, you practise heroism. Your life has purpose, routines and responsibilities. In the ordinariness of everyday life, you are establishing a sense of meaning and self-worth. A simple task such as bringing your children to school in the mornings can have a meaning that gives your life a noble and heroic purpose. Of itself, it may be nothing; but in the context of the 'wound of life' it can be an act of *symbolic living*. In fact, almost all of your daily actions have a higher meaning and purpose that lay beyond their mundane appearance.

We develop plain, earthy heroism every day. Think of the father who works nights at the plant for his family or the mother who awakens twice a night for her small child. Every person walks a path of private meaning and heroism. Everyone seeks to earn a feeling of worth, meaning and significance.

The beauty of imagination is that you can rise up out of the limits of yourself and give meaning to everyday acts. Things can be more than they are. We all have this wonderful ability to defy the potential anonymity of life. We did this when we were six years old and we still do it now!

If you are committed to heroic love, you are at home in the struggles of life. You know how to greet a friend at a funeral. You know what to say to a small child who has been hurt. You know how to act when a loved one rejects you. You know what to do when death visits your door. You know all of these things because you have already lived through them in the intimate details of your life. When you are open to the wound of life, you are being asked by life to face your own death with courage in small, everyday ways. You can draw inspiration from the human stories of heroic living because you know that you face little deaths every day. You know intuitively what real courage entails.

I came to see and know real courage when I watched my father's battle with terminal cancer.

> *My dear father*
> *sits up in bed, at death's door,*
> *and still butters his brown bread,*
> *smears jam purposefully to the edges,*
> *heroically defying, to the last second,*
> *nature's indifference.*

My father's dignity and courage remained utterly intact in the face of death. He was defiant, with a heroism that took my breath away. Socrates could not have done it better.

> *My father,*
> *with the snake of cancer coiled around him,*
> *turned in his bed to compliment his grandchildren:*
> *Brendan's new shoes,*
> *Christine's beautiful hair,*
> *Joseph's height for his age.*
> *With death closing in on his stuttering life,*
> *he built up their significance.*
> *He passed what he had left of his strength onto their innocent*
>   *shoulders.*
> *Though dying, he thanked his grandchildren for the honour*
> *of their visit.*

These are the acts of a spiritual being, a soul and heart that defies the body. There was no turning in to the wall; just wakeful and courageous waiting. That takes character.

Meditation

What is at stake for you in a marital fight?

When you are hurt by your spouse, it can feel like it threatens your significance. This hurt can be a dent in your sense of self value. When your partner shoves you off your hero path (by suggesting that you are a bad parent, for example) then something in you feels threatened—perhaps even violated. There is really nothing more devastating than to feel that your sense of significance is dismissed or taken away from you.

How often have you said: 'I am doing the best that I can'? Try to be aware of how it is a summary of your heroic struggle in life. You do your best to overcome obstacles. In doing so, you have a small heroic purpose. When this is taken from you or threatened, something in you rises up to protect that. You protect the unseen meaning that lies behind your effort, which you believe is threatened and at risk. This is the only way one can understand the ferocious intensity expressed and displayed by you when slights, offences or insults occur. You make objectively trivial issues important because they symbolise your heroic efforts.

You may cling intensely to your arguments because they seem to prove your importance. They are your security blankets. Your arguments, defences, irrationalities and angry outbursts reveal how tentative your inner hold is on yourself.

What undoes you may be no more than a smart comment by your partner, an unintentional put-down or a dismissive attitude. But what it does is attack your precarious sense of yourself. It makes you ask: 'What is the point of trying?' This, in truth, is the struggle for a heroic life.

The tragedy in relationships is that this is rarely seen and rarely admitted. It is so difficult for you to admit that you hold onto your irrational arguments because they keep you afloat. It is difficult to admit that you need to be right because if you are not, it will feel like your very purpose is called into question.

However, there are better ways to find your integrity and significance than through righteousness! Instead of fighting over the issue, try to reveal to your beloved what is at stake for you. Explain why you are irrational and why your response seems over the top. Expose the real concerns: your heroic purpose in life and what is at stake for you. Your point of view is often your symbol of your status in the world. As a flag is to a nation, a point of view is to a person. Burn them at your peril: they mean more than they say.

WE ARE IRRESISTIBLY RELIGIOUS

We are by necessity driven by religious impulses to find some meaning and heroic purpose in life. By 'religious' I am not referring to formal institutional religion, but to the ancient and most primitive of impulses in humanity to find symbolic ways of coping with our precarious situation and mortality. By 'religion' I mean: coming to terms with the vast unknown; giving expression to existential emotion; and finding symbolic gods through which one resolves the unanswered questions of humanity. These essential impulses contribute to the creative process, formal religion, philosophy and the arts. In a much less formal way, these impulses influence how each person choreographs, creates and acts out their own life in behaviours, rituals, symbols and imagination. 'Religious impulse' is my preferred term because I want to highlight how deep-rooted, intense and far-reaching these impulses can be; and how powerful these urges are when expressed within the confines of a committed intimate relationship. In fact, it is my belief that it is within the family home that humanity reveals its true nature. From the intense triad of mother, father and child are revealed the ultimate truths about humanity.

Our behaviour in emotionally committed relationships is determined less by our personal psychology and more by these primitive religious impulses that determine the intensity and direction of our actions. These impulses are common to every single person and have been characteristic of humankind for thousands of years. Religious responses become the source of the person's creative, adaptive meaning-making. More important, they become the organising principle for personal behaviour that is geared towards motivation, survival and inspiration.

Each person builds their life around their rituals, attitudes, beliefs and symbols. In fact, these become the equivalent of a private religion. We are guided not by rigid logic or our personal scientific research but by beliefs and attitudes from our earliest years—beliefs that have developed into a kind of private mythology. This is what we draw on when confronted with the challenges of life and our wounded mortality.

We act out this unconscious religion in the three areas of behaviour, beliefs and emotion. We each develop everyday routines, beliefs, attitudes, compulsions, obsessions and fears. We have a host of small, idiosyncratic ways of living; and they function to help us survive, find meaning and deal with mortality. Although we claim to be driven by reason, we are really motivated by security symbols, such as the behaviour of another person or measures of our social status.

The problems that affect our behaviour, thoughts and emotions in intimate relationships are never really problems of logic or reason. They are problems caused by our struggle with the conditions of life. The quality of marriage is determined by our solutions to problems that arise from the conditions of life and existence. Each of us is driven by very definite religious impulses that seek to address and overcome the human condition. Because of this, our behaviour during interpersonal conflict is rarely rational and always emotionally disproportionate. This is because our response to perceived threat is always emotive and symbolic, rather than rational and literal. Our defensive reactions to our partner make sense when we realise what is really going on.

You must see your partner not as someone influenced by 'unreasonable attitudes' or a 'screwed-up family', but as someone who deals in the currency of symbols of vulnerability, woundedness, helplessness, inadequacy and anxiety. Their arguments with you have nothing to do with the issue itself but with what it *symbolises*.

We must learn to appreciate that the struggle to find safety and significance in life and in relationships is a religious kind of struggle. Once we see this, we get a dramatic sense of what is really at stake for couples embroiled in the bitterness of marital conflict. We can come closer to understanding the spouse who is always on the defensive or the spouse who terrorises their family.

You can use the safety of a committed relationship as your measure of your success as a person. The beloved can become the high ideal through which you can seek to fulfil your life. Your urge to overcome the confines of your mortal life can be brought down to earth and fixed in your partner. Your drive to find meaning, significance and passion in life is condensed into intimate love. As we have seen, this can be transformational and free—or reductive and controlling. If you can sense the transcendent element of the heroic impulse (the impulse to be somebody of significance), you can imagine how precarious and convulsed it can become if it is dependent on the response and co-operation of another person. In other words, when your self-esteem becomes too tied up with your partner's moods and reactions to you, the validity of your very existence is at risk. Therefore, you can become distraught.

*

Although we take pride in our technological achievements, accumulation of wealth and intelligence, the human brain has changed very little over the past 100,000 years. We operate, in large part, under the influence of the same brain as Homo sapiens who walked the plains of Africa at that time. What motivates and sustains us is not much different now than it was then.

Consider, for example, your daily habits. Your daily routine is repeated by you not for entirely logical reasons but for reasons related to your need to do things that ensure your safety, security, status, significance and certainty in a world and life that is inherently uncertain. You shower in the morning, groom yourself, put on clothes, drive to work, obey the traffic lights, get to work, go through your duties, have lunch, etc. All of us engage in a series of rituals that are just as much about *soothing our mortal anxiety* as they are about serving practical, everyday functions. Every person has a unique set of behaviours, priorities, beliefs, feelings and assumptions about the world. These have not been created by their logical brain but by their existential preferences for self-soothing.

Most of us keep these fantasies, personal myths, illusions, beliefs and behaviours hidden from the world. This is because we know, subconsciously, that they reveal the real truth about ourselves. We disguise them in everyday arguments and convictions that try to prove that we are reasonable and sensible. Yet we cling to our arguments and rituals like our lives depend on them. This is because *they do*. Our arguments, beliefs and righteousness are the life-rafts we cling to in the chaotic sea of existence. This is why people everywhere have such difficulty in admitting they are wrong. They will argue defensively even the most irrational of beliefs.

We cling to our beliefs about even the most trifling of matters because our beliefs cover up our anxieties about our status, power and worthiness. We hold tight to our little beliefs and attitudes because of our dread of rejection, belittlement and the humiliation of being revealed as the anxiously insecure creatures that we really are. Yet, in this process we conceal not only our terror but also our vulnerable *beauty*.

Our beliefs become our protection against feelings of meaninglessness and helplessness. Most people I have worked with in couples therapy hold onto attitudes and beliefs that are fundamentalist in character. I see men and women clinging tightly to ways of being, with a ferocity that has nothing to do with logic or reason. It has everything to do with a hidden religious terror of a consequence they have never been able to look at, i.e. death and the conditions of life. We each fear a consequence in life that lurks in the darkened corner of our psyche like a hooded figure that threatens some unspeakable horror. We cling with fundamentalist fervour to our ways of behaving, thinking or feeling. Of course, the horrors of the hooded figure are only imagined. It is a vague dream from childhood, a shadow that, when it walks into the light, is nothing more than the face of life. This hooded figure, when it is welcomed at the table of your life, can become your guardian angel. We imagine that vulnerability is dangerous, so we turn it into a dark figure in our dreams. We think that righteousness protects us. Really, the opposite is true.

Partners stand and rage at each other, fighting to the death over flimsy principles and convictions. We all do this. Fearfully and righteously, we hold tight to our illusions about the world and ourselves. At times, the strength of our hold is like the vice-grip of a survivor clinging to a sinking raft. Our beliefs and behaviours are like national flags or symbols that we hold onto for dear life. They reveal our need for a security beyond what we truly have. Our beliefs and arguments can become a fortress. The cost of breaking them down is at the price of one's existential significance. It is for this reason that couples going through divorce are capable of destroying everything around them, even their children, in the service of their righteousness. This is a religious disposition to life.

The battle or war becomes religious and, in doing so, is frequently done to the death, towards the annihilation of the other. The other's arguments are taken as hostage. The other becomes a conquest. Victory over the other becomes essential for basic and primitively religious reasons.

People sometimes choose *psychic suicide* over the survival of the other. For these reasons, violence and abuse are endemic in domestic life. In couples therapy we witness sadism, cruelty, control, domination, murder, suicide and extreme brutality. Despite the beliefs of both popular and professional psychology, these are rarely acts driven by just psychological motives. They are deeply religious, in the pagan sense of the word.

Most societies create rituals for dealing with enemies who threaten their beliefs, status or security. Each person in a relationship does the same thing. We sacrifice, reject, attack, ignore or banish the enemy that is our partner. Our beliefs and behaviours serve the purpose of securing our private redemption, salvation, victory, forgiveness, blessing or atonement. We make them our sacrifice, our offering to our god, i.e. to ourselves.

Therefore, when I work with couples, I am attuned to the necessity of creating a sanctuary, a place where the sacred beliefs of each person are held and examined with honour and respect. Unless one appreciates how primordial, primitive and religious are the attitudes and behaviours of a couple, one can miss the point and be taken aback by the forces unleashed when one fails to honour these attitudes.

Hidden from the world, your secret inner life and its associated collection of idiosyncratic convictions and dispositions are like rituals, prayers, spells, magic omens and affirmations. They serve to protect you, make you feel safe and reassure you of your worthiness. With them, you act out a primitive, ritualised dance that gives a foothold in the invisible anxiety and love of life.

The behaviour of couples in emotionally committed relationships is irrational when viewed through the lens of logic or psychology; but it is consistent and meaningful when viewed through the lens of anthropology or theology. Based on this new understanding of marriage and intimacy, we will go on to prescribe radically new solutions to common dilemmas experienced in relationships.

As a consequence of our innately religious and emotional disposition in life, our interior world has a magical quality. Our attempts to deal with life draw on beliefs that are sometimes more fanciful than real.

LIFE IS SYMBOLIC

Symbolic living is an essential part of our existence. This is evident in different cultures, social customs and in individual behaviour. Our medals, cups, photo albums, degrees, rings, cars, homes and clothes are all symbols that we use to define our place and status in life. The truth is that, through these things, we seek some form of ritualised symbolic status. Our symbols are actually symbols of some form of victory in life—things that suggest that we can and do rise above our ordinary mortality. The real meaning of all of these things is that, in acquiring and admiring our symbols, we actually get a little taste of what it would be like to be free of mortality. We taste immortality. We achieve a victory over mortal weakness. In these moments of success, we forget ourselves a little. We feel like someone special.

The little boy who runs towards the touchline after scoring a penalty and imagines he has won the World Cup rehearses something about life. He shows his desire to have a feeling of status, victory and competence. He spits out the bad taste of human frailty and swallows the symbolic experience of his status, success and significance. It is actually wonderful to behold when you appreciate what it really means.

In everyday life, the symbols of your status, significance, worthiness and immortality are not literally found in medals, cups and degrees; but they are found in any currency that seems to enhance your self-value. The measure of your worth can be made up of a host of things which appear to be trivial, but which are given enormous symbolic weight. They can include: the tone of voice with which your partner speaks to you in the morning; the tidiness of the kitchen after the night before; the willingness of your children to do what you tell them; the degree to which you are getting through your 'to do' list; whether or not your boss seems to be happy; the quality of your hair; your comfort in your clothes; your feeling of competence as a partner; signs of affection that are shown to you; your mother's approval… The list is endless. The point to be emphasised is that all of us have a core list of behaviours which are given enormous weight in symbolising our worth and value as a person.

Just look at your spouse or partner. Notice how they have their own rituals, i.e. things that have to happen in order for them to feel secure and safe in the world. Notice how they can become very upset by some small irregularity or unexpected event. In such ways, they cling to obsessive little certainties or codes. 'Who deleted that match from the TV recorder?' he bellows. This may be how he measures and proves his status in the home.

Unfortunately, we all have misguided ways of showing our status in life. Little things become the symbols and transitional objects of security: 'I may feel insecure and powerless in my life but at least I have all my DIY tools stacked neatly away; I know exactly where each one is.' This is typical of a hidden, life-soothing belief.

Each of us finds symbols of our significance and security that actually serve a spiritual function. A stay-at-home mother might keep her kitchen spotlessly clean so that she can stand back and experience delight in her achievement: 'Yes, I am somebody.' For somebody else, it could be: their 'to do' list; the number of texts they get; the stylish car they drive; the quality of their clothing; the success of their children, etc. We all have little invisible ways in which we measure our status and achievement. They are utterly trivial in themselves but, to us, they are how we find some sense of significance in life. They are rituals and signs that we are somebody. They are our medals.

I cannot overstate the fact that the value we give these things is entirely symbolic and arbitrary. When things are given this symbolic value, they assume an exaggerated importance in our everyday life to such a degree that they can cause us great distress. For example, winning an argument with your husband, getting your way or having your view of things approved can become literal symbols of your worth, status and significance. So much so that if these things do not happen as you expect, you find yourself reacting with a desperate intensity. Notice how often you may find yourself upset during an argument only to forget completely at a later time what the argument was actually about. All you know is that you were fighting for something that seemed to mean something to you—but you don't really know what it was. You were, in truth, fighting about symbols!

So the repetitive fight you have with your partner often has nothing to do with the content of your disagreements. It is often a lot more to do with perceived slights to your status and significance.

We need to have our significance, worth and status re-affirmed in life because we know that the brutal truth about life is that it does not guarantee any of these things. In fact, because of death, dying and the tragic possibility in living, we are forever seeking to rise above our animal and ordinary mortality. Conflict and abuse in everyday marital life is the disguised struggle against one's mortal inadequacy and the other's mortal flaws.

Because we are powerless over our ultimate fate, we have an ongoing, fear-driven tendency to become powerful over whomever or whatever is closest to us. And when our ultimate vulnerability and impotence is revealed by the very people we think will conceal this from us, we often respond with such overwhelming aggression or intensity that our true motives are revealed.

When we appreciate that much of the currency in everyday marital and family life is symbolic, we begin to see the potential for intimate relationships to become vehicles through which people expand their self-importance in symbolic rituals.

We are symbolic people. We are all behaving religiously, superstitiously and irrationally. We express our most basic desires, needs and thoughts through symbolic, physical behaviour and not through literal or rational declarations. In fact, it is not possible for us to be totally literal about anything. Everything we say and do is a symbolic external expression of an inner reality. Intimate human behaviour at its most noble is always symbolic, religious and imaginative.

We are a body *and* a mind. Our thoughts and decisions do not guide us completely. This is the desperate myth of modern man. Our acts and decisions are *shaped by our bodies* in fundamentally symbolic and profound ways.

Symbols

When you are dealing in symbols, you are dealing with very powerful forces and representations. People surrender themselves to all sorts of symbols: the wedding ring, the flag, the religion or the ideology. As we have seen throughout history, the force of these symbols can be used for great good or horrendous evil.

People often fight to the death over something small. A husband batters his wife to death because of some perceived resistance to his demands. We cannot understand the behaviour and emotions of couples unless we understand them as being symbolic. And we cannot understand what they symbolise unless we see ourselves in the full-round of our being and existence. We convert the most primitive of our human anxieties into symbolic problems or phobias and then seek to address them there. Your worth in life and your sense of security on this planet can, for example, be measured by the degree to which your partner treats your points of view with respect. If they seem to disregard or dismiss your response, it can feel as painful as if you had the feet cut from under you.

It is for these reasons that one of the most common complaints expressed by couples in real distress is simply this: 'He/she does not take me seriously.' Our need to have our requests, needs and arguments treated with respect cuts to the core of our need to experience some form of symbolic status in our ordinary and seemingly unremarkable lives.

LIFE IS MAGICAL AND SUPERSTITIOUS

The superstitious basis of so many of our everyday beliefs is more pervasive than any folklore about black cats, ladders, broken mirrors or magpies. What I want to illustrate here is something that might be quite surprising: we are extremely superstitious in our own private psychological life. We all have secret mental superstitions and rituals that we use all the time to soothe our inner anxieties. Most of our obsessive ways of thinking and compulsive ways of doing things have a basis in superstition.

A superstition is the irrational belief that future events can be influenced by specific, unrelated behaviours or occurrences. The earliest superstitions were created as a way to deal with the fear of the unknown. Superstitions are a way of attempting to regain control over events in one's life. Most of them are harmless and can be helpful in encouraging people to cope with life. However, attributing results to an unrelated cause can be somewhat dubious.

The term 'superstition' refers to the remains of behaviours and beliefs that continue in our life long after they have served their usefulness. However, we still believe that these behaviours or patterns will work. Many of our personal beliefs, habits and behaviours are actually relics from our childhood that we still cling to, as a child clings to its blanket. Many of our interpersonal habits represent an outmoded way of behaving that we want to *believe* is still effective—

despite evidence to the contrary. We are superstitious without even knowing it. We continue to believe things (about ourselves, others and life) that are exactly like normal superstitions. We usually cannot bring ourselves to admit to this. In fact, the suggestion may seem preposterous to many.

Our superstitious beliefs and behaviours originated during our earliest years as a child. Faced with natural anxieties and fears, as well as the unpredictability of life, we created an understandable belief that these things could be influenced by our behaviour. This is the origin of obsessive habits, over-thinking, guilt, self-doubt, etc. Our earliest superstitions, thoughts and reactions were created by us as children in order to deal with the unknown. We created lots of ways that gave us a feeling that we controlled the unknown and the unpredictable. 'If I keep my feelings to myself then Dad won't get mad,' says the little boy who thinks his behaviour is the cause of his father's aggression. Later in life, the boy grows up to be a man who also believes that expressing his feelings will result in bad things. Most of us grow up with a need for approval: 'If I please Mam, then she will approve of me.' We can only feel good about ourselves when we get this approval.

Superstitious behaviours and beliefs were our innocent childhood ways of attempting to regain control over little and big events in life, particularly at times when we felt helpless. The greater the level of trauma we experienced, the more likely we had to create somewhat magical behaviours and beliefs in order to cope. Children of traumatic families have to create superstitious ways of coping; this is what psychologists call *magical thinking*. People who survived the concentration camps found innocent, soothing rituals and beliefs to help them survive. This is perfectly normal. In fact, it is wonderful.

However, it is inaccurate to claim that these beliefs and behaviours in life are rational, logical and factual. Most of our current adult behaviour has developed as a combination of the magical thinking of a child, superimposed with the reasoning of an adult. This results in our idiosyncratic ways of behaving. (I am sure that those close to you, those who know you best, can testify to many idiosyncratic, imaginative peculiarities in your thinking and behaviour.)

Our superstitious beliefs, behaviours, habits and rituals are sometimes born from casual coincidence. For example, if you found that when you kept your bedroom lights on it appeared to soothe your anxiety, then you may have begun to associate warm lighting with safety. If you discovered as a child that once you concentrated obsessively on homework your parents loved you more, then you are likely to grow up with compulsive habits that you believe are essential. As a child, maybe you had to run home from school in order to ensure that your mother had not passed out from alcohol consumption. If this was so, you may then have begun to magically associate your vigilance about others with her safety. Later in life, you may turn out to be an over-protective parent, who worries about everybody because worry was what gave you a feeling of control.

The truth is that there is a superstitious basis for a huge amount of our adult habits, traits and ideas because they were formed originally out of the magical thinking of a child.

*

As a child, you developed strategies for keeping your self-esteem intact in the face of all the little challenges of life. So that you could cope with the uncertainties of life, you developed micro-beliefs, behaviours and rituals that helped you create some certainty in this unpredictable world. As a baby, you learned: to cry or not; to suck on your soother or not; to demand food or not; to be active or passive; to wait or to go ahead; to accommodate or demand; to introvert or extrovert; and to oppose or conform. These patterns became your unique coping style. This was based on beliefs that if you did X, then Y was more likely to happen. You began to believe, like every little child, that what you did controlled the world. If you were good, then your parents would not be angry. If you accommodated, you would get what you need. If you were vigilant, maybe your Dad would not get drunk. If you rocked yourself to sleep, maybe the shouting downstairs would stop. If you tidied your room, you'd get praise. If you counted sheep going to sleep, maybe Mam would come home. If you daydreamed, the anxiousness stopped. These were your necessary superstitions.

As you grew, these beliefs, responses and expectations developed into a coping system. This coping system became an automatic way for you to deal with reality. It became a tool-kit that worked to some degree; but because it was limited, every life problem became the nail to the hammer of your coping style. Your coping style was an armour that both protected you *and* kept you prisoner.

You had *faith* in your way of coping. You had faith in your invisible system because it gave you some feeling of power and influence. Your assumptions became more certain and began to grow into the sensation that *what you did* controlled your world. 'If I am bad, Dad will hurt me. If I am good, I will be praised.' Your world view became your *gospel*.

As an adult, you do hundreds of strange, idiosyncratic things that reveal your undisclosed beliefs. You spend hours taking care of your hair because you have linked it to your self-status. You anxiously rehearse what you will say when you meet someone important to you. You get offended when a waiter does not do what you expect. You rise up in anger because one of your children does something incorrectly. You bathe in private, obsessing about your body parts. You have unique and peculiar ways of dealing with life's anxieties.

*

Our superstitions are unconscious. We invariably deny that they exist at all. But this denial would be wrong. We are far more irrational, emotional and influenced by outmoded habits and beliefs than we ever care to admit. We believe that life is controlled and made safer by our idiosyncratic responses. It is not unusual that in family life others challenge our behaviour and attitudes; even though we defend our positions, we know deep down that we hold onto them not because we are certain we are right but because if we did not we would be exposed for what we are. We anxiously hold tight to our superstitious beliefs in a vulnerable world.

The truth is that we are all superstitious beyond credibility. Just watch the idiosyncratic way that anyone does anything. Notice the meaning people give to how they sit in a restaurant, how they care for their garden or how they choose their clothing. We live in a world of magical thinking.

The best approach is to always admit that you are uncertain about your beliefs. Fundamentalism, which is the belief in one's own certainty, is terribly destructive in family and social life. Admit that the belief you have and the importance you attribute to it stands on at least one wobbly leg!

*

On planet earth you are a castaway, without power over fate, without ultimate significance, and largely helpless. Yet you somehow transcend all of this and achieve some heroic purpose. Even though I do not know you, I know that your personal story is inevitably inspiring in ways you have not yet acknowledged. How you have imbued your ordinary life with extraordinary purpose and themes has been quite *magical*. It is what makes your story *ordinarily magnificent*. This is how you have been able to rise above the ordinary. The initial shoots of human religion, philosophy, spirituality, imagination, magical thinking, poetry, art and creativity have broken through the soil of your life.

Imaginative feeling and magical thinking are what we do. We are always in a state of half-dreaming. The spells, omens, wishes, longings and ancient memories of life swirl around us all the time. Our most ordinary of routines can have a magical quality. Poetry, theatre, movies and dramatic art all reveal this to us.

*

I hope that I have shown that, in order to deal with the uncertainty and mystery of life, with its inherent suffering and tragedy, you actually draw from a private mythology that directs what you should do. From an early age, you develop what you might call your own private religion about why things happen, the kind of person you are and the consequences of certain behaviour. This private mythology was developed and refined over many years as a consequence of your unique development. Later in life, you superimposed an adult logic on top of this to make your beliefs seem reasonable. But the truth is that the assumptions you made (and still make) about life were not built around reason or logic but around the scaffolding of beliefs you formed in the earliest days of your attachments and life experiences. The structure of these beliefs about people still holds up today.

It may sound strange to suggest that we have our own private mythology or even private unique religion; but it is irrefutable. This mythology that guides us through life can be a source of liberation or imprisonment.

Unknown to yourself, you have been creating your own mythologies about your life, just as primitive man did around the fire and on cave walls. Each person has the equivalent of a private religion or spirituality that actually choreographs their behaviour through the emotional dramas of family or work life. The thing is that most people are not aware of this. When they become aware of it, they deny it vehemently and claim that their behaviour is based on reason and logic.

The truth is that each person's view of others is, by and large, subjective and shaped by a collection of idiosyncratic beliefs, rituals and attitudes that are an expression of a belief system that is largely emotionally-driven and more like a private mythology or religion than a logically developed way of life. Research in social psychology continually shows that our firmly held beliefs really stand on sand.

Every day, you ritualise your life and sacrifice yourself or others so that you can create control and order in an emotional world. Beneath the modern exterior of your everyday life, behind the curtains of your poise and composure, you are no different from a primitive woman repeating chants and rituals in order to come to terms with life. We all wish to soothe ourselves in the face of life's terror and dance in the aftermath of its joy.

Of this I am certain: you do what you do, you feel what you feel and you believe what you believe because you have a set of attitudes about yourself and you act out a set of rituals that affirm and consolidate an identity that you created on the anvil of your imagination. In truth, you are what you have imagined yourself to be.

Perhaps you are approaching the second half of life now; and you have discovered that your world view is based on a subjective (rather than objective) interpretation of life. Yet, you remain devoted to it. You argue some of your points vehemently, even though you know they are weak. You know no other way and still, like a child, you are terrified that if you let go of the certainty of your beliefs, you have nothing. You are left helpless, an open target for everyone. And so you hold on.

In your world, you believe that you are somebody, that the world is manageable, that there is a reason for your life and that you have a justification for your actions. Yet you long for freedom from your private superstitions and religiously-held world view. You know it is limited. You want to *break the spell of the magical trance* that holds you. At times, I am sure, you even get tired of being yourself.

Chapter 4
Denying Love

LOVE EXPOSES YOU

All was well until you entered into a relationship, wasn't it? You got together with someone who seemed to promise that they would secure your sense of reality and confirm the faith you had in yourself and in your superstitions. But it didn't work out that way, did it? You ended up with someone who could see through you; someone who held up a mirror to you. You ended up with someone who could: easily dismantle your armour; reveal your magical and irrational thinking; and expose you to uncertainty (if not terror) that you thought was long since defeated by your powers.

If you are to live an unexamined life, you are assured of remaining a prisoner. The prison of your superstitions is built to deny one terrifying reality: your ordinary helplessness and inadequacy. Self-awareness includes the awareness that you are a self-conscious *animal* and not the god or angel or other important being that you so much want to be.

In a strange way, your personality (your coping style) creates a kind of illusion about your own powers. It creates a necessary deception about the nature of reality. You develop a kind of pretence that you are invulnerable.

However, in the back of your mind a voice whispers another possible truth: that your life may not be more than a meaningless event in the drama of flesh and bones that we call evolution. Perhaps the Creator does not care about your destiny. Because of this truth, a truth that has haunted humanity since the dawn of self-awareness, humanity has created magic, imagination, transcendence, art, literature, world religions, cultural myths, flags, anthems and civilisation. These make up a magical, superstitious, religious way of being. Your own life mirrors this exact process.

Religion has less to do with God and more to do with creating a way to transcend ourselves, to make meaning and purpose, to find immortality in this life. It is necessary illusion. But when we lose a sense of humility, when we elevate our superstitions into facts, when we turn our way of looking at the world into our own fundamentalist religion, when we consider the magical in our life to be scientific, and when we consider our illusions to be reality, we lose touch with our most essential humanity. We lose touch with our imaginative way of responding to our vulnerability.

*

The strange thing about believing in one's superstitions, religions and deceptions about oneself and the world, is that it works to the degree that it avoids the inherent conflict of life itself. It helps you to avoid the anxiety, uncertainty and precariousness that is inherent to a full-blown heroic exposure to life. This approach to life has an unanticipated outcome. To the degree that you rely on your superstitions and magical beliefs and you develop a certainty about yourself (and others), you do not need to rely on anything outside of yourself. You no longer need spirituality. You have become self-sufficient.

You conclude: 'I may not be in control of my life but I am in control of my weekly schedule and that is sufficient for me.' You think: 'I know that my hold on life and others is weak but if I hold tight to my opinions and force others to comply with my way of doing things, then my lack of control is hidden.'

However, to have the masks, deceptions and magical expectations and assumptions stripped away from us exposes the raw nerve. This is evident in the men and women who come to my clinic. By the time they see me, they are at risk of losing everything. Often, these people have maintained their deceptions about themselves through a relationship to such a degree that they almost destroy the relationship in the process. And when one partner threatens to leave, the lie is exposed. The partners return psychologically to childhood and all the old fears return. For the first time, they have to admit to the illusions they have created. They also discover that, without these illusions, they are strangely relieved. They begin to experiencing themselves as being real and integrated into life—perhaps for the very first time.

So what is the alternative to illusions? It is opening oneself to existence and anxiety; experiencing uncertainty; and feeling ambivalence. On that ground can be built a courage, an integrity, a spirituality, a faith or an imaginative approach to life that is religious, poetic, and open. Herein, surely, is the life of passion and fulfillment.

All of this is critical because it is the basis on which we realise that what is at stake when you are engaged in intense conflict with your spouse or ex-spouse is not reality but the dominant *lies about reality*. It is about whose religion is most fundamental, whose superstitious beliefs remain, and whose rituals have to survive.

*

The Deception of Co-Dependence

Patterns of dependency and co-dependency are an example of this sort of interior religion. You keep seeking the approval of others. The origins of these patterns arise from the response to terror and anxiety where the child 'discovers' the truth that if they appease and please others then they are more likely to feel secure and safe. This impression that they can control their world by pleasing others becomes a religious belief and a religious reflex.

The constellation of rituals (trying to make everything perfect), beliefs (I can only be safe and happy if those close to me are happy) and feelings (I am guilty until I prove myself worthy) become a secretly religious approach to life.

This magically-thinking child grows up to be a so-called reasonable adult but they have only *disguised* the magic in a sort of reasoned certainty. So they seek approval everywhere. The emotional–religious–superstitious lie of co-dependence is an insidious one. You get so absorbed in trying not to upset people, trying not to offend anyone and trying to keep others happy. You go on to convince yourself that this is a meaningful approach to life. You are fearful of seeing that it is a *lie* that protects you from the passionate dangers of life.

The co-dependent person spends their time worrying about everything to the degree that their life becomes a chronically anxious one. In their enclosed life, they worry about everybody else and assume total responsibility in solving the problems of their family. The power they assume is a false one based on subjective impressions, ancient reflexes and superstitious beliefs.

The anxiety about all these other people is *displaced* anxiety. It is displaced from the person's original discovery (at a young age) that they were powerless. It is displaced from their more recent developmental discovery that they cannot control future outcomes. It comes from an immediate realisation that they cannot guarantee that they will find approval.

*

THE DECEPTION OF SELF AND OTHER

I must lie down where all the ladders start,
In the foul rag-and-bone shop of the heart.

W.B. Yeats

Deceit is part of love. The question is not *whether* you deceive your partner—but *how*. There are many ways you disguise your anxiety, helplessness, dread, terror, insecurity, despair, need and dependency. If deceit is accepted and understood, then love can rescue each person from their white lies about themselves. By turning over stones, looking behind doors, rummaging in the basement of the self, one can find forgotten memories, little children from one's past, shames and secrets hidden from oneself.

Love understands deceit and never feels betrayed at its discovery. It welcomes it. It knows that, behind the disguise, the terror of one's smallness makes this deceit inevitable.

Tell me of your lies,
tell me of your secret shame,
tell me of your suffering,
tell me of the vengeance you seek.
And I will not judge you in your errors.
No, my heart knows this woodland of hidden places,
traps, illusions and tricks of the self.

In love there is always a form of deception: a concealing of one's full truth made necessary by the terror of being humiliated, trivialised, admonished or rejected. You can hardly help yourself. Guilt knows that the self *revealed* is one member of the family of selves *concealed*. Paradoxically, deception ultimately reveals itself—either as a secret too big to hide or a truth flushed out by the stare of your lover's eyes.

In committing to a relationship, you naively thought you had found someone who would help you button down the deceits you held about yourself. Instead, not only did your partner hold a mirror to your face, they also reported what they saw. And in their witness you feel betrayed.

It is in mid- and later life that the weariness of trying to create the meaning of one's own world from within yourself gets revealed. I have been quite astonished at the throng of couples who come to me caught in the exhaustive and frustrating trap that is the lie of their relationships.

People fabricate a relationship that is a deception. It disguises their motives, power, fetishes and superstitions. They refuse defiantly to see how they cling to a relationship in order to support the fabrication they have made about themselves. And when the lie of their relationship begins to collapse, and can no longer hold itself up, the enormity of the rage and despair that results illustrates how the lie had become the very purpose of their existence. To let go of the lie is to be exposed to the storm of one's vulnerability, long since avoided. This reduction, this shrinking of life, is shattering in its cosmic proportions.

In domestic abuse, we see how love turns to hate when the victim exposes the vulnerability of the abuser. By the victim's very existence and proximity, they reveal the abuser's dependency and inadequacy. The abuser hates the victim for this. Faced with the truth about themselves, the abuser takes the coward's path and seeks to intimidate the victim into behaving in ways that confirm the abuser's lies about themselves.

We see also in the process of separation and divorce how, when the other does not confirm the lies about the self, the offender engages in a battle or stand-off with their ex. In divorce, this can escalate into awful battles where the terrified self takes down the entire family in seeking to tie itself to the dead tree of its righteousness. In divorce and separation, the great forces of life are unleashed and can wreak havoc, unless the participants can hand over to a process that is larger than them. This is the spiritual challenge of a break-up. It brings people as close to psychic death as many people can get. Many end up on the brink of literal suicide or even homicide.

On the very day that I write this text, I must appear in court to describe exactly this scenario. I have to testify that a man, in his righteous need to maintain control and hold onto the only certitude in his life (himself), has alienated all of his children. In this crisis, the only certainty is the man's narcissistic self-belief. It remains his shield against helplessness and vulnerability. In holding up this shield at every encounter, he has banished the vulnerability of his life and love. This is all about his terror of death, his inability to relax into the arms of life. Life will expose him to helplessness and vulnerability and, by such, will make him open to love. Only when he can face life and become open to love, will his children love him in return.

We do not want to admit that we are fundamentally dishonest about our relationships; that we do not really control our own lives; that we have no grip on what our true motives are. We confidently proclaim ourselves while trying to draw all our strength and power from an intimate relationship, even if that power is derived from the destruction and degradation of the other. Some people need to abuse in order to feel right about themselves. People sometimes have to repress a great deal of reality if they want to feel a sense of inner value and security.

CREATING AN ILLUSION OUT OF LOVE

How is it that most people only become aware of the intensity of their love at the point of losing the relationship? How is it that so much need and passion can remain hidden within the body of a relationship? How come men (in particular) can banish their vulnerable need for their partner until the partner withdraws from them? Why do these things happen with such regularity?

Why these things happen can be best understood when placed in the context of much of what we have addressed so far in this book. When a person is left alone and abandoned, there rises up in them a taste of fear, loss and powerlessness. Herein, they encounter death; and in being forced to embrace this abject mortal vulnerability, there rises up in them a forgotten longing that is love. It is not uncommon to hear a person who has neglected their partner for many years exclaim aching and tragic regret. 'I adore the ground she walks on', 'I will die without him', 'My life is not worth living without her', 'I love him—*now* I see it!'

So often, in long-standing relationships that break up, one or both partners are shocked that the assumptions they made about the safety and predictability of the other were flawed. They discover that their so-called dull or disappointing or distant partner had a secret life: 'They are not the person I thought they were.' The truth is that we often reduce our partners to stick-figures, eradicating the complexity of their secret life. We do this because we are actually fearful of it. And we do the same thing to ourselves.

We create a false ID in order to maintain a relationship that seems to promise victory. We become the false identity. We begin to live out of a role and sell ourselves to our project. But it wears thin eventually.

The assumptions we make about 'not needing' the other turn out to be illusion. In loss, we discover how much we loved and needed them. This is because we invariably kept the possibility and reality of all deathly omens locked away at the back wall of our psyche. It seemed like it was too much to bear.

Post-Separation Hatred

After separation, it is staggering to observe how the perception of the other changes so dramatically and so quickly. How fickle the so-called love seems to have been. The beloved is now turned upon as a dangerous enemy. Everything we believed and espoused about the other partner now seems to be an illusion. 'How could I have been so stupid?' we ask.

When a relationship ends, people reveal extraordinary things about the love they championed as being so virtuous at the time. What they pretended was secure and stable was inherently insecure and unstable. In fact, not only was the relationship unstable; but so were they. They discover that they also *presented themselves to their partner* in ways that were false and reduced the complexity of who they were. Sometimes people claim that they feigned security in order to protect their partner, but it always has a strain of *self-protection*. We back away from risk in favour of comfort.

Sometimes people seem to keep a secret log of sacrifices and betrayals. After separation, it appears as if years of sacrifices, suspicions, grievances and mistrust burst open like a wound. The

entire pretence—the entire deception of the relationship—is exposed
for what it was. It was a house of cards.

The realisation that committed, intimate relationships are
inherently *unstable* may be initially frightening. It actually seems quite
groundbreaking and it shatters our views of what is really happening.
The problem is not with the relationship itself but in our attitudes
and beliefs *about relationships*. The issue lies in how we manage them
psychologically (from within) and socially (from without).

It is surprising that even up until the last breath of a relationship
one or both partners still refuse to yield their illusions, fantasies or
convictions about their perceptions. The defiance almost supersedes
their psychic life. And when the relationship dies, they die, holding on
tightly to their convictions in a storm of anguish and bereavement.
It is quite extraordinary. Then what follows is so predictable: after
the annihilation comes extraordinary bitterness and cruelty. This is
the repressed hostility and aggression of dependence. The bitterness,
anger and paranoia that become part of the territory of separation
and divorce reveal starkly how complex and contradictory are many
of the forces of romantic love. It is a sad fact that when the illusions
of security fall away, hidden and denied bitterness rises to the surface.

The truth is that you want a sanctuary because you know inherently
just how ill at ease you really are. You know in the quiet of your heart
how precarious is your sense of yourself. You know just how hard you
must strive to hold on to yourself.

Passion

Out of sheer terror, people remain stuck and abandoned in the cold
corridors of a lifeless partership. The terror of a direct encounter with
death and one's wounded humanity is so fierce as to allow people to
waste away.

Better the dying that I know than the death I fear.

Passionate intimacy is experienced when the vulnerability of life
and death is exposed during the life of a relationship. Intimacy dies
when this vulnerability is denied and closed off. When relationships
end, the vulnerability can be exposed in a storm of rage or grief.

A man has taken his wife for granted. Throughout their marriage, he has treated her with disrespect. He contacts me in great distress because his wife has decided to leave the relationship. The distress he experiences is his awful realisation of how much he needs her and how much he really loves her. He falls apart in a turmoil of regret, grief, anger and heartbreak. He says he will do anything to get her back: 'I have treated her so badly over the years. I have neglected her and did not listen to her. I was such a fool. She does not realise how much I really loved her. I need her. Please, you must tell me how to get her back. I don't think I can cope. I can't live without her. She is the only one that has ever loved me. She is the only one I want. Please, help me.'

> *And he pours out the years*
> *of repressed love, admiration and need,*
> *for which he ridiculed himself*
> *and for which he punished her.*
> *Belittling her for exactly this:*
> *evoking the need in him.*
> *So he forgot her,*
> *dismissed her,*
> *humiliated her,*
> *blanked her*
> *because he could not tolerate*
> *love's abject vulnerability.*
> *So he punished love.*
> *And in his efforts to escape the man he could have been*
> *he became the man he was.*
> *He sacrificed her body*
> *as a symbol of his power over death.*
> *In doing so,*
> *he burnt at his stake*
> *the vulnerable, broken beauty*
> *that is Love.*

THE DENIAL OF LOVE

Sometimes it is only when we experience loss that we can find the courage to reveal the true nature of love. The deeply felt love that brings people together in romance is exactly the same that is revealed at the point of death or bereavement. What is so disappointing is how, throughout the duration of a committed relationship, so much love is repressed. It appears to be impossible for us to keep open the wound that makes love necessary. If you remember that love exists purely because we are mortally vulnerable, our phobic avoidance and denial of death is an avoidance of love. Our denial of human vulnerability tries to escape the urgency, intensity and fragility of life. We cannot escape the truth that death and love are inextricably entwined.

Grief is the heart's response to sorrowful death.

Love is the heart's response to vulnerable life.

There are times when we get glimpses into the heart of things, when the anxieties and trivialities of everyday life get swept away. We then see with clear vision, just for a moment, the truths of death and love, sorrow and joy. But they are just glimpses, brief revelations.

It appears that in all our relationships we deny (despite ourselves) the love we feel. In fact, the love is below the radar of experience for many. It often lies hidden in the long grasses of the self. It is rendered obsolete by the ego's concerns with survival and control. It is boxed and put away, as if in an attic. Like a box of Christmas ornaments, it is only brought out on occasion.

Sometimes it takes moments of real family definition—funerals or crises—for love to be brought out. At times like these, love gets unpackaged and displayed. It reappears in too-late eulogies of regard. And then it can be quickly wrapped up again and stored away self-consciously.

The fact is simply this: in order to resist passionate vulnerability, we try to maximise our safety and security in the sweep and drama of life. We hide, repress and deny the nature of love we hold for life and, more particularly, for those close to us.

Every day I see this denial revealed. It is at moments of loss, breakdown or unexpected vulnerability that the longing in a person's soul has a reason to be set free. Often, an emotional dam breaks and tears fall like precious waters drawn from the well of a once-closed heart. At these times we can see that love has not died: it has simply been repressed.

Romance, often vilified as illusion and deception, is another way that the wound of life opens up. It is what happens when we are gripped with the urgency of life, when we have one foot in the soft grass of the meadow and the other in the clay and dust of our destiny.

Romance, too, does not fade.
Like love, it slips away into the darkness
to arise from its cold-storage
when the heart is opened to loss.
The beauty of sorrow is that it uncovers love
and drives it from its seclusion.
Genuine sorrow is not self-pity or despair:
it is compassion for life.
Love is its expression.
Joy is its consequence.
It is along these by-roads we should walk,
among the forgotten bohreens and lanes,
through the quiet countryside of the heart.

The fingerprints of the soul's longing are everywhere. Repressed love shows its face in many ways. Love that is denied leaves a trail of breadcrumbs back out of the forest into the light. Somehow, we hope that our trail will be followed and yet we persistently deny the crumbs are ours.

And all the while the child of your soul lies wordless,
draped in your denials
like a great Van Gogh or Michelangelo,
a masterpiece hidden from your lover's view.
You distract your lover with everyday irritations.
You do not show them the sorrowful Pieta
of your heart's unlived life.
You show them the trivialities of what is lived.
And so, you lie in bed, your heart aching
from your fear of revealing yourself,
depressed in isolation.

Love waits to be called; it will never pursue you. It will never demand your attention. It can die or be suffocated or repressed by your fear.

So, call it forward! Bring down the Christmas decorations and keep them up throughout the dark winter. Do not be love's executioner. Do not imprison love. Do not fear love. Love is an embracing of sorrow and the vulnerability of death.

To give expression to love means to give expression to longing, need and desire. We desire because we are hungry. Hunger is a physical sensation of dread: an anticipation of death and a promise of survival. Love is similar: it combines the experience of abject vulnerability and the promise of fulfilment. To experience hunger and need is to become aware of vulnerability.

Without your decay, there is no longing—because whatever you have would be sufficient to survive. Without a mortal life, there is no inclination to love—because survival would be guaranteed. Without the vulnerability of fear, there is no love.

Love is a need and is always incomplete. To acknowledge and show love is to admit the vulnerability of life and to open the doorway to brokenness.

We survive in many ways by denying love. We have evolved into beings where the survival of our species is dependent on each organism's ability to carry on functioning oblivious to its precarious mortality. Yet, thankfully, the sensitivity to life's precariousness is visited upon us at times of great loss or of great blessing. At these times, a door into our heart is opened.

Chapter 5
Misusing Love

RELATIONSHIPS AND SELF-IMPORTANCE

It is in intimate relationships that your struggles with life are played out. Here you have to deal with your untidy, awkward and inadequate attempts at trying to overcome your limitations. It is in intimate relationships that you tend to set a test for your success or failure in life.

There is considerable protection in surrendering yourself to a flag, a movement, a crusade or an ideology; but there is little protection in surrendering yourself to a relationship. It is in your intimate relationships that the fundamental issues in life are dealt with and resolved. At home with one's partner in a loving relationship, the protective blanket you have placed over yourself is pulled back. It is only your partner or children that really know the truth of your anxious vulnerability. If you have kept this vulnerability hidden, your partner or children will be the ones to see your angry defensiveness.

Being in an intimate relationship means that you give allegiance to the relationship and to the other person. But you also give allegiance to your self-importance. Everyone prioritises their self-importance to greater or lesser degrees; this is one of the neglected realities of relationships. They serve three functions for us. They allow us to experience love, experience control and secure a sense of personal status. It is this latter need that I would like to focus on. This need for self-importance is our response to our subconscious awareness of our insignificance.

It is worth being curious about what is happening to you when you need to use the relationship to maintain your self-importance. This is when you need to prove yourself, to justify why you are the way you are. There is usually a tipping point where you realise that the primary purpose in the relationship or the marriage is no longer to love, but to serve your self-importance. Sometimes, a relationship has become the only place you can achieve any sense of enduring significance in life. When this happens, everything that occurs in the relationship takes on a critical importance. It becomes vital that the relationship confirms and supports your image of yourself. It is no wonder that you go into a rage over the most trivial of conflicts! If your spouse wins the argument, everything you stand for—and all of the self-importance that goes with it—dies. This is why you sometimes respond to conflict or the possibility of being rejected *as if your life depended on it.*

To some degree, every person tries to control their partner in order to get what they need. This is usually subconscious and not at all as deliberate or cynical as it may sound at first. However, our lack of awareness that this is what we are doing creates increasing difficulty. The real trouble comes when our partner begins to fight back. This is not unusual: you will certainly have moments when your self-importance goes into direct battle with that of your partner.

We find security in the everyday certainties that sustain us. We can cling to our attitudes and arguments like life-rafts in a storm. To lose an argument can feel as if a part of us has died. In these situations, it is our fear of death that is really the issue. That is why a domestic fight or stand-off can feel so terrible. The feelings evoked by rejection can be powerful. The intensity comes from our terror of annihilation—but we dare not name it.

It is beyond most of us to acknowledge the fear we have that drives our anger, irritability, moodiness or depression. The chronically angry partner imagines themselves to be fearless. However, their endless anger reveals their desperate need for control. This control is essential because it distracts them from their own powerlessness and tries to serve a self-importance that compensates for a vague, unacknowledged sensation that they are of no consequence.

For many people, their intimate relationship is the predominant way that their existence in the world has significance and meaning. This is as true for men as it is for women. In very dependent relationships, we witness the intense clinging of one to another, regardless of the effect on the relationship—or on the self.

In patterns of paranoia and jealousy, we see *control* exerted by one partner over another in order to ensure that the controlled partner and the relationship remain fixed and rigidly secure. The controlling partner aims to guarantee their status. In patterns of abusive personalities, we witness a ruthless control aimed at maintaining a relationship in order to experience power and status. In violent relationships, we see the violent abuse of one partner by another; this is done to feed the self-importance of the abuser. In masochistic patterns, we observe the co-dependent surrender of the self to neglect and abuse from another; this is done so that the abused partner can experience relevance. In all of these situations, the purpose of the relationship is primarily to provide evidence of the self-status, significance and existential importance of the partners.

An intimate relationship can be a key refuge from unease in oneself and the terror of one's mortal vulnerability. I see everyday how the breakdown of relationships threatens many people's *psychic security* in the world. In fact, given the power of human attachment and bonding (and how its success relates directly to human survival), I would suggest that it threatens *everyone's* psychological survival. A relationship serves a vital role in securing people's self-importance and safety. People are in relationships so that they can tie down the certainties that they need in order to endure. Sometimes these certainties stand on shaky ground. Sometimes these certainties are feelings of dependency, suspicion, control, mistrust or jealousy; and people tie up all of these things in their most intimate relationships.

The Price of Using a Relationship for Self-Importance
When the need to prove and justify the self overrides the need to be flexible and available to the other, then there is a price to pay. There are a number of consequences for this in a relationship.

Your attempt to use your relationship to escape your vulnerability and brokenness can only succeed if the *other person* sacrifices themselves for that project, too. In other words, *your self-importance needs a victim.* In every intimate relationship, there is an unwritten acceptance that one willingly does sacrifice oneself for the other *at certain times*; this is a quality of love. There is give-and-take in this and, while each person needs it from time to time, the expectation is neither persistent nor intense. However, some people are so needy that they must make a victim of the other. This can happen to the degree that the freedom and dignity of the other person is sacrificed. Unfortunately, this 'colonisation of the other' is not uncommon in relationships.

A person's need to use the marriage to escape something disturbing in themselves can result in the *emotional imprisonment* of the other person. The other does not sacrifice themselves; rather, they are captured, terrorised and imprisoned. They are held hostage to the offender's sadism. You are familiar with tragic stories where such horrors are revealed after a murder, suicide or exposure of child abuse. Sometimes one partner will gradually humiliate and demean the other partner to such a degree that the other has to sacrifice their self. Sometimes one partner will terrorise and frighten the other partner to such a degree that they are bullied into emotional submissiveness.

In using a relationship as a mirror for the self, offenders have to surrender their *own freedom*. Abusive partners become trapped and imprisoned within their own validation system. They toss away the keys in favour of the secure certainty of a prison within which they feel justified, important and significant. Even though they are imprisoned themselves, they prefer to remain there because it is there that they can control their partner and family. Even though they are in a prison of their own making, they tell themselves that they are king.

*

Intimate relationships are imbued with an enduring significance far greater than what can be objectively observed.

> *Good relationships endure because*
> *vulnerability is loved,*
> *sacrifice is not ever sought,*
> *righteousness is never assumed,*
> *and freedom is cherished.*

These issues are revealed during relationship breakdown because, while conflict may threaten one's mortality, relationship breakdown announces its arrival. At the time that relationships break down, it is not uncommon to find that a person begins to collapse physically and emotionally. One's will to live begins to die and one is overwhelmed with grief, helplessness or a terrible physical dread. People who have been through this know it well. The trauma can last for some time; and if someone is not defeated by breakdown, they can find that they are still at war with their ex long afterwards. They still feel the pain of break-up. They find themselves still holding up their arguments and positions. They do this because their positions are their symbols, their security stickers, the things that they believe guarantee them. Without them, they imagine they might be nothing.

In my work with people experiencing separation or divorce, I frequently have to give them permission to *let go*. I have to remind them that they do not need to hold on to their anger or bitterness because the so-called enemy they think they are fighting has long since left the field! They are just fighting against their inner fear of self-reduction.

We all have this inclination to elevate ourselves beyond what we are. We have a false sense of specialness, of being invulnerable and immune. This enables us to proceed confidently into an uncertain future. We deny our vulnerability until we are forced to face it: we become ill, suffer a loss, are hurt by someone or just have to deal with the unavoidable disappointments of everyday life. Each of us has a defensive system that, up until those points, makes us imagine that it would 'never happen to us'. We all have this false confidence of being above the risks and vulnerabilities of normal life. Though we see illness all around us, we are shocked when it visits our family. When these things happen, our denial and avoidance are shattered. Life breaks in on us with a shocking brutality and we are left to ask: 'Why did I not expect this?'

ACCREDITING THE SELF
There is a terrible deception of placing oneself at the centre of one's life and heroic quest. Putting one's own needs at the centre of one's life is a dubious practice. When you place yourself—rather than another, a virtue or the relationship—at the centre, then your heroic mission is a flawed one. Your purpose then is more cowardly than heroic. You need the marriage to buffer you from your woundedness and vulnerability—from the taste of your passionate mortality. Your

relationship then becomes all about *you* and you alone. It becomes your mission to destroy something. It can be cast in garments that make your expedition look loving, caring or family-centred, but it is your impotent plan in disguise. It is your attempt to achieve some experience of godly power by virtue of taking another as a victim. It becomes that which defines your very significance in the world.

Your marriage then becomes your private religion—and it strives to become your salvation.

You pretend that the meaning and miracle of creation is reduced to how your partner treats you. You assume that your partner, through their compliance, has the power to beatify you. The relationship really becomes a monument to a lie. You see the relationship as *your* success, *your* conquest.

It is many an innocent person who commits to a relationship in wide-eyed hopefulness only to find their life being drained from them by a partner whose need for endless validation leaves them exhausted.

The potential fulfilment of a relationship is that it gives you exactly what you need to resolve your conflicts with *yourself* and with *life*. Because relationships provide a very definite, intense and captive location for undertaking your safe heroism and for redeeming yourself. You have exactly what you need to solve your existential and 'religious' problems. There is no other location quite like it for addressing these issues. In effect, your longing for something transcendent, for some quality of being able to master the conditions of life, is brought within your sphere of influence. It is brought right into your own home.

Although you cannot avoid your sense of powerlessness over the course of your life, you can borrow your power from the other and the status bestowed by them. Though you cannot escape the sense of inadequacy you feel in the face of the majesty of life, you find some temporary relief in submitting to your beloved. Here you can sense the addiction of relationships as much as the healing power of love.

We prove ourselves there.
We validate ourselves there.
We establish our worthiness there.
We alleviate our guilt there.
And we find relief there.

TURNING A RELATIONSHIP INTO A LIFE PROJECT

As we have seen, we all use intimate relationships and our partners for purposes that have little to do with love. This is okay and necessary, though it's rarely admitted. We have seen how our need for self-importance, self-security or self-justification can take precedence over the needs of the other person.

We have seen how a relationship can actually be hijacked by a controlling person, in order to meet their need to domineer, manipulate and accredit their power and status. A *controller* can coerce their partner into a role where all the partner does is prove the strength, power and significance of the controller. The *controlled* partner submits, agrees, supports and complies with all of the expectations of the controller, however unreasonable they are.

This hijacking and co-opting becomes a kind of 'life project' for the controller. They devote so much of their energy to this control. It serves a very deep, primitive need in a person to achieve some kind of power in their lives. The controlling partner feels like a god in their domain. They ensure that their arguments, beliefs, behaviours and personality traits are never questioned. If they are built up to be strong in this way, if their weaknesses are never exposed, then they do not have to face their mortality.

Intimate relationships are co-opted as life projects. A life project is something you use to defeat the symptoms of your mortality: woundedness, vulnerability, helplessness, inadequacy, etc. Your project serves to make you feel powerful, invulnerable, unafraid, adequate and righteous.

I bet you have seen and witnessed this in your own family or families known to you. You discover very quickly that the forces at work in relationships and in relationship breakdown have nothing to do with broken love. They have a lot more to do with control and power.

The gravitational attraction of marriage or other committed relationships is that they can provide us with that sense of significance, power and relevance. A relationship can be intoxicating in the romantic stages because a person can feel this powerful sense of influence and purpose that has been absent in their lives up to now. To be loved by someone is indeed to experience a sense of visibility, relevance and stature that nothing else in life can provide. Relationships bestow both significance and security. Therefore, issues of power, significance, control, status, justification, redemption, accreditation and recognition are powerful forces affecting how we are in relationship.

It is somewhat disquieting to admit that we enter love relationships to meet these needs. But it is okay. It only becomes problematic when this need is denied and then exaggerated at the price of genuine love and the serving of the other. Our denial that this process is always at work creates real difficulties for us. Acknowledgment and acceptance of this need actually disarms it and converts its energy into a humility and love that has courage and integrity.

By now, you probably have a feel for how anxious, insecure and vulnerable we really are; and how compulsively we seek to overcome this unavoidable human trait. How we reconcile ourselves with helplessness is an essential spiritual and psychological struggle for all of us. Every religion down the ages has addressed this fundamental problem of how we deal with human helplessness, how we deal with the fact that we do not control life or suffering. The family home is the place where the themes of religion come into being and are lived out.

When a relationship becomes a life project, we use it to try to shield us from these truths. We want the relationship to provide us with an experience of ultimate security and validation. *The more one seeks to achieve this outcome, the more one strangles the potential for courageous love and intimacy.* The more we co-opt marriage into this devious purpose, the more we inhibit and ultimately extinguish love. We are then left with a marriage that no longer serves as a harbour for love. At its best, it becomes a safe and secure relationship. This is not such a bad thing when both partners mutually meet basic needs. It can be a lifeless, but nonetheless safe, way for a family to be.

At its worst, it becomes a place of abuse, self-sacrifice and self-justification. It becomes a siege against life itself. Partners can actually join together in this mission. I work with couples that are mutually abusive in their desperate efforts to establish control. These can be characterised as 'can't live with you, can't live without you' relationships that involve the sacrifice of both partners to achieve the needs of both.

VIEWING A RELATIONSHIP AS A 'SECURE REFUGE'

The range of bad jokes about marriage is endless. Popular culture, folklore and humour all exaggerate the notion that marriage is a killer of romance and that it becomes boring and predictable. You may recall wistfully the passion of earlier days and blame the predictability of your marriage on the passing of time. Let me suggest that the predictability has actually been created by yourself. It has been created by you, as you have sought security. Though you may complain that you are imprisoned, you are terrified of release! The 'prison' you have created becomes essential to your experience of security and sense of worth. You corral the mysteries, conflicts and ambitions of life down into the small cell of your relationship, where you think all of these things can be controlled.

When your relationship becomes a 'prison' or 'trap' it is because you repress your childishness, sexuality, terror, longing, desire and fantasy; and you fasten down the obligations of the relationship into something you can control. It becomes essential to you for reasons other than 'true love'. It is your shield against the vulnerable mortality that disturbs your sleep and haunts your daydreams.

We seek and maintain stability at the cost of passion and romance, at the cost of our frail and transient beauty. More particularly, *we exaggerate constancy and safety* in an intimate relationship in order to compensate for its emotional danger. There is *danger* in an intimacy that acknowledges anxiety, deceit, vulnerability, self-righteousness and all the things that happen but go unnamed. We repress and deny the dangers of tender love in order to maintain an unstable stability— one that may ultimately collapse beneath us.

Your need for stability tends to overpower your need for vulnerability. Your fear of rejection overcomes your longing for intensity. The mistake that you make is not that you got into a stable and predictable relationship, but that you *shoe-horned* it into stability. *You* built a relationship that became devoted to that illusion. We *all* do it. We all need the reassurance of predictability, role fulfilment and security.

If we make things secure and stable for our partners, then we get their approval. You want approval because it is critical to your wellbeing. We inevitably reduce ourselves to something that secures such approval. Despite our claims, we resist the unpredictability of mortal love because, the truth is, it scares us. We do not want to be these things.

We need to become more aware of the inherent instability of relationships. The social illusion of marital stability contributes more to its demise than anything else. Pull back the curtain of this illusion and we feel passion, love, romance, light-heartedness, compassion, longing and everything that is real.

The failure to acknowledge marriage's precarious vulnerability means that expectations of security get emphasised. No wonder couples then begin to ask: 'Why do I feel so trapped?' Partners search for ways to keep themselves, the other and the relationship locked in the security prison of that relationship. And so, passion dies, spirituality gets trivialised, romance gets banished and security gets tightened. The ironic thing is that you feel imprisoned by the very walls you erected to make you feel free of what threatens you from the outside—passionate, wounded, broken, anxious vulnerability.

The tragic irony in our attitudes to intimate relationships is that in our flight from death (insecurity, uncertainty, passion and unavoidable danger) we strive to create a refuge that actually makes us even more depressed. Our striving for security makes us more vulnerable to collapse.

On an everyday basis, we choose the predictable and secure while bemoaning the lack of creative intensity in our lives. The depressiveness of a trivial life begins to set in, along with the felt powerlessness that goes with it. Desperately trying to secure stability and protect us from emotional danger and vulnerability, we end up experiencing a gradual emotional death.

Throughout our lives, we will feel powerful forces to be reckoned with. We will face heroic challenges in coming to terms with the conditions of life. We will try to turn intimate relationships into security-enhancing life projects. We will struggle with separation and connection. We will have a relentless need to embrace the passion of life. We will strive to find freedom, emancipation, novelty, excitement, sexual fulfilment and cathartic release. Given all this, it is ironic—even comic—that we seek such psychological refuge in such a dangerous entity as intimate relationships! The promise of sanctuary seems to outweigh the threat of insecurity.

THE INEVITABLE FAILURE OF 'RELATIONSHIP AS REFUGE'

Your relationship cannot fulfil the task you sometimes assign to it— to affirm your significance and protect you from the frustrations and vulnerabilities of life. Many of our traditional structures have changed: religion, gender roles, family, marriage, culture, etc. Modern society is searching for an ideology, theology or technology that will provide meaning and certainty in the face of so much change to the traditional structures.

If you don't believe in family virtues, a personal God, a social system, a religion, a personal code of ethics, then you will need some symbol onto which to project your suffering and fear. You have to attempt to resolve these bigger concerns through your everyday endeavours. I think it would be fair to say that most people draw their energy from the symbols and myths that have emerged from their family of origin. In everyday life, our reference point for how to live is always what we grew up with. It is our default position, whether we like it or not.

As I have discussed earlier, when you seek salvation through another, when you pursue a sense of purpose and mission through another, when you utterly depend on another, when your spiritual heroism gets lost in personal love, you are in grave danger of losing both the *other* and your *life assignment*. Many relationships are doomed to fail because it is impossible to be a partner who is granted heroic status and bestowed with too much significance. People seek to be redeemed by a relationship or get spirituality from the other person. Such idolatry ensures that one is left bereft. This double failure is what triggers the terrible pain that gets unleashed in many modern relationships.

It's not hard to understand how you end up becoming a product or an effect of the other person. You can become inextricably bound with the people on whom you are dependent: needing them as either a source of strength or as an object of control. In either case, the other restricts our self-development. It is too narrow a constriction of meaning and we may come to resent and fight against it. The abusive personality becomes more abusive, controlling and aggressive. The co-dependent becomes more self-sacrificing and deferential.

If the other becomes the sole measure of what is good or bad in oneself, we become simply the effect of the other person. At the deepest level, we resent it even though we surrender to it. We become depressed because of our dependency on them for their approval or for their acquiescence. It is no wonder. No human relationship can bear the burden of all of life.

LOVE OF VIRTUE
When we aspire to a virtuous life, a spiritual life or to a life of charity or compassion, we draw on these aspirations to enable us to function in the relationship. This is because the thing that makes transcendent

sensitivity and spirituality valuable is that it is *beyond* the physical reality of the relationship. In other words, we draw on something other than the other person. We choose to be good or loving because of a value system, virtue or character orientation that we *bring to* the relationship rather than *draw from* the relationship. For this reason, Nietzsche said: 'Love your virtue.' Because it is all you have to draw from.

We must acknowledge that when we draw on a relationship to enable us to function in life, we place too great a burden on the relationship. We want the relationship not only to relieve us from the burden of life's conflicts, conditions and responsibilities—but we also expect it to inspire us to be free and safe!

This is not possible. Instead of being a mirror of one's magnitude or importance, the other inevitably reflects our earthly mortality, decay and imperfection. To the degree that we are dependent on our spouse for everything, we become threatened by their shortcomings and by how they reflect back our own. Our partners reflect right back to us the very imperfections, inadequacies and vulnerabilities we have sought to avoid and deny.

We feel we are left with no choice but to either punish ourselves for our weaknesses or to attack our partner for theirs.

The truth we must ultimately face is that the greatness of the mysterious universe, the enormity of life's wonderful challenges, the palliative care of one's life, can never be resolved through the pettiness of relationship squabbles.

Our relationships must not be the only well from which we draw the sustenance to find meaning and significance in life. They must not be the only place within which we encounter the divine. They must not be the only vessel within which we empty the anxieties and terrors of life.

We must draw from other sources. The qualities, inspirations, virtues, visions and imaginings from these other sources are poured over the angst of relationship like a balm. Tolerance, compassion, courage and humility must be what we bring to our beloved. To come with empty hands expecting redemption is to expect too much.

MARRIAGE, POWER AND CONTROL

If we have repetitive experiences of power over our partner, we get a taste of what it might be like to be free of mortal vulnerability. We can spit out the bad taste of our human ineffectiveness and swallow the symbolic experience of our success through the submission of our partner to some trivial demand. This banishes terror away, as we taste some sweet relief.

I have worked for many years with violent abusers and have discovered that a person who is in the throes of abusing their partner (either physically or emotionally) experiences the thrill and relief of violence without consequence. While the abuser beats their partner (literally or metaphorically), they experience an exhilarating relief from the burden of their own self. This is what is chilling about domestic abuse—be it physical, emotional or sexual. It has this *addictive* element. During the moments that the perpetrator is violating, they feel a god-like, intoxicating power.

But one does not need to look at the extreme situation to discover this. Look at yourself and how you forget yourself when you are arguing, criticising, verbally attacking or berating someone you love. Step back and realise that what you are doing is not proving a point, but rather justifying yourself. It may not be too harmful to the other, but you know that it has a sinister feeling to it.

You can feel a certain shame afterwards because you know that your critique is dishonest. You hide the real truth of your insecure righteousness. You know that you are involved in a deception that your anger and outrage hides. Your victory never tastes right. This is why you apologise later. You are not sure why but you know that what you were doing was something symbolic, something self-serving, something that turned your beloved into a victim rather than an equal. You know that, in those moments, you dehumanised them. It is not good but it is something we do all the time.

I know it seems far-fetched and strange to say this, but at the deepest level this is true: *marriage can become a way for us to defy death.* As such, it can become a way to feel godly. It allows us to counteract being a victim of life, a slave to life.

It is not unusual for you to leave home in the morning with this question in mind: 'I wonder what life has in store for me today?' You might ask this question with dread or anticipation but, either way, it is an acknowledgment of both helplessness and receptivity.

Because we are powerless over our ultimate fate—and impotent in our attempts throughout life to be its master—we have a fear-driven tendency to become powerful over those who are closest to us, those we are supposed to love.

And when our ultimate impotence is revealed by these very people, when we discover that they are unable to co-operate with our agenda, we often respond with such disproportionate, emotional intensity (anger, anxiety or despair) that our true motives are revealed. This can, for example, be seen between parents and their children. Children get abused and humiliated because of their inability to exist *for* the parent—to prove and justify the parent's control and power. So children are yelled at for nothing more than doing things that interfere with the parent's need. This could be as simple as accidently knocking over a glass of milk. It appals me to witness how children get abused for accidents and mistakes. The parent's irritation arises from the inconvenience of accidental life. This is anger at life itself for not co-operating with them, with not being there *for them*. The child then becomes a casualty of the parent.

Relationships can serve to keep the everyday reminders of our subterranean anxiety at bay. We want to experience some sense of power, adequacy, control, influence, significance and meaning because we inhabit a life in which these are in such short supply. So the repetitive fight we have with our partners often has nothing to do with the issue at hand but it is a symbolic struggle to wrestle back some sense of status and power.

THE IRRITATION OF HUMAN INADEQUACY

The human inadequacies of the other person can be experienced as a very distressing reminder of our own impotence. If the relationship is co-opted, the flaws of one person become infuriating to the other. In a loving relationship, the flaws of the other may be temporarily annoying but they never threaten the relationship because it has not been hijacked to submit to someone's expectations.

Sometimes, when one partner discovers that the other has important priorities outside of the relationship, they can feel betrayed and enraged. In the healthy relationship, each person fosters the freedom of the other. They know that their partner's role in life is not just to be there for them—but to become their own person. In the unhealthy relationship, the dysfunctional one does not foster the freedom of the other. On the contrary, they seek ever-increasing control and enmeshment.

DOMESTIC FUNDAMENTALISM

When we use our relationship to experience a sense of self-justification and significance, then our partner gets co-opted into proving our status in life. When this happens, we employ tactics of power and control, sadism and cruelty, manipulation and deceit. We do this in order to preserve and secure our status, significance and god-like control of the trivial.

Sometimes, in unintentionally abusive ways, we react defensively against our partner because we know they have the power to expose us and therefore to humiliate us, denigrate us, dismiss us, ignore us, shut us out, blame us or control us. We can react viscerally, emotionally and righteously to these everyday experiences.

We have the freedom to choose how we handle these everyday stirrings. We escalate these feelings into a righteous defence of the self or an angry reaction against the other. We know that in these situations we move closer to the rejection and abuse of our partners. Here is where the first seeds of human evil actually take root: when we seek to expand our self-importance and self-esteem through the diminishment of the other.

Control as Religious

As we have discussed earlier, the exertion of power over another, the control of another, and the diminishment of that other are a kind of ritual to find significance and release from one's innate powerlessness. *We diminish the other person because they have failed to elevate us.* The abusive tirade that one partner regularly inflicts on another is, in many ways, the same ritual as a tribe burning a tribe member on a sacrificial altar. The impulses are exactly the same. The one who engineers the sacrifice elevates themselves by degradation of another.

It is necessary to keep emphasising this because it is such an elusive truth. It is a truth we seek to avoid at all costs. There are many different tactics of control: coercion, threats, manipulation, verbal assault, rejection, isolation, blaming, put-downs, name-calling, cynicism, stonewalling and defensiveness. There are many indirect ways to control: sulking, throwing tantrums, disengaging and passive-aggressive silence. It could be said that most tactics of control are, at their root, *pagan–religious* impulses. They are the reflexive response to encountering one's mortal powerlessness and vulnerability. They are the low-key, everyday derivative of *primitive needs to take human sacrifice to confirm one's godly status*, to experience power and to defeat mortality. To have power over another is to begin to get a taste of what it might be like to be immune to the effects of wounded humanity. Make no mistake: the forces at work in domestic life can be powerful, basic, pagan, religious and existential.

Everyday Life and Symbolic Immortality Projects

This is what you are doing when you 'innocently' criticise your partner. You convince yourself that it is just a rational response to their incompetence. What is provoked is your unconscious discomfort with earthly imperfection. Excessive criticism or excessive defensiveness reveals our dependence on our relationship to validate our arguments, eliminate ordinariness and buffer us from mortality's messengers. Excessive criticism proves to us, in the most primitive of ways, that we are achieving some kind of victory.

Do you ever catch yourself, in certain moments, erupting into an emotion that takes you by surprise, shocks or disturbs you? You fume under your breath at your partner's behaviour: 'God, they're so sanctimonious!' You let fly with a hostility or sarcasm that later has you apologising. 'I don't know what came over me,' you might say. There are those moments when you get a visceral sense of *what is at stake* and *what does come over you* in your relationship. What comes over you is the realisation of your condition, an awareness of impotence and ineffectiveness. What is at stake is whether you can actually live with this, whether you can face life with courage. These experiences reveal the way we try to prevent some dreadful thing from happening. The dreadful thing that *does* happen is that the other is seen to fail our project to eliminate the unattractive. Every time your partner lets you down, they expose you to the truths of life. The uneasy truth is this: both of you are ordinary, fumbling and beautiful mortals.

Every day I encounter the anguish, pain, terror, horror, grief, rage, bitterness, loss, fear, anxiety, cruelty, abuse, violence, self-rejection, despair, humiliation, frailty, tears, brokenness and death that is experienced when it appears that a partner has failed the other in this way. When this happens, the house of cards begins to fall. The partner reveals the lie that has been lived. There is no escape. There is no secure harbour where you are protected from the storms of life. There is no safe place where your status and your private exertions of power and control are confirmed. Instead, your partner—as the face of mortal love—reveals all of your brokenness and impotence.

At times, they seem to mock you; at other times, they seem to love you. Remember this duality: you are just as capable of *striking* that face as you are of *caressing its beauty*. It is for this reason that I emphasise that there is nobody on the planet with the same power to expose you to life and death than your intimate partner. There is nobody else who can introduce you to the broken, wounded and fractured beauty of your self.

Chapter 6
Trivialising Love

*In your life it may be
that if things are so,
it does not matter why.*

We are protected from anxious uncertainty in our intimate relationships by the unimaginative alternatives we make available. We obsess about the small events in our lives. We wake up at night and worry about locked doors, bank balances, hair colours, golf handicaps, work relationships, sexual prowess, unfinished reports, dysfunctional family members, children's needs, imagined insults, personal inadequacies and endless doubts about ourselves. The list of things we become pre-occupied with develops a dull but ever-distressing predictability.

It is interesting to realise that you worry about the same things you have always worried about: status, competence, control and security. The unpleasant truth behind all of this is that you live your life with a disappointing inevitability. Devoid of spirited imagination, you anaesthetise yourself with preoccupations about the trivial, terrified of the full impact of your apparent insignificance.

You prefer to turn your face away from the cliff edge, from the terrifying and majestic landscape of creation, towards the small corner you have secured. There, you arrange and rearrange your achievements, gathering honours, successes and mementos, lining them up to display them to the passing world with pride.

Why do people accept living a life that prioritises the trivial? Why do people sink into a passionless boredom in their intimate relationships?

Why does the danger of romance give way to the predictability of stability? It is because the danger of a full landscape of experience is too much for all of us. Self-revelation exposes one to potential annihilation, humiliation and rejection. To *not live* a trivialised life is to live a *mortal* one, to engage with the essentials of life.

Maintaining the predictable patterns of your personality is a hollow victory. It celebrates your triumph over emotional emancipation, which you have probably concluded is dangerous. This is defensive living. In it, you find meaning by thwarting danger, borrowing your purpose from something else, minimising vulnerability and denying death.

This kind of defensive living is everywhere. We see it in people who: measure their life's purpose in a bank balance; define their worth by the number of people who love them; feel victorious in having power over others; or find value in keeping up with the Joneses. It is natural that we find safe ways to feel heroic. We strut and prune ourselves in the confines of our little cell, actually afraid of early release into the conditions of the vast world.

For the solitary person, it is safe enough; but when our 'hero' seeks to confine *others* to the same prison they inhabit, we see the measures of tragedy. This is the first sign of control and abuse of others; it is born of the perpetuation of triviality. In seeking to justify ourselves and perpetuate our defensive heroics, we end up needing others to applaud and ratify our project.

ANAESTHETISING PASSION

Once you explore the intimate details of the ailing marriage, you discover that the boring or dull predictability alluded to is, in fact, manufactured rather than being a natural consequence of the marriage. Psychologist Stephen A. Mitchell expressed this dramatically: 'The familiarity [is] not based on a deep mutual knowledge but on collusive contrivance, the predictability not an actuality but an elaborate fantasy.'

Therapists often talk about the concept of 'fixed distance' between spouses in a relationship. This refers to the notion that in a relationship both partners contrive and collude in creating a set emotional distance between them that becomes fixed. This fixed distance becomes the safe distance they always return to. If one pursues, the other distances. If one withdraws, the other follows. It is as if there is a set distance that, though often temporarily changed, is reset like a thermostat.

There is a homeostatic mechanism that operates in marital relationships to ensure that the relationship continues to function within set limits. The sensitivity of couples to these limits, and their collusively agreed honouring of these limits, is remarkable to behold. In fact, our predictability within our relationship would be quite shocking for most of us to witness from the outside.

An effect of this contrived agreement is that a convincing and compelling fantasy is developed in a mutually reinforcing way. The more couples quietly agree on how they behave, the more they can develop imagined certainties about their stability. So the fixed distance is reinforced not just by our behaviour but also by our beliefs and fantasies. As a consequence, our sense of certainty and stability gets reinforced and solidified. But it is built on shifting sands. It is based on an invisible agreement. It is reinforced by wishes and hopes, as much as by truth.

Each person in an intimate relationship will adjust themselves—out of love, sacrifice, compassion or fear—to preserve something between themselves and their beloved. In interactions there is a constant process of adjustment, accommodation, negotiation, withdrawal or pursuit that maximises safety and security. This is not unusual in any way because it is part of the give-and-take and accommodation that occurs in every relationship in order to create that unique third identity—the relationship itself.

CLINGING TO EMOTIONAL DEADNESS
We have made clear how we have a tendency to create and structure our intimate relationships as a refuge from our wounded mortality. What we have not examined so far is how it is a defence against risky, unpredictable, self-diminishing, virtue-centred love. So when we complain about our relationships being dead, passionless, predictable, limited, banal, lifeless, boring, monotonous, tedious or tiresome, we have to courageously take on board how prized and precious these very predictable qualities are to us. We must acknowledge how essential these qualities have become. Our routines and agreements become like religious rituals, relics, spells and curses to ward off the terror of death.

In fact, we cling to this imagined security as if our life depended on it. Not only do we cling to it but also we cultivate, mind, refine and maintain it with an obsessive devotion and diligence that would be most discomforting to fully realise.

When you react defensively to your partner's dismissing of you, when you get upset when your routine is altered, when you feel outraged by your partner's forgetting you, when you get angry at your partner's ignoring you, you protest. You raise a voice that is just like a primitive religious outlet that seeks to get life back into alignment. Your anger is a curse, a spell, a chant to the gods.

In order to avoid this perceived loss of alignment, you try to keep your emotional love-making within fairly predictable limits. It is enormously difficult for any of us to change our security-enhancing means of guaranteeing our emotional survival and securing us from the premonitions and omens of death.

Constructing an Illusion of Safety

Because relationships mirror the passion and conditions of life, it is within relationships that we encounter life's full passion with vulnerability, woundedness, inadequacy, insignificance, anxiety and sorrow. Because life and love are inherently dangerous, we secure a sense of symbolic immortality if we construct and exaggerate an illusion of safety and certainty.

We prefer to believe that relationships are inherently safe. In believing that relationships are stable and fixed, then we must use our imagination to elicit desire and danger.

For this reason, people going through mid-life often have a desire to 'chuck it all in' and escape from the dull, secure certainties of everyday life and seek something more adventurous. Here again, relationships are believed to be safe and secure, while adventure is something that needs to be created.

Society, culture and popular myths suggest that one gets trapped in the boring certainties of a committed relationship and one must fantasise a more passionate one—or seek a more passionate one elsewhere. Nothing could be further from the truth.

OBJECTIFYING THE OTHER

Your notion that you actually know your partner is seriously flawed. The belief that you really know your partner as a predictable, safe, reliable or even boring person is a false illusion.

We want our partners to be safe and stable because we depend on them for so much. For many of us, our partners are our anchors. They are our shields. They are critical to our survival. We therefore need and want them to be reliable and safe. This may be achieved through accommodating compliance, coercive power, compulsive control, clinging dependency or passive-aggressive manipulation.

Recall those times when you have been out to dinner in a nice restaurant and you notice different couples sitting at other tables. One couple may be chatting in an affectionate and clearly pleasant way while another couple sit in silence and eat without eye contact and with only brief mumbled comments. Which couple, you might ask, are the couple that are married? Assuming you think it is the latter, you base this assumption on a belief that married couples have reached a point where they imagine that there is not much more to be known about the other. This assumption could not be further from the truth. There are so many thoughts, feelings, needs, fantasies, anxieties, poses, roles and secrets that relate to our partners. We know nothing of them, partly because they keep them concealed even from themselves. Our so-called 'objective' assessment of our relationships is really an invention.

What one sees in another person depends a great deal on *who* one is and how one *approaches* the other. All of the great traditions in psychology have discovered these facts in different ways. The nature of intimate relationships has been explored in great depth by psychodynamic, ego-psychology and object-relations theorists and researchers. All of them have discovered and analysed this simple process: the intimate other is the recipient of a range of projections that turn this other into someone almost magical, someone created, someone far different from who they might objectively be. When one fully grasps the implication of accepting this truth, the possibilities that open up are indeed awesome.

Your relationship is *invented* by how you envision, imagine and think about each other. Your relationship is impassioned not by measuring objective reality but by your *ability to imagine beauty and possibility*, and to see into the magical life of another person. One can have a cynical or hopeful view of love. A good-natured, trusting person will see different things from a paranoid or suspicious person.

What I want to emphasise here is that what you see in your partner is what you *creatively imagine them to be*. What you see in the other is a consequence of your artistic, spiritual and imaginative faculty. The faculty of imaginative thought and feeling is not easily learned; but it is universal. It is poetic, creative, spiritual and compassionate.

If you were to imagine painting a colourful portrait of your lover that displayed their inner life, what would it look like? Your answer would come from your imaginative love and not your objective assessment. To be able to imagine the other person's inner life sustains love.

The relationship we have is invented as much as it is real. And given our extraordinary ability to be able to project onto the world what we want and need to see, we *create the partner we love*. This is radical but inevitable. It is bound to be the case because of: our ability to create the reality we engage with; our extraordinarily rich and fertile imagination; and the degree to which we engage with our world in symbolic and mythic ways.

We prefer to give these qualities to affairs and secret lovers. However, your dull spouse is another person's romantic hero! *We imagine what we need*. Romantic heroes are mortal. Although you don't care to admit it, you prefer to keep well clear of such vulnerability. This is why you deny love.

We urge our partners to be safe and known; to confirm our assumptions about life; and to be refuges, asylums and immortality projects. We do this because of our fear of powerlessness and of this frail, transient, unstable, magical, mysterious, accidental, tragic, zestful and beautiful life.

Meditation

Imagine having an affair with your husband, wife or partner. Think about what you would have to believe or imagine about them to make this a passionate experience. For this day, conjure up those ideas and feelings and begin to see your partner differently.

FREEDOM AND DEPENDENCE

Relationships are not just about love. Relationships are a way that we look for a secure and safe home in life. We look for this safe home because life itself is not so safe. Putting it very simply, we are vulnerable because in life we do not know what is going to happen. Nobody can tell the future. Every person has felt this anxiety in them; it is there from birth. Sometimes the anxiety gets extreme and can feel like terror. Other times it can be smothering and can feel like depression. Other times it is hardly detectable. It can also become a form of excitement, an anticipation of what is going to happen. That feels good and it prompts a disposition towards possibility and change.

Relationships, though, are one of the main places that people look for comfort and safety. It can be very thrilling for people when they first seem to find this. They fall in love and feel that they have found what they have been looking for all their lives. What often happens in relationships is that the other person appears to have the power to make you feel good about yourself. In falling in love, the other person gives you acceptance, approval and safety. It can feel like you have arrived, you have been freed or you have been saved in some way. As the other person becomes more important, you realise that how they treat you becomes a key measure of how good you feel about yourself. Love does this.

The success of the relationship is that it becomes a safe home for you. You feel 'at home' in the relationship. This is obvious in the level of anger, rage, violence, paranoia and utter despair that is unleashed during and after a break up—this shows the enormous importance that is placed on a relationship. You can begin to get a feeling for how, in an enmeshed relationship, the other person can come to represent the *essence of your fate* or destiny in life.

Of course, I must add that falling in love and being in love—where one needs and relies on the relationship to feel right about oneself—is a wonderful thing. The doting husband, the admiring wife, the idealistic newlywed and the hopeless romantic all move towards the other with an optimism and enthusiasm that is real and right. It works in the long run, once you do not use or hijack the relationship for your own need to feel loved. What makes love dangerous is that you can transfer the authority to accredit your significance in life to another person. You do this because your beloved is now your most compelling and immediate psychological surrounding. The other becomes the location and the arena within which you now live out your life. It is therefore not an emotional mistake when we refer to our lovers as our 'whole world'. This applies as much to a young couple in the throes of romance as it does to a middle-aged couple feeling trapped in a boring relationship.

We bind ourselves to others to control terror, mediate wonder and defeat death by the strength, security and predictability of relationships. However, what happens then is this: we experience the terror of not being able to live without them. We experience fury if they choose not to live with us. Because they represent our life and fate, they then call into question our very freedom. We are left to wonder if we have any freedom any more.

The abusive partner batters the other because of the other's freedom. The co-dependent partner surrenders their freedom to the other partner. The passive-aggressive partner punishes the other partner for their freedom. Even the average spouse, who isn't abusive, can 'pick away' at the other's confidence because of this 'binding' in a relationship.

COERCION AND INTEGRITY

One of the unspoken expectations that people have of their partner is: 'Here is someone who should make me feel more secure, confident, important, significant and worthy than I am. Here is someone who should help me forget my inadequacy, isolation and sense of confusion. Here is someone who should help me to not feel so vulnerable.' The narcissist might seek a trophy partner to achieve this; the dependent might seek a partner to hand over responsibility; and the control freak might seek someone to submit. To greater or lesser degrees, we all seek someone who makes us feel good and right about ourselves.

The extraordinary thing about intimate relationships is that this is never really acknowledged. There is a common, unspoken demand: 'I need you to behave in a way that helps me feel good about me— sometimes despite the cost to *you!*' Day after day I see couples with the wrong intention: the intention of going to the battlefield of their relationship to find victory, to coerce the other into submission and to wrestle from the other a surrender or an apology. Every couple in chronic conflict does this. Each partner thinks that what *they* want is right, just and necessary. They need it in order to feel more secure.

Partners in a relationship often have this belief: 'If I continue to point out my partner's flaws to them, a time will come when they will thank me for it and realise that they have to change—because I am right.' Many partners find it impossible to let go of this position because, in their righteousness, they are convinced of their own point of view.

True love and respect requires something entirely different. It requires the ability to be a separate, dignified self that might *want* but does not *need* the other person to be any other way than they are.

As soon as a want turns into a need, then one resorts to tactics that become coercive or manipulative.

The heroic lover must be able to state a different belief system:

You are a separate person from me. There is an inevitable distance between us, which we must not avoid. There are things I want from you. My hope and want is that you can respect and respond to these. However, you are a free person and your role in life is not to meet my needs.

Equally, I do not need you to validate and approve of me. I am strong enough to do that for myself. I affirm and encourage your freedom to reject me. Our relationship has to be built on this freedom and respect. However, I expect you to have the courage to reject me with dignity, to say: 'I honour and respect what you want but I cannot meet that for you.' Then I can freely choose what I must do. But I ask you not to manipulate me, ignore me, dismiss me or control me. When you do this, you reject me with fear rather than with courage.

Let us learn to tolerate the inevitable distance that is between us and speak of it without fear or anger and most of all without a desire to blame each other for it.

Fear and Guilt in Rejecting the Other

An extraordinary thing I see in relationships is people's fear of rejecting the other person because of how exposed it makes them feel about themselves. People are always trying to disguise the fact that they are rejecting and hurting their partner. People reject each other through manipulation, sarcasm, pressure, ignoring, sulking, silence and abuse. These are all ways of making the other person feel bad *without taking responsibility for it.* Each person rejects the other with these toxic and often cruel tactics because of their terror of the isolation that accompanies self-responsibility and admitting that 'I need to reject you'.

A partner will rather abuse, humiliate or entirely blank the other rather than take responsibility for their impulse to reject. They will do anything rather than say: 'When you do not meet my needs I feel I have to punish you for it. It is my perverse way of re-establishing some control over you. If I do not have that control I am actually terrified.' It would be far more accurate and truthful if they could say: 'I do not love you. I find all sorts of ways to blame you for that. I have this perverted need to actually punish you because of my inability to love you or to be tolerant of the fact that you are so different from me. How crazy is that? No one deserves that. So let me have the courage to speak the brutal truth: I do not show love to you because my need to be right is more powerful than my need to love.'

Mature love actually includes the ability to reject the other person with respect and compassion.

MAKING A FETISH OF EVERYDAY ARGUMENTS
The diagram below shows how so many of us funnel the essential issues of life into the manageable nonessentials of the everyday.

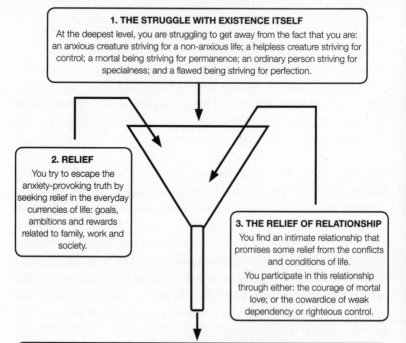

1. THE STRUGGLE WITH EXISTENCE ITSELF
At the deepest level, you are struggling to get away from the fact that you are: an anxious creature striving for a non-anxious life; a helpless creature striving for control; a mortal being striving for permanence; an ordinary person striving for specialness; and a flawed being striving for perfection.

2. RELIEF
You try to escape the anxiety-provoking truth by seeking relief in the everyday currencies of life: goals, ambitions and rewards related to family, work and society.

3. THE RELIEF OF RELATIONSHIP
You find an intimate relationship that promises some relief from the conflicts and conditions of life.
You participate in this relationship through either: the courage of mortal love; or the cowardice of weak dependency or righteous control.

4. EVERYDAY CONFLICT IN RELATIONSHIPS
All of the above get reduced down to everyday conflicts and struggles. You seek to win these conflicts because to lose them would threaten the illusion that your partner will relieve you of the burdens of living.
You may engage in: endless efforts to keep your partner happy; coercive efforts at getting your partner to change; or conflicts about freedom and responsibility.
Fights ensue about: who does what; who goes where; and why people are the way they are. These are all manageable fights that one can win. 'I might not be able to ward off the inherent inadequacy, vulnerability or powerlessness I feel, but I think I can ward off the closest reminder of this—my partner.' This impulse results in relationship conflict and everyday squabbles.

In many cases, the only way that we have of experiencing a sense of significance or importance is through negative criticism or hostile defensiveness. I have argued that domestic disagreements are the spilling over of primitive religious impulses to have power over a relationship within which you are reminded of your powerlessness.

Sometimes you counter your existential helplessness by attacking the spouse who has dared to expose you in some small, everyday way. You prove your significance by displaying some power over another. You can be superior to another through criticism and contempt. You argue, attack, blame, ignore and control.

Despite your best attempts, the dark side of your needs and motives seeps under the door of your deception. You argue vehemently in an attempt to coerce your partner towards submission. These arguments are your response to your inability to draw your family into your personal salvage expedition. The terror that takes over the adult is no different from the screams of a child that thinks they are abandoned.

Think for a moment about the ways life or certain people have hurt you. Very often, what gets bruised is your self-esteem. When your self-esteem is hurt, it feels as if something fundamental in you is threatened or violated. It is your sense of importance. There is really nothing more devastating for any of us than to feel that our sense of significance, no matter how small, is dismissed or taken away from us. Nothing else can leave us so utterly naked and exposed.

This is the only way one can understand the ferocious intensity expressed and displayed by people in relationships when slights, offences and insults occur. The life-defining importance we place on what are objectively unimportant issues actually reveal our true concerns. *The motive for your frustration and defensiveness is never what you say it is.* Your motive is actually your real dread of insignificance. Your everyday defensiveness is revealed as your compulsive urge for some heroic standing in life.

So you cling to your position and arguments with ferocity and intensity because these positions seem to offer some protection from your solitary vulnerability. They are your security blankets against powerlessness and death.

When you begin to fight with your partner or your children, more often than not, your arguments, defences, irrationalities and outbursts are the domestic version of a despot who proves his status by belittling another. In winning the argument, in proving yourself right, in attacking the other person, you are, in effect, warding off a demon that reminds you of your smallness and your vulnerability: 'If *they* win this argument, then a part of *me* dies. And if a *part* of me dies, then *I die*.' Your subconscious self feels and your conscious self acts out. And all the while, your thinking self *denies*.

To have one's efforts dismissed is more than just a rebuttal of one's efforts; it can feel like an attack on one's efforts to remain equal to life. It may be no more than a smart comment by your partner, an unintentional put-down or a dismissive attitude. But what it does is attack your precarious sense of self. It makes you ask: 'What is the point? What is the point of *trying*?' This, in truth, is the struggle for a heroic life.

Part of you wants your partner to be a symbol. You do not want them to be a symbol of death, decay, vulnerability and frailty; you want them to be a symbol of a triumph over all of these things. They do this by: being perfect; anticipating your needs; conforming to your beliefs; and soothing your anxieties. But what happens when your partner falls short, becomes imperfect, is unable to meet your needs, grows old, has bad habits or develops the images of decay? Then there rises up an awful terror and betrayal. This can be damaging, unless you can infuse it with spirituality, virtue and a love of life that loves all life.

TRIVIALISING RELATIONSHIPS

We are all guilty of trivialising our lives and relationships. You lose your temper because your spouse fails to comply with your expectations. You become irritated at your spouse's handling of the children. You sulk for days because you did not get your way. You fight over the smallest of things. You get silent for reasons you cannot remember. You hurt your partner out of spite. You punish your partner simply for being themselves. You gradually try to mould them into being the 'proper person you deserve'. You want to improve them and get them into shape. Perhaps you secretly feel superior to your partner?

Why do people accept to live a life that prioritises the trivial? Is it because the danger of a full circumference of experience is too much for all of us? Is it because the vulnerability and sheer terror of revealing oneself fully exposes one to potential annihilation, humiliation or rejection?

We find security in the familiar and trivial. Change, as we know, is enormously difficult for most people. Even changing everyday habits is difficult: losing weight, exercising, being organised, communicating properly, etc. We develop patterns of behaviour that create a world for us that is manageable, predictable and relatively controlled. The majesty, enormity, chaos, wonder, passion and possibility-filled life and universe are distilled down by each individual to a routine way of existing and participating in this infinite cosmic drama. We focus on how tidy the house is, how we care for the children or how we fulfil our responsibilities.

In a world filled with possibility, we reduce ourselves to a *manageable world*. We do this in order to establish some secure foothold. In many ways, we have no choice.

Safety, Security and Romance

Once you have secured your marriage as a refuge, maximised safety, anesthetised love, objectified your partner and created the illusion of safe love... then what is left to do? What happens is that the relationship becomes a prison of *safe obligations and responsibilities*. You follow the guides of what is socially acceptable. You take control of intimacy. You tame the dangers of desire and longing and place them under house-arrest.

Casting your romantic passion into the dungeons of yourself, you keep yourself safe from its distractions. It breaks free only when the wounds of life force you to lift the gates to your inner heart: at times of loss, death, vulnerability, trauma, tragedy or breakdown. Otherwise, the anxiety of life is apparently tamed and eliminated by being channelled into trivialities and away from the essentials.

Our lives become limited to functions that are necessary to sustain this superficial arrangement. We do what we can to keep up with the Joneses, climb the ladder of success, keep our relationships within limits and conceal our secret life. We conclude, unnecessarily, that there are no other options other than to live a trivialised life.

We avoid the possibility of rising above the limits we have put on the relationship. We avoid the possibility of an intense life because it threatens us with destruction. We realise this when it comes time to make substantial changes in life. We might want to, but our body and emotions don't want to follow. So we take many of our good intentions to the grave.

So we hold onto our predictable way of relating. We hold onto our partner, who we have co-opted as a key player in our network of reassuring responsibilities and belittling interactions precisely *because* our spouse is our protection. We are sheltered then by all the securities, predictabilities and trivialities of our relationship; and we are willing to accept it.

> *But now our tragedy is exposed:*
> *all of the things that we feel are essential*
> *to our relationship's stability*
> *have become petty;*
> *and so we have become a slave*
> *to the trivialities we depend upon.*

If your relationship has lost its passionate and spiritual meaning, it is because both of you have become dependent on it and, as such, have been depersonalised. You surrender to your relationship because, in its trivialisation, it is safe. However, as a consequence of this trivialisation, it loses its essential meaning. And yet you find yourself afraid to move out into it. *It is as if you are dying in the relationship but you remain physically committed to sustaining it.* You are faced with your own torment and shame: the tragedy is that you find yourself justifying what you know to be cowardly. You feel somehow important and worthwhile because of your superficial and trivialised life!

This is the dark side of your personality. This is how you continually end up in the same dead-end streets. You remain addicted to your way of being, your way of relating, your way of trying to love, even though it frustrates you and heightens your weakness, impotence and helplessness. You eat away at yourself from the inside. And your frustrations come out against all the reminders of your inconsequential living. You are consumed by inconsequential things. You spend your life measuring your significance in terms of status, power and vanity. You need it; and you hate yourself for it.

MAKING A FETISH OF TRIVIALITIES
Attempting to build up your heroic quest all by yourself becomes exhausting. The world and your family will not always co-operate and you end up seeking solutions to the great mysteries of life in the small fetishes of social approval, measured success, money, houses, social status and successful children. Such a successful life becomes increasingly neurotic and anxious. Mid-life disillusionment is a

consequence of your attempt to create your own world from just within yourself.

You are forever trying to inflate yourself up to something more powerful than you really are. The more you separate and inflate yourself the more anxious you become. You swing between the extremes of being everything to being nothing.

Whether through old-fashioned sin, psychological neuroses or rigid personality, there is this unreal self-inflation in the refusal to admit to the truth of existence. The truth is that we are all inadequate, fearful, vulnerable and powerless. In refusing the existential conditions of life, a couple cannot be consoled by shared mythologies about life and love. The lie of the marriage will often hold together; but this does not console the heart or replenish the soul. Joy, bliss and rapture die in the hollowness of the relationship; and they are replaced by addictions, compulsions and trivialised happiness.

THE HOSPICE OF EVERYDAY LIFE

Through the beloved, we encounter the beauty, safety and passion of living. Through the beloved, we also meet the limitations and tragedy of life. In the face of our beloved, in the cradling of a small baby, in the stewardship of parenting, in the wonderful drama of family life the deepest truths about life and love are revealed. This does not happen in any other social context in such a deeply revealing way. Its emotional origins are in the original experiences of early childhood bonding with parents and family. The early experiences of bliss and sensual joy are ones our unconscious mind never forgets.

The attempted solutions to the problems of life are first experienced in the family—where love and loss, life and death, tragedy and sacredness are experienced in the flesh. The flesh of our existence is found in lovers, children, siblings, grandparents, extended family and newborns. Here we find the original experiences of love and violence, sorrow and joy, light-heartedness and bliss. The great mysteries and dilemmas of existence are made incarnate in family life. The flesh of family life is its emotional life. The flesh of intimacy is the bond between partners.

When your sense of power, control, significance and invulnerability is threatened, then this is the distant bell that tolls in your life. When you experience a loss of status, it is the evocation of death at your door. When you are made to feel insignificant, it is a reminder of your vulnerable place. When you feel helpless, it is the cold wind of mortality. When you feel inadequate and incompetent, it disturbs your sleep. When you feel vulnerable and exposed, it is mortality burning at your fingertips. When you feel isolated, it awakens your fears of abandonment. When you feel trapped, it is a life sentence.

Everything you fear is derivative of the progressive disease that is your inevitable dying. Without death, there is nothing to fear. With death, everything in nature shakes with an anxiety to survive. More important, it is *with death* that nature pulsates with longing, desire and love. Death should not be portrayed as the Grim Reaper but as the God of Possibility. Death should be seen as an ancient god that makes life possible; and that makes everything about humanity possible.

But our body knows both anxiety and desire. What we do as humans is to convert anxiety of life-and-death into everyday life. We express it in our relationships. This allows us to distract ourselves and focus our attention on the proximate. 'I am not afraid of death,' your subconscious might argue, 'but I am afraid that my partner might be upset if I tell them how I feel!' We play out our deepest dramas on the stage of our intimate lives. We condense the mighty challenges of living down into seemingly pointless battles with the trivial. But this is the only place in which to do this. This is why the great works of literature are stories about people and relationships. Great songs, films, novels, operas, plays and TV shows are dramas about the ordinary through which the extraordinary is revealed.

The same things happen in every home in Ireland. Big themes and existential issues are fought out in the medium of the mundane. One partner rages against the other for failing to keep the cooker clean. One partner berates the other's incompetence in their attempts to handle the children correctly. A couple stands in the middle of the street, arguing over just how long this shopping should take. Are these trivial, pointless exchanges of anger and frustration? No: they are each person's attempt to project the largest of human issues onto the smallest and most manageable space.

*

You are afraid of disapproval because it is important to your self-esteem. Your self-esteem is important to you because it makes you feel strong. It is important to feel strong because it makes you feel powerful. When you feel powerful you can survive. When this happens, it feels like your survival is assured; and death is kept at bay for a time. Now you convince yourself you are secure, safe and impenetrable. However, everyday reality seeps in under the door of your delusion. Your dependency then mocks you. Grief ultimately breaks down your walls.

Your immortality project can never succeed. Some people struggle to accept this fact. This is why the abuser beats their partner. The abuser knows that they are vulnerable and that they need their partner; and they beat their partner for this.

When you fight with your partner, this is what you are fighting about. 'Don't you dare make me feel insignificant!' is the cry. 'Don't you dare take away my control! Don't you dare cancel me out by your silence! Don't you dare take away my sense of immortality because as long as I have power, status, competence and invulnerability, I am victorious. Without them, I am left exposed to the terrifying conditions of my decay.'

You would be better off speaking the truth: 'I am afraid. Can you soothe me with your love?'

Chapter 7
Diminishing and Elevating: Self and Other

DIMINISHING THE SELF AND ELEVATING THE OTHER

Existence presents us with very particular problems for which we seek solutions. These problems encompass how we cope with our helplessness, impotence and smallness. One specific way that people cope is to surrender themselves and their lives to such things as gurus, gangs, religions, ideologies, fashions or fads. This solves some of the problem of the burden of self-responsibility. We hand over the responsibility to another.

There is something in human nature that seeks to submit to something bigger, beyond or outside the self. There is a certain psychological relief that is felt in being answerable to something other than oneself. This outside source can help us to decide what to do and how to be. Of course, this can be done for purposes that are noble and for purposes that are evil. To see a person fighting for freedom is inspirational; to see a person follow an evil dictator is chilling.

Relationships are another place where this process is achieved. Through the other, we believe we can find both relief and inspiration. We indirectly escape the feelings of being ordinary, vulnerable humans. We can unburden ourselves of anxious uncertainty. In extreme situations, we surrender ourselves to a relationship that guides us in what to do and how to do it.

Extreme situations aside, there is not one of us who is not prone to wanting someone else to carry some of the responsibility of life for us. I would suggest that each of us does this to greater or lesser degrees at different times. This is not at all unusual because we are dependent creatures. From the moment of birth, we latch onto others and we need others in order to survive. Unlike most other animals, we remain dependent on our families for many years—often throughout the entire life span. This lays down the blueprint for emotionally committed relationships. You become dependent. Notwithstanding your emotional and economic dependence, it is hard to be isolated with the entire responsibility for figuring out how to be in the world. In can become exhausting.

In the absence of any rulebook for life, in the midst of not knowing why we exist or how we should live, every person leans on external resources to figure this out. People find all sorts of activities to give themselves to: politics, sexual conquests, religions, football teams, gangs, addictions or shopping. Some sort of external measure of one's worth and value is needed, however crude it may be. You do this in ordinary, unremarkable ways, too. Your needs to be praised, admired, approved, complimented, encouraged and affirmed are little ways that show your need for outside validation. This is part of being human. However, this tendency can become exaggerated when we elevate the other and diminish the self in our search for something important.

Every day in my clinic, I encounter people who have gradually abdicated the burden of self-responsibility and handed it over to another. One partner devotes their life to making the other partner happy and, in the process, diminishes and surrenders themselves. One partner controls and dominates the other partner and thus experiences superficial power and a relief from their own estrangement. The process can work both ways.

One way to co-opt your partner to guarantee your significance, potency and meaning is by diminishing yourself and elevating them. In this, you sacrifice yourself and (whether you admit it or not) you surrender to the other.

It is through this elevating of the other and diminishing of the self that some people find a relief from their anxious life. The elevation of the other invariably involves the diminishing of the self. I can look for relief from my solitary fears by elevating you to something bigger than you are, so that I can surrender myself to you. This is what Freud called *transference*.

This is how you can overcome your private sense of inadequacy. You can establish a sense of competence by successfully surrendering yourself to someone else. You elevate the other to the status of a parental figure. By relating to the other as a parental figure, the burden of vulnerability in your life is lifted in some way. By transferring onto someone else the power to approve of you, you do not have to summon this power for yourself.

I have little doubt that you do not even have to go beyond your own family to spot a relationship like this. The significance that is promised by such a relationship is achieved through dependence, submission and lack of the will to assert the self. One submits, defers and surrenders to the other. This is the surrender of the self to the need for approval and recognition. It says: 'If I gain my partner's approval, if I please my partner, if I avoid personal rejection, then I am significant and living a meaningful life and I will avoid the terror of vulnerability, helplessness and inadequacy.' This might sound extreme but observe in yourself how much you need approval. You will see this in how upset you feel when you are rejected.

In such relationships, people are freed of the burden of self-development. They can sacrifice themselves to the identity of the *relationship*. This is true of the man who surrenders himself to a relationship that has emasculated him, in which he still craves the blessings of his cruel and indifferent wife. This is true of the woman who is drawn to abusive relationships in which she drowns her own autonomy almost from the moment of first contact. This is true of abusers who seek out partners who are willing to accommodate the abuse. Many abusers become dependent on their victim, since the victim proves the abuser's potency.

In the more ordinary and everyday kinds of relationships something similar happens. You strive to fit in. You bestow on your relationship and on your partner this emotional task of confirming your significance in life. In this way, your safety seems assured. In projecting your yearning for belonging onto your partner, you create the satisfaction of being approved. I cannot overstate how profound a need this is for so many people. To get approval from someone important to you can mean the world. It can light up the faces of young and old alike. It is food for the soul.

You locate in your lover the power to provide love, admiration and redemption. Why else such huge distress, despair, anguish, rage and desolation when these enterprises begin to fail? Why else the joy, happiness, pleasure and satisfaction that come from feeling loved and accepted?

Co-dependency is the term used to describe people whose own happiness is dependent on other people being happy. I am sure many of you will identify with this common and sensitive trait. In co-dependency, security and significance is achieved by keeping other people happy. It can be an endearing quality but it has its downsides. The co-dependent gets so absorbed in trying not to upset people and in trying to keep others happy, that they forget *themselves*. They are fearful of seeing how this behaviour protects them from the dangers of living a full life. The neglect of the self, in favour of an over-concern about the other, creates an imbalance that can diminish and erode the fabric of the singular self. We see this not only between spouses but also between parents and children—where a needy parent can even become dependent on a child's approval.

Guilt

There are other feelings at work in all of this: guilt and self-rejection. The surrender of oneself to another's project is to sink into silent self-rejection. We may depressively *deflate ourselves* in order to keep the relationship. In some way, we give up on ourselves and on our own unique destiny. Though we think we escape vulnerable life when we give up on our unique self, we can begin *to die* as a result of this. Many people begin to fade away in the shadow of such relationships and they can become lost or depressed. They may feel there is something wrong with them and they end up on antidepressants. This, for many, can be the symptom of sinking into a relationship from which they cannot escape.

Many put up with bad relationships and unfulfilling lives because this compensates for some natural guilt. Many people feel they are not worthy of much more than they get in life. They feel that there is something wrong with them, that they are inadequate and that they should feel bad for wanting more out of life.

Everyone feels that they are 'not worthy' at some point. Issues of self-esteem affect every person on this planet. This guilt is a free-floating inadequacy and poverty of esteem. We each hand ourselves over and diminish ourselves before another. We merge into the other.

There is some indescribable need in humanity to be victimised in some way. This is some little streak in us that allows us to be treated poorly. We are all affected not by the guilt of having done something wrong, but by a free-floating, vague guilt. We have a sense of unworthiness that is an ever-present background emotion. It can be most annoying! In such reluctance to stand up for ourselves, we accept bad treatment; in effect, we feel we deserve it.

ELEVATING THE SELF AND DIMINISHING THE OTHER

The diminishing of another can achieve the same objective as elevating or idealising them. It is a self-protective function. In diminishing another person, we seek to externalise our deepest fears and impotencies onto someone other than ourselves! It is a chillingly effective psychological strategy called *projection*. The 'bad' in me is projected out into you and I can then attack you for it.

Instead of hating my own weakness, I disown it and locate it in you. Then I can magically hate it there! This is the basis of all prejudice and discrimination. To be honest, we all do this to some degree at times. Bad moods and bad humours that cause you to hit out at others are everyday illustrations of this. You are in a bad mood because life seems to be going against you, as it does. When someone close to you then does something wrong, you let fly with your existential resentment. You convince yourself in that moment that *they* are the cause of your irritation and distress. If you catch yourself in that moment, you can identify the early seeds of human cruelty.

Through diminishing that person, we can find some relief. It works! People unburden themselves of individual angst by attacking the other for being unable to give them the validation they long for. Each of us is prone to such behaviour. We want someone else to carry the weight of our frustrating and irritating life; we want to blame them for it.

These processes are sometimes necessary and desirable to achieve some kind of comfort and soothing in life and in relationships. We have to find something beyond ourselves on which to discharge these tensions. One can do it through simple activities such as sport, art, gardening, exercise or hobbies. The challenge for someone who has narrowed their life too much is to find a way that does not require the elevation of themselves above another. Achieving this involves expansiveness, imagination, creativity, integrity and courage.

Human Sacrifice

How often have you let fly at your beloved for some small infraction? Have you blamed and criticised your partner disproportionately? Have you sulked, withdrawn and ignored them? Have you felt resentment and anger, caused not by their betrayal of you but by their imperfect, sometimes irritating and always real *humanity*?

If your sense of security in life is dependent on controlling a relationship, you will exhibit a self-serving pattern of behaviour. Your need for superiority is so critical to your self-esteem that empathy, compassion and sensitivity for your partner's experience is diminished. You degrade the other in order to establish self-importance.

What might this look like? It shows up in so many coercive behaviours: complaining; criticising; using put-downs; placing your needs ahead of your partner's; intimidating; threatening, etc. In extreme cases, one partner seeks to establish some heroic significance through the hostage-holding of the other. This is how so many people prove their status in life. Many a family has been held hostage by a violent and abusive father. Many a family has been terrorised by a tyrannical and angry mother. Many a child has had to build their little life around the self-absorbed entitlement and rage of an alcoholic who destroyed any semblance of normal family life.

When a person diminishes their partner to elevate themselves, they are saying: 'If I get my partner to do what I want, meet my needs and protect me from my own experience of inadequacy and powerlessness, then I will be safe and will have proved my authority.' The exertion of tactics of power and control maintains command of the relationship. This illustrates how relationships can be the hiding place of the fearful, terrified or cowardly. The ambition is that one can, through the exertion of force and power onto another, secure happiness. If they cannot secure happiness for themselves, at least they can deprive it of the other. Herein the offender plays God.

It is quite a natural motive to inflate one's size, importance and potency. Once we understand this, we can understand how it is in intimate relationships that one gets the daily symbolic measures of one's importance. Only by comparing and contrasting yourself with your partner—and the outside world—can you judge if you have some extra claim to importance. This can be achieved through the love and validation you receive from your partner, which makes you feel good. Or it can be achieved by your diminishing of your partner, which makes you feel powerful. Relationships are ready-made props for self-exaggeration and inflation of oneself to something important. Intimate relationships are fraught with the potential for the diminishment of the other to exalt the self.

Your relationship gives you exactly what you need to solve your emotional problems. In your relationship, you have found a definite point of reference for your courage and redemption. Your longing for some ability to be able to master the conditions of life is brought within your range of influence. It is brought right into your own kitchen. Although you cannot avoid feeling powerless over the destiny of your life, you can experience power over another. Although you might not escape the sense of inadequacy you feel in the face of the majesty of life, you can find some adequacy in controlling and diminishing your partner. It is awful, but it is true.

> On this altar one can sacrifice the other,
> one can feel one's godliness,
> one's victory over the emotions
> of vulnerable humanity.

In all of these ways, we can see how the modern love relationship as imagined by culture (art, religion and mythology) can be hijacked and used as an interpersonal solution to a fundamental existential problem.

This is the reason there is so much bitterness in family and marital life. The imperfections in those close to us seem to reduce and diminish us to a size we cannot tolerate. For this reason, we attack loved ones and try to bring them 'up to size', as it were. We see that they have clay feet, so we chip away at them in order to save ourselves. We try to deflate the unreal over-investment we have made in them in order to secure our self-esteem.

EVERYDAY SADISM

This might seem like a strange thing to say but, let me say it anyway… *Honest love owns its inevitable destructiveness.*

In other words, the courageous lover claims ownership of their inevitable insensitivity and cruelty. This meanness or hurtfulness is often subconscious. Therefore, it feels unintentional to the perpetrator. It is rare to ever hear anyone say: 'I hurt you because I want to cause you pain.' It would seem like an awful admission, wouldn't it?

So there is always an excuse given,
an explanation provided,
a good motive ascribed.
But the victim feels it.
The lover knows it.
So often you apologise for it
without ever being able to admit it.

Sometimes, cruel acts towards a partner are served up as a form of love, within which the giver denies any mean-spiritedness or retribution. In twenty-five years of counselling, I have not encountered a couple where there was not some form of rejection, criticism, withdrawal, hostility, punishment, revenge or defensiveness. Therefore, I am convinced of this: *mature love includes being able to acknowledge and own that one inevitably hurts the other person; and that one inevitably does some of that with subconscious intent.*

Couples get into great difficulty because this reality is continuously denied; and in the denial, there is real conflict. After inflicting some hurt on the other, you say: 'That is not what I mean', 'You are completely misunderstanding me', 'I don't know why you are getting so defensive', 'You are completely overreacting', 'I don't know what your problem is', 'I am just being honest here', 'You are imagining things', etc. So many people come into my clinic and inflict wounds on their partner, simultaneously denying that it is happening: 'I am just trying to get to the truth here,' they say.

The art and courage of love is being able to reject your partner with *integrity*. It is being *honest* about one's rejection of the other. It is admitting, if possible, to one's mean-spiritedness. Admitting to the faint strain of sadism—the satisfaction felt in making someone else feel the pain that you do. In fact, a lot of conflict involves this need to create equal distress for the other so that they feel what you feel. There can be some relief in this, perverse though it sounds.

I have worked with thousands of couples. For most of them, it is very difficult to say the following things:

• Yes, I am hurting you because it feels good to me, given what you have done to me.
• I withdraw from you in order to inflict pain on you.

- I give you the silent treatment not because you have hurt me but because I need to punish you.
- I get angry with you because I can see in your face that it frightens you, and that makes me feel in control.
- I criticise you because it makes me feel better about myself.
- I criticise you because I know it makes you feel small, and I take perverse pleasure in that, in pointing out your flaws.
- I rage at you for no reason other than the pleasure I get out of discharging my frustration.
- I am on your case all the time because, in some way, it gives me a feeling of power I never had growing up.
- I neglect you because I want to upset you.
- I am filled with irritation at life and I enjoy venting it on you.

To say these things would feel like admitting to something awful that is repressed from consciousness. It would be admitting that, at times, you get satisfaction from causing distress to the other person. You might say that you never do that or rarely do that. If you do, I would suggest that the satisfaction you get remains subconscious. In other words, you get that satisfaction but you say to yourself it is only in the service of justice. Or else you deny entirely that there is satisfaction in your behaviour. You suggest that it causes you terrible upset and it's the last thing you want to be doing! Of course, these are rational denials and excuses. Every day I see people hurting each other as a means of achieving some form of release or relief that subconsciously feels good, as if something has been squared up and balanced out in life. Very often the intended target is *life itself.* Your partner symbolises all of the symptoms we spoke of earlier (vulnerability, insignificance, etc.) so they are on the receiving end of your indiscriminate irritation, crankiness and moodiness. Sound familiar?

It is important to bear in mind that to reveal one's *occasional* meanness, cruelty or projection—and to admit to it—is a brave act of vulnerability. The vulnerability is in showing one's neck, exposing one's weakness. It is in the vulnerable courage of revealing one's own spitefulness, revenge and stealth.

It is the courage to be shamed.

Love runs into all its problems because these impulses are denied. Now they may only constitute 5 per cent of one's motives but the *denial* of them can cause 95 per cent of the problems. One of the most common complaints from partners in therapy is that the other partner is causing real hurt and pain to them—and the perpetrator is in complete denial that they are causing this pain. 'You don't seem to realise the hurt you cause me,' says the injured party to the other who seeks to diminish or deny the hurt. What we have here is a second level of sadism—that is the denial that one has a negative effect on the other, the indifference shown to the other person's wounds and pain.

Not taking the other person seriously is another passive way of inflicting distress. Again, the perpetrator holds their hands up and says: 'I don't know what you are talking about. I do know that it upsets you but you just don't seem to get what I'm saying to you. This upsets me more than it upsets you!'

This impulse of self-relief does not necessarily come in big acts of betrayal or violence. Rather, you hurt you lover in much less visible acts of diminishment. It takes courage to admit that, at times, you engage in invisible little acts of revenge. You play innocent under the disguise of the 'good partner' but you subtly inject traces of poison into your words or deeds. Sarcasm, cynicism, negativity, irritability, 'innocent' accusations, smiling jibes, cruel jokes, camouflaged meanness, false hurts, exaggerated offence … all these things are done subtly in your words or deeds every day or week. You play the role of either hero or victim, occupying your moral high ground with feigned regret!

> *Marriage is never brought down*
> *by great acts of defiance*
> *but rather by the thousand cuts,*
> *the chipping away at the foundations,*
> *the scraping at the walls of the other's self-confidence.*
> *The gradual, inevitable pulling*
> *of each blade of grass*
> *brings forward the mud slide*
> *of destruction.*

Communication and Deceit

We must not be fooled by the word 'love' and imagine it to be something soft and woolly, something to do with hugs and reassurances. No, love is made of clay. It can soil the hands that mould it. So one of the real problems in relationships is the expectation that love is pure, that it does not have contaminants or additives that can poison its taste.

In fact, love has two ingredients: control and love. The controlling element to love always casts a slight shadow. For example, one inevitably uses the other to relieve or resolve issues in one's life that have nothing to do with that other person. It is inevitable. The ghosts of many people from your past drift around your house, affecting what you say and what you do. Voices from the past whisper things to you about what is happening in your life—voices that are mute to your partner or spouse. Sometimes you hit out at these ghosts who seem to have entered your spouse's body. Love, therefore, has inevitable disappointments and rejections.

Most acts of love are served with traces of control. Positive love is sometimes contaminated by punishment. Affection may be contaminated by expectation. Protectiveness may be contaminated by traces of dominance. Most acts or gestures serve different functions and are rarely pure but rather cocktails of different kinds of communication. Gestures and statements are often inconsistent and contradictory. The other person intuitively knows this and is caught in a bind. They *feel* this bind but they have no evidence for its existence.

They pick up the hidden lie imbedded in communication. They may feel the inherent hostility or deception but are unable to expose it. We are talking here about the deceptions of intimacy, the necessary illusions of love. Anxiety creates deception because the one you love is also your potential assassin! If the one you love is your life project, you need to take great care.

These are the inconsistencies and deceptions inherent in marital communication. Every communication *reveals and conceals* the truth. Over time, the other person learns to react to what is *concealed* rather than what is revealed. You begin to discover the hidden agendas, the trickery at work and the denial of the undeclared truth. There is a kind of implicit agreement that the deceits and deceptions of intimacy will never be named. There are things between the closest of couples that, for good reason, remain unnamed. An extreme example of this is the unholy alliance of George and Martha in *Who's Afraid of Virginia Woolf?*

This is why you can experience very frustrating feelings in relationships. You can feel as if you are 'going mad', 'desperately frustrated' or 'walking on egg shells'. You can feel desperately self-doubting and lose confidence. Often, this happens because what you are dealing with is the drip-feed of invisible deception.

What is that deception, inconsistency, lie or bind? The cruel 'love' of the offender reveals the deception that lies within us all. Love is never utterly pure. It can be cruel love, avoidant love, whinging love, blind love, needy love, painful love, righteous love, hostile love or defiant love.

The avoidance of the offender is mirrored by the avoidance of the victim. This is a revelation of what we all do in more subtle ways.

He slaps her in the face
and she says sorry.
Her lie is to herself when she says:
'I am sorry, I did not mean to provoke you.'
His lie is to both when he says:
'I only did it because I love you.'
The victim apologises,
the perpetrator complains
and in that there is a grave reversal
of the truth.

Part II

Heroic and Inspirational Love:
Relationship Solutions

The solution to all of the relationship predicaments described in Part I can be found through heroic virtue and imagination. I am referring here to qualities and dispositions that are much more than strategies, problem-solving techniques or communication skills. Heroic virtue refers to qualities that lie within you that enable you to rise above your life conditions and relationships. These qualities enable you to find meaning and purpose in more than what is objectively before you.

The people who inspire you are not those who deal rationally with life but those who, despite what reality has set before them, rise above it and find a way to overcome that reality with imagination and courage. Such qualities inspire you to be better than you think you are. In a similar way, through imagination and virtue, we can transcend or rise above our condition. We can enliven it with hope, humour and possibility. In fact, this ability to rise above ourselves is that quality of self-awareness that defines us as people. It gives us the unique ability to see ourselves and others as if from above.

When we do this we are able to see the bigger picture. We can see life in the round and our place within it. Not only do we see the bigger picture, we *feel* the bigger picture, we experience this bigger picture, and we are intimately connected to it. This ability to experience ourselves and others in the context of the arc of life makes love and compassion possible; it makes inevitable our sympathy for another's pain. Whether it is through bereavement, new birth, loss or unexpected joy, we weep, celebrate and express love because of this. In the bigger picture, our sorrows and our joys are connected.

These qualities of imagination, virtue, light-heartedness and sympathy cannot be easily taught. However, they can be inspired and evoked from their dormancy in a human heart. With spiritual discipline, they can be nurtured. In much of my work with abusers, I find myself appealing to the better part of them. I find myself urging them from the prison in which they have confined themselves. I find myself calling them towards their tear-point—the point where the tears of vulnerability flow when the cloak of denial is pulled aside. I intuitively know that this point lies within them. This is the point where their controlling self meets their compassionate self. I find myself raising the bar for them, rather than dropping it lower. I challenge them to be bigger than who they are. When the wound of life is opened in the human heart, change and conversion are possible.

In order to do good and be better people, we must not only know what we want to do (i.e. be kinder to our partners), we must access the source of energy that *makes* us want and need to do this. At the risk of repeating myself, such desire is only experienced when we inhabit the twin passions of mortality and creative life.

When we can bury our own parents with uncomplicated grief and we can cradle our own children with uncomplicated joy; when grief and joy are purified by our openness to life and death; then the ordeals of marital breakdown, family illness or financial distress can be managed in proportionate ways. Spiritual heroism and courageous love prevent you from deteriorating into righteousness or self-pity. People with these qualities have, as a result, a dignity and integrity that ensures that love survives in its most essential form.

Heroic and inspirational love is underpinned by many qualities. These qualities will be explored in Part ii of the book. This section is not a list of things to do or a set of gimmicks to use to get what you want. Rather, it refers to virtues and metaphors that describe this imaginative life. I write them not to tell you what you should do but to remind you of how you can be. I want to inspire you to remember who you already are. I want to prompt you towards your inevitable heroic destiny: a passionate life.

Chapter 8
Integrity

I n Chapter 2, we explored the inevitable symptoms of vulnerable love:

- Woundedness
- Vulnerability
- Anxiety
- Insignificance
- Helplessness
- Inadequacy
- Guilt

These represent the key experiential effects or conditions of life itself. Human beings, by virtue of mortality and mystery, all experience these emotional realities. These emotions are a central and unavoidable dimension to our emotional and spiritual life. It has been the role of ancient religions and rituals to give repression to these facts and to find solutions to them. Cultures and societies have tried to give expression to—and find relief from—these human experiences. So too does each individual. We do this particularly in our family and intimate relationships. You will have found your own way to try to deal with these experiences in your love relationships. Putting it simply, you have either sought to control life and each of these elements *or* you have learned to integrate them naturally into your life in ways that have released the joy that is within you.

Traditional religions have recognised the helplessness and vulnerability of humanity; and they have created imaginative ways to cope with this life without rejecting it. For example, ancient practices of meditation and prayer sought not to escape life but to be *equal* to it. Doubtless you have your own inner practice and rituals that inspire and encourage you through your life and day. Heroic and inspirational love integrates these symptoms of mortal life into everyday life. Compulsive and controlling love does not.

*

Integrity in relationships can be understood as the ability of a partner to honestly integrate all these qualities into themselves, and to relate to the other from this perspective. This kind of integrity creates a love that is void of righteousness and self-justification. It is a love that is in sympathy with the other person's plight while holding onto one's own plight.

In seeking relationship fulfilment through integrity, a person embraces and fully inhabits these unavoidable conditions. The lover integrates the dread of mortality with the joy of living. The lover does not take flight from helplessness, vulnerability or anxiety. Rather, they accept, tolerate and befriend them. In this way, the person calms the inner conflict. Rather than trying to be victorious over the other, they display a certain humility, grace, tolerance and flexibility. In assuming this attitude, a person finds peace, competence, influence, openness, connectedness, capability, transcendence and self-worth.

It goes without saying that this is not a constant state: it is experienced to greater or lesser degrees by each person throughout their day—and throughout their life. The path to a rich and fulfilling life demands this integration of the self and the ability to rise to the occasions of life. The symptoms of mortal life and love are transformed when they are embraced with courage. They become the qualities that we admire most in those close to us. They become the symptoms of an integrated and courageous life.

When we are able to appreciate life and love, we understand and accept its inherent vulnerability—which is the very source of our passion and compassion. When we walk this path and find that we do not flee from natural anxiety, we can become peaceful and light-hearted. We feel capable and adequate without having to prove ourselves or overcome natural inadequacy. Rather than being controlling in relationships, we become influential and confident. We are open and accessible and comfortable with our vulnerability. We become connected and compassionate precisely because we experience our own natural isolation. We become transcendent: with imagination and spirit we can rise above the ordinary foibles of our partner and we can love them in the bigger picture of life. Finally, in being true to our vulnerable human nature and our passionate love of life, we overcome guilt and find a deep sense of self-affirmation and worth.

In doing this, we can experience:

- Peace
- Light-heartedness
- Capability
- Influence
- Openness
- Connectedness
- Confidence
- Transcendence
- Worthiness

*

Love built on integrity will integrate the symptoms of vulnerable love into everyday life. Compulsive and controlling love will not. When someone seeks to reject their woundedness, vulnerability, etc. they then begin to develop a counter-phobic reaction to these experiences. Their fear of these unsettling emotions results in a denial or rejection of their vulnerability through over-compensating for it. This person is then motivated by the need for ever-increasing control and success over the other person and their relationship. The person then chooses the *opposite* disposition of these core emotions. Rather than being able to tolerate anxiety, they become aggressive. Rather than being able to tolerate inadequacy, they become perfectionists. Rather than accepting helplessness, they become controlling.

We all seek refuge in these positions in domestic life and relationships. However, this becomes problematic when it becomes an *overall attitude to life* and others. Some people will relate from this position in a consistent way. It makes a genuine, deep and intimate relationship impossible because the person is at war with life itself. In seeking to control life, they diminish and control the other person. They take their spouse as a hostage or victim, as a false symbol of their own success. An abusive, violent or controlling personality exhibits this pattern. Sometimes they do it to such extremes that they destroy (even murder) those close to them as one final act of 'godly power'. It is as if they wish to show life and the world that they have been victorious.

The symptoms of counter-phobic and controlling love are:

- Detachment
- Invulnerability
- Aggressiveness
- Status-obsession
- Control
- Righteousness
- Self-justification
- Self-pity

Chapter 9
Courage

*It is a relationship
of selflessness
without reference
to profit or loss.*

Courage is the attitude from which most of your solutions to relationships emerge. Courage has been present in the whole breadth of your existence. You can see it in your parenting, work and loving. Your life can be described in terms of courage—the striving and persistence to succeed against many odds. In fact, the history of evolution is itself a narrative of physical courage. Relationships need to be understood not just in terms of love and commitment, but also in terms of courage. In getting to know a couple in therapy, I want to know what inspires them to endure. I ask one question of every partner I counsel: why is it that, despite everything, they remain loyal to the irritating person that is their partner?

To suggest that love involves courage seems to suggest that it is some sort of ordeal rather than a form of bliss. Well, noted anthropologist Joseph Campbell has said exactly that. He argues that love is like life itself: life is an ordeal and love is an ordeal. It is passionate and exhilarating precisely *because* it is such an ordeal. If there were no ordeal, there would be no life, no drive and no passionate response. In a strange way, it is the ordeal that makes life worth living. It is worth living because the reward that comes from everyday triumphs inspires and sustains us.

As I write this book, the 2012 Olympics have just come to an end. The games and athletic achievements have been inspiring and enthralling precisely because they model the drama of life itself. It is all about the *ordeal* and the *application of the self* towards it. We cheer athletes not just for victory but for *effort*. This is why 80,000 people in a stadium respond with such emotion when they see someone push themselves to their limit. It is also the ordeal that makes the spectators weep when they witness the athlete stand before their flag or anthem to receive their medal. This is because the athlete has shown great courage and they have done so for something larger than themselves. Sport, in this way, is a mirror of everyday human courage.

Courage is about fortitude and endurance. It is about not giving up. It is present in how you are true to yourself in spite of those elements in your relationship that work against you. It bridges the gap between what you long for and where you are now. It makes the link between what you expect and what is. It exists in the space between the ordinary and the extraordinary. It is that quality in you that keeps trying. Every day in countless ways, you keep on trying. What exactly it is you strive for may not be clear to you but you do not give up. You may feel like giving up at times—but you endure.

Love demands sacrifice. If you are a parent, spouse, partner, adult child or grandparent, you have to suspend yourself to be available to others. In courage, however, the most essential part of you prevails over the less essential. In other words, your courage is your commitment to something more than yourself; it is a commitment to something bigger than yourself.

Courage is not something you think of much when you think of love or family relationships; but it is actually the very essence of existence. When your striving disappears, you disappear. It is what makes a living thing what it is. When, for example, depression takes over your life, you know that desperate feeling of *losing* that striving within yourself. The hopelessness of depression is the awareness that one has lost one's courage.

The courage of love is the acceptance that the frustrations and disappointments of relationships are part of life and the human condition in particular. It is the affirmation of the deeper meaning and purpose beyond what seems trivial, irritating and random. Wisdom in relationships rises above anger, distress, disappointment and irritation. Courage involves being able to affirm yourself despite the fact that your partner, child or parent *appears* to reject you.

Ancient wisdom and common sense tell us that the pursuit of always-being-satisfied, always-feeling-loved and having-my-needs-met leads to disappointment and frustration because this can never be achieved. This is the longing to return to that blissful state of childhood when there was no conflict within us—just pure freedom and delight.

The deep affirmation of oneself in spite of the inevitable disappointments of a relationship creates the space for love and contentment. This is not the satisfaction of fulfilled desires or of getting what you think you need; this is the lifting of oneself above difficult circumstance. It is the courageous *yes* to one's deepest self, regardless of the understandable *no* to some circumstances.

Courage is being able to experience the tensions, disappointments and frustrations of relationship without letting it overcome what you might call your essential self. Irritation, frustration and stress are really a consequence of what you might call the accidental in life rather than the essential. However, if you imagine it is essential (as we often do), then you feel as if the integrity of your self is at risk. As I have found with couples, many people mistake the accidental and circumstantial for the essential; and they over-react with righteousness or defensiveness.

We should now see that the landscape of love has a river of courage running through it.

There is something about love that will see you not loving the person but loving the *courage* in them. You love the courage of your small child—you see this when the very small five-year-old runs onto a very big soccer pitch. You love the courage of your partner, who carries a great burden without complaint. You love the courage of your mother or father, who keep hidden the pain of illness.

The person may be weak but their virtue is strong. Nietzsche said that it is our virtue that is dearest to us. Your lover's virtue should also be dearest to you. You must love their efforts, not their success. In your relationship, it is virtue that you should love and affirm. Virtue is your dearest lover. To love your partner because of what they *do* is the flipside of rejecting them because of what they *do not do*. You are virtue. If you love your partner's virtue, you love the eternal in them.

Deciding that 'what they do is good' is just cold admiration.
Rather, judge not the goodness of their acts
but the manner and motives of their doing.

This is courage.

To be in a relationship with courage and honesty is to be able to inhabit, tolerate and ultimately befriend the threatening primary emotions. Though these emotions may seem like steps towards despair, they emerge as being the stepping stones towards a joyful and uninhibited life. It is from within these waters that the abandoned soul can find transcendence. In mythological and religious terms, the hero is not one who experiences invulnerability and fearlessness but rather one who experiences vulnerability and fear courageously!

The courageous spouse might say something like: 'I am afraid. I feel really exposed at this point. But nevertheless I must say these things to you because if I do not I will be a fraud. My heart is racing with anxiety but you must know the true me. I am afraid of losing you but if you have me in your life you must know me fully—in my frailty as much as my strength.'

Here this person expresses elements of fear, vulnerability, inadequacy and helplessness. It is from this engagement with the other that the symptoms of mortal life become the base from which the true impulses of love, compassion and an undefended approach to life emerge. From the existential emotions (of woundedness, vulnerability, etc.) arise the emotional longing, the religious impulse and the heroic urge towards love that is spiritually and psychologically meaningful. Here, love is the ordeal it should be. Ten times a day you are faced with the choice of courageously embracing your vulnerability and inhabiting the essential condition of your life and your relationship— or else denying and turning away from it by way of pretence.

Courage is the gateway to the undefended life—the door to the soul. It is the path of descent. These emotions involve a certain 'bearing of one's neck' to the world. It may look like surrender but it is ultimate bravery and honour when one does not hide from the terror of life but stands out in front admitting to one's fear but not accepting defeat. The greatest inspirations in life are acts of heroism. The ultimate proof of the hero is seen in how they welcome adversity, in how they inhabit these difficult emotions. To face difficult emotions is to face the death of your ego, to cast aside the security blankets of trivial importance, to step down from the compensation of righteousness. It is to rid yourself of the superstitious stones and pagan rituals of your compulsive status-seeking and self-justification.

Heroic love can be seen in so many places. It is in the kindness of people who care for sick loved ones. It is in the determination of single mothers who do their best to raise their children alone. It is in the will of the bereaved to use their grief as an opportunity to give back.

Leave your anger at the door. Leave your self-pity at the door. Leave your self-justification at the door. Leave your self-absorption at the door. Leave your self-importance at the door. Leave the crutch of your convictions at the door. Leave your polished opinions at the door. Leave the trophies of your treasured beliefs at the door. Leave all the attitudes you have refined into the armour of your self-protection at the door. Stand naked in all your vulnerable smallness. Speak your fear and inadequacy. Speak your desire and longing. Speak your integrity, self-belief and courage. With a sense of virtue, say no to what depletes you. Say yes to what inspires you.

Touch the garment of sorrow and the veil of your helplessness. From here your hand will reach out with integrity, strength and the freedom of no longer carrying the burden of your own pretence. Now you can play in the meadow of natural exuberance.

This emotional disposition is characterised by humility, gratitude, tenderness, respect and compassion. It is known by those who have suffered, those who have sought to live a virtuous life and those who have maintained respect and dignity for the plight of others.

We see these people everywhere: the battered spouse who brings Christmas gifts to the neighbours; the separated father who speaks well of the woman who betrayed him; the wife of an alcoholic who does her best to show her children the beauty in the world; the partner who loves you for your efforts.

True joy and contentment in intimacy (and in life) can only be achieved if we walk in the way of passionate life. Out of this journey, true rapture, bliss and passion can ensue. Religion and psychology speak of this in many different terms. The dark night of the soul, the valley of darkness, the Via Dolorosa… They are all part of the path to transformation. There is no transformation without a casting off of the garments of power.

The real act of courage lies in tolerating worry, anxiety and despair. The revelation of one's vulnerability is courage. Courage includes tolerating your own inadequacy, accepting your own limitations, inhabiting your helplessness, befriending your limits—and still having confidence in your own self. It takes courage to stop self-rejection. It takes courage to stop thinking that there is more you should be doing, there is more you should have, there is more you need to chase.

Tolerating your limits involves celebrating your limited competence and being thrilled at your impotence! It is not just acceptance: it is celebrating imperfection and being enthusiastic about failure. It is the courage to fail gloriously.

Chapter 10
Trust

Simply trust your spouse.
The autumn leaves
flutter downward
with that same trust.

Trust is surrendering to life and death with gratitude and faith. Trust is at the heart of every act of courage. Trust is the source of our persistence. If you are trying to get out of a relationship with dignity or wanting to become engaged with sincerity, you need to trust that the impulses within you are related to the desire in you *to live*. To have this trust, you need to overcome self-doubt because it has the power to drown you in guilt.

Trust bridges the enormous gap between eternal life 'out there' and the mortal body 'in here'. Trust exists in the gap between your soul and your brain. And despite this gap, the power of existence itself is present.

Life is a pure flame, and we live by an invisible sun within us.
Thomas Browne

It is invisible but we know the flame is there. We do not see the light, we see by it. We do not know life but we trust it. The spouse who needs to escape from an abusive relationship must have that trust. They must trust that the power of life, the power of their children and the power of the gods are with them. If they can access this, their move comes less from panic, worry or defeat—it comes from the power of their own being.

Their trust knows that to walk this path is to walk with guilt, doubt and helplessness. Their courage means that they can do this in spite of all the difficulties. Trust accepts that you must exist in spite of— and not instead of. You must love in spite of its failures, pains and betrayals.

Life asks big questions of you. Trust means accepting that there is something that lies beneath ordinary experience. It is the state of *being carried in the river of life* that participates in everything. You can affirm yourself because you are affirmed by life. Here the mystical and the personal are identical. The ordinary is in the extraordinary! In both, trust is the basis of courage.

Here is the heroic act of living within oneself. When an abused spouse is ready to leave, it is because they have accepted something in themselves that is beyond their current living situation. They begin to trust something beyond their abuser's definition of them. They trust something beyond their definition of themselves as failure. They trust a connection with something eternal. They trust that they have something in common with all of human life. They affirm themselves in the midst of their abuse because they know they are affirmed by life itself and nobody can take that from them. The mystical and the personal join in their life. They see through the mist of their diminishment. Trust is the basis for their courage.

All these acts of survival are acts of heroic transcendence. This is decisive: we live in a time when the anxieties of self-doubt, helplessness and guilt are everywhere. But the anxiety of self-doubt seems predominant. We are terrified of losing the meaning of our existence. This is why we find it hard to trust.

Chapter 11
Affirmation

A good man [is] one who accepts with cheerfulness his lot in the sum of things, and deems it bliss enough if his own deeds be just and his nature kindly.

Marcus Aurelius

I want to try and describe something called self-affirmation. Self-affirmation is the ability you have to affirm your very existence. It is something that is so fundamental to your life that it is hard to define. It is that quality in yourself that enables you to endure, to keep going, to survive. It is that quality of courage in you that gets you up in the morning and gets you to sleep at night knowing that tomorrow is another day. It is that quality in you that, despite everything, insists on you being supportive of yourself. It is that quality in you that wants to be true to yourself, that needs to be true to yourself.

It is deeper than self-esteem or self-confidence. It is in your very name. It is in your body. It is the affirmation of yourself that is beneath words. It is that quality in you that says: 'I arise today.' It is the self that was always there. It was there when you were born; it was there when you were two years old; it was there when you were twelve years old. It is there now, as you read this.

Beneath your thoughts, you keep going no matter what. Your deepest self affirms you. This affirmation is the acceptance, support, encouragement and physical determination to exist as yourself. It is that extraordinary quality in you that gives you courage. At its purest point, it is the joy in being alive. In its everyday form it is the life that is living you.

It is that deep, distant voice in you that encourages you to get up out of bed, keep going, eat, talk and engage. It is even deeper than an inner voice. It is a self-affirmation that enables you to sleep, breathe and love. It is that thing in you that is for you. It is almost like the 'God' within you that supports you. It is at the level of your very existence.

It is how your body affirms you, your breathing breathes you and your uniqueness unfolds. Self-affirmation is not an act of thinking but a disposition of self-acceptance and a humility that is full of grace. It is the rock within you. It is the river that flows through you. It is your strength. It is your inner character.

In your relationships, self-affirmation perseveres in spite of being treated badly, being abused or being rejected. Your affirmed self does not need to defend itself against attack; nor does it need to prove itself. If someone tries to put you down, your ego gets hurt but your affirming self actually does not understand. The affirmed self is not wounded by someone else's anger or disrespect because it does not rely on others for approval or affirmation. It is that core in you that *affirms itself by itself.* You can therefore exist above the horizontal troubles of everyday life. In many ways, it is the *divine love* in you that persists despite even yourself. It is the courage and will to be in your own skin. You could be kidnapped and imprisoned by terrorists who might beat and abuse you; and yet, underneath all the fear and terror, there would still be an *untouched you* observing all that happens to you. It would be the 'you' that was born and grew up and has remained you no matter what has happened to you. Victims of abuse and trauma have all identified and held onto this truth.

When you have the courage to be in your own skin, rejection by another is not fatal because you affirm yourself. When you are being in your own skin, your self-affirmation is not selfish because you do not need to have your superficial needs for approval or applause met. Having the courage to be in your own skin is physically heroic, emotionally virtuous and mentally wise. It is that awe-inspiring quality in people who can, as the philosopher Nietzsche put it, *love their fate.* It is the gift that enables you to willingly participate in your imperfect and, at times, troublesome life.

This is why happiness in life is an expression of courageous virtue. It is not the result of a profit and loss account of all the good things minus all the bad things in your life. It is that amazing potential in people to find happiness and purpose even when the bad outweighs the good. Having the courage to be in your own skin is *beatitude*—a serene blessedness.

For this reason, all the books that speak about how to have a successful life are doomed to fail because there is no such thing as 'a successful life'. The so-called successful life is measured in terms of profit and loss. The affirmed life is lived through courageous self-affirmation. The patients who line the wards of any hospital this very day are possibly more successful in their courage and self-affirmation than any line of successful businessmen. So-called success is as much accidental as it is intentional; and to the degree that it is intentional, it is fake. Real success is not a technique. It is beatitude.

Being in your own skin comes from a willing participation in the mystery, in the divine and the eternal. I do not use these words in either a religious or mystical sense but in a very real way. The very source of your courage in life springs not from your thinking mind but from a spring within you that comes from a life source that you might call divine. It is also a life source that connects you with the generations that have gone before you and the generation that has already begun after you. There is an eternal heartbeat that sustains and guides you.

Having the courage to be in your own skin is a participation in the universal, eternal, divine act of your own life. It is a self-affirmation that permeates all of nature and humanity. It is felt and seen by the poet. It is the melody of the musician. Self-affirmation is the source of love.

Chapter 12
Virtue

God will not have his work made manifest by cowards

Ralph Waldo Emerson

The source of passion, commitment and strength of character lies *beyond* the physical reality of a relationship. When we aspire to a good life, we draw on virtue and a purpose beyond ourselves so that we can function in the relationship. However, when we draw on the relationship to enable us to function in life, we place too great a burden on it. We transfer onto the other person the responsibility to provide us with the experiences we seek. We want the relationship to not only relieve us from the burden of life's conflicts, conditions and responsibilities, but we also expect it to inspire us to be free and safe!

Relationships must not be the only well from which we draw the sustenance to find meaning and significance in life. They cannot be the only place within which we encounter the divine; nor can they be the only vessel within which we empty the anxieties and terrors of life. No—we need to draw from other sources so that these qualities, inspirations, virtues, visions and imaginings are poured over the angst of relationship like a balm.

Tolerance, compassion, courage and humility must be what we bring to our beloved. To come with empty hands expecting redemption is to expect too much.

Chapter 13
Spirit

Love is non-moral.
It lives a deeper life
that is not cast down by failings
nor elevated by virtuous action.

Hopefully you will have come some distance towards appreciating that modern marriage and emotionally committed relationships, though cast in secular clothing and spoken about in terms of personal emotional needs, are actually undertaken as spiritual, heroic, transcendent and religious quests. Our exploration leads us to the realisation that the immortality-related, anxiety-driven demands placed on the modern love relationship are often so great that the relationship caves under the weight of this expectation.

The consequence is that relationships become de-spiritualised and de-personalised. The coin gets flipped over from wanting too much from one's partner to wanting too little; from wanting too much for oneself to wanting too little. Virtue is transformed to vice. Good is transformed to evil. Hope becomes cynical despair. All around us are examples of the tragic deterioration and degradation of love built on subsiding sands. A couple so deeply in love can, five years later, find themselves fighting over custody in the courts. A couple who were happily married for twenty years are now not talking to each other; they correspond only through solicitors.

Therefore, our conclusion must be that our heroic urge, our spiritual longing, has to transcend our intimate relationship. We need something that is beyond and ahead of ourselves. When we seek fulfilment through the other, when that other becomes the sole source of meaning and significance, it limits and enslaves us.

Our growth and strength have to be gathered and developed as we progress along the hero's journey, towards a meaning and purpose that calls us forward. But this purpose must be above, ahead and beyond one's partner. In fact, both partners must walk towards the same light—and less towards each other. This is the value of virtue, faith, spirituality, compassion, charity and courage. The courageous person sees beyond the frailties of both the self and the other.

This might sound airy-fairy but most of us choose safe heroics. We want the gain without the pain. We want to peg down life through our immortality project. We want to stake down our lives by establishing security, safety, power and control. We all play it safe.

In terms of marriage and intimacy, we choose the ideals of the standard cultural prescriptions of heroism. We try to be a good provider, a good parent, a good partner. In this way, we earn our significance through child-rearing or being part of a social group. There is nothing false or non-heroic about this standard cultural solution to the problems of life. It represents both the truth and tragedy of our condition: the responsibility for the sanctification or justification for one's life is delegated to our partner, society or popular culture.

Virtue, values, faith, imagination, spirituality or a belief in God can be sources of inspiration. This is because they are abstract in some ways; they are beyond the physical reality of the relationship. If you are committed to a particular virtue, then the virtue inspires your everyday living. It guides you from beyond. However, if we look for someone else to inspire us totally, then we are in danger.

One of the inescapable truths of everyday life is that life asks one to endure one's littleness and one's daily insignificance. In relationships, life is reduced to fixing gutters, organising lunches, having petty disagreements and taxiing children and teenagers here and there. One gets stuck with the annoying idiosyncrasies and trivial demands of one's partner. The consequence is that the everyday trivialities of marriage and relationships become intolerable unless they are inhabited and experienced as being part of a larger, higher meaning.

What is it that enables a parent to get up in the middle of the night for their crying child? How is it that we can tolerate the irritating habits of a spouse? How can we bear to pick patiently through a pile of our teenager's laundry? We can do these things when they are translated into a meaning that lies beyond private needs. If you try to find this meaning within *yourself* or within the dull routines of everyday life, you will ultimately grow weary and fatigued.

Meaning is found in compassion for another's suffering. It is not found in controlling others to minimise one's own discomforts. Compassion involves a heroic sacrifice that is very different from the fetish of control. For this reason, it is critical to appreciate and understand the meaning of heroism. Heroes give themselves passionately to what may appear to be an unimportant event: the heroism lies in the *character of that surrender*. Therein lies courage.

Rather than looking to the other to give, grant, award, prove, justify or bestow significance or power, try to *bring* spirituality to the other. When you bring imagination to the other, you can love in a way that seeks to *bring* life's mystery rather than *find* it. Love is ignited by imagination.

My dear mother, though walking a road of bereavement, never failed to continue love's mission after my father died. This was because her love was true and could continue through to her children and grandchildren. That would not have been possible if her love was purely dependent. I see in her every moment the reality that my father accompanies her through her ongoing mission in life. She did not let my father's virtue die with him. In other words, their relationship was not just about him but about the *virtues* they chose to live by. So, even though she is heartbroken and grief stricken, she has continued their mission. She knows that which is bigger and beyond herself and the marriage she had. She knows how to live a life of service and virtue.

Love is not morality.
God makes no judgment
of your spouse's imperfections,
but you do.

Meditation

The salmon was in much distress and had lost hope in his life. He went to the pond where the wise salmon spoke to him: 'You are a salmon. You struggle with your life. You feel much distress about your life. Your anxiety is coloured by three questions: "Is this what I should be doing? Am I good enough? Why can't I be in control of where I go?" When all these things build up in you, you lose hope. You get down on yourself because there seems to be no escape. You feel that this river is a prison. You feel trapped in your own destiny. There is no point in talking about your complaints about your life—the water being too cold, the current being too strong and your companions being too difficult. Your stress has nothing to do with any of these things. It has to do with whether you want to be a salmon or not!'

Because of our unique ability to transcend any situation in any direction we create goals beyond ourselves. The salmon lives for 'the beyond'. It is miraculous even to biologists how that inner 'beyond' takes the salmon across oceans back to the same still pond. It exists for something beyond itself. In marriage and intimate relationships, our purpose must be towards something beyond. It becomes our inner intention. Vitality is the ability to live beyond oneself without losing oneself.

Chapter 14
Transformation

*Grateful acceptance
co-operates with your partner's imperfections,
knowing that they are no different from your own.*

Spirituality suggests that, if we want to achieve transformation in our lives and in our relationships, we must walk away from what is established and begin to search at the edges. The traditional symbols of spiritual success are not politicians, monarchs, leaders or business people; they are the figures of the forgotten child, the sinner, the slave and the broken people.

It is important to remember that all of the substantive moments in life are about death. All of the people who symbolise change and transformation are close to death. They are sensitive to the powerlessness and vulnerability of the life we have. All of the symbols of transformation in spiritual texts are those people who walk through what we might call the death experience.

You do this also. You have had experiences in life where everything you believed or held onto was called into question. This may have come about through the death of a loved one, the illness of a close friend, the accident that changed your life or the falling out of love.

What does this mean for intimacy and relationships? It means that we must move away from a centre that needs power, control, victory, significance and approval. We must move to the edges *where one imagines one loses these things.* To find one's soul, one must turn away from the established securities of marriage, towards its unavoidable insecurities. One must recognise the evil that goes by the name of self-rejection.

To enter the garden of intimacy is to accept rejection and exclusion. There is no mature love that does not carry the scars and wounds of rejection, sorrow and inadequacy. All the great spiritual teachers seemed to know this. The *excluded one* is one who understands. The only meaningful spirituality is the spirituality of the castaway. Soul work involves walking through your sorrow, pain and exclusion until you have something to contribute.

Richard Rohr emphasises this concept throughout his work. He maintains that we must know rejection in order to have experienced life. We must know isolation in order to love.

It is hard to realise that the conflicts, arguments, loneliness and despair of relationships are less to do with yourself or your partner and so much more to do with *life*. You are entwined with the universe and your breath is the breath of life. Your fear is humanity's fear. Your sorrow is the sorrow of living. There is great sorrow and fear in all of life; of course you experience your piece of it. Yes, you blame it on the people and events in your private life; but it is a wave sweeping forever through all humanity. It is not really yours. It is the feeling of being.

Chapter 15
Acceptance

To ask why about life and your relationship
implies there is something outside it.
It is because it is.

The real root of your marital distress and anxiety is not your partner; it lies in the conditions of your life. It is your struggle against life. The universal anxieties are converted into conflict in all relationships. Tillich suggested that there are three things that cause us all the distress we have in life. These are the anxieties of:

- Not knowing our fate
- Feeling guilty about how we live
- Doubting the meaning and purpose of our life

Our anxiety about our fate is our subconscious realisation that we do not control fate and that we are at its mercy. It creates this compulsion in us to want to control everything. In fact, this is the impulse of life that drives you forward every day. This is the impulse that makes plans, takes precautions and seeks safety in physical and emotional life.

Our anxiety about guilt is our subconscious realisation that we are totally responsible for how we live, which creates a compulsion to succeed. We have this ever-present wish to be doing something of worth and value. We urge our children to better themselves. We are acutely aware that we have complete responsibility for what we do with this precious life and we are haunted by this vague guilt that we are not doing that well. This prompts us to do more and to try harder.

Our anxiety about doubt is our realisation that life has no meaning unless we create it. This impulse creates our compulsion towards certainty and righteousness. We create our own narrative, story and purpose. We define ourselves, make plans and construct a life that has an inner coherence and consistency.

Let us look again at the first anxiety—our anxiety about our fate. The distress caused by our realisation that our fate is not entirely within our own hands flows beneath our life constantly. Despite the popular belief that 'your dream can come true if you try hard enough', we are haunted by the awareness that this is not really true. Everyday life, like a suspense movie, is filled with this anticipatory uncertainty about what is going to happen next. The events of life are so often accidental—whether they are tragic or fortunate. As the humorous 'de-motivational' poster put it: 'In every race there is one winner and hundreds of losers. Chances are that you are one of them!'

We listen to the news every day, which tells us the same things over and over again. If you listen to the themes behind daily news you will realise that it gives just two pieces of news every day. The first is: *people die.* The second is: *bad things are happening.* In other words, the daily news bulletin tells you the same thing every day: *your fate may not be good.* News bulletins are, in essence, psychological reminders of this and 'the news' becomes compelling to people because of our innate anxiety about fate. The news is our wake-up call to fate and our simultaneous relief that it has not been our loved ones who have been killed in some accident on this occasion.

Fate is your destiny that is not determined by you alone. Although you are giving directions, you are not the one driving your own bus. You know where you want to go and you have your goals and objectives. However, even though your driver appears to listen to you some of the time, you still do not drive the bus of your own life. Like taking a taxi in a foreign city, you give the directions but you have no idea where you are going or how you are going to get there. Despite what all the motivational books say about following your dreams and realising your destiny, you are not in full control of your own fate. You know only too well that illness, accidents, tragedies, traumas, diversions, mistakes and so many unforeseen things can happen to you at any time.

Because of this, you move through the hours and minutes of your life with this vague anxiety and stress. It comes and goes. At its best, it is experienced as excitement and anticipation. At times, you feel the excitement that comes from realising that fate is working in your favour. You experience the bliss of enjoying the moment because you know it to be the moment. You find pleasure in realising that the gods seem to favour you, for now. This is the excitement experienced when you feel you can trust fate. It is that feeling that whatever happens in your life will be okay. It is a kind of inner confidence that life will be good to you; and if it is not, you will be able to deal with it.

At its best, this natural anxiety about fate can be soothed into a delight and peace with life because you know that these times are blessed; and whatever happens, you have this sense of gratitude. You strive to live for the now, for the moment, because when you take your eyes off the moment, the distant heartbeat of stress or anxiety is heard.

However, no matter how good you feel about your future, the anxiety of fate never fully goes away. If you are a parent, you know this feeling only too well. This ever-vigilant sense of danger that lurks around the corner of your child's innocent exploration. You know, as a parent, that the fate of illness, accidents, unexpected events is never but a few steps away from your vulnerable child.

We can find some relief from our anxiety about fate through *control*. We don't just sit back and wait for fate. We try to counter fate by simply making plans and setting goals. We operate on the assumption that we are driving our own bus and try to live accordingly. We counter the dread of fate with our efforts to control our lives and the behaviour of those close to us. Exerting control gives us some passing sense of being in charge of our immediate life. We ease the anxiety. It is necessary and essential in order to live and make our way forward through life. Having a sense of agency and control is the fire of life. However, this temporary control is set against the background of the unknown fate that life has in store for us.

The danger of control is that we take it a few steps too far. We can become control freaks. We can become so controlling that we freak out when people do not conform to what we expect—be it our children or partners. When our need for control takes over, we can become aggressive and demanding.

Sometimes we turn this control inward. We scheme and plan on a daily basis how we are going to cope with and outwit the day ahead of us. We make obsessive plans to ensure we have some kind of controlled victory over our work, our boss or our family.

Instead of trying to find relief from the anxiety about fate by trying to control everything, we can find resolution to the problem through *acceptance*. Acceptance affirms the fact that you are not in control of life and you do not need to be. Acceptance sees that the very essence of life is its unexpected nature and that your task in life is to enjoy the scenery on the daily detours away from your best-laid plans! Acceptance of the vulnerability of life can bring a humility and ease. It can bring a realisation that you do not need to be in control because you never *can* be in control. Your partner and children are free entities with their own destinies separate from your plans.

Acceptance helps you to access the divine freedom of life. You can find that your *love of freedom* is the antidote to your *fear of fate*. And the gateway to this freedom is through hope—the naive hope of the child.

The sparrow in my garden, whose nest has been destroyed because the thicket within which he has lived for many years has been cut down, is not crestfallen. He has not become distressed or hopeless. He has not been filled with despair. He just gets on with it. He starts to build another nest. He has no self-doubt, no guilt and no fear. He is courageous in accepting fate and life and he is heroic in persisting with a physical optimism. His family home has been destroyed. Does he feel like a failure? Not at all. He just moves to the next stage of life with courage and enthusiasm. His fate is not denied; it is accepted. But in his acceptance, there is a pulsating self-affirmation. There is no surrender to fate. There is *hopeful participation*. It is delightful to behold.

*

When I go,
guard my tomb well,
grasshopper.

Issa

The fear of being trapped in a marriage gets aroused on a regular basis. The fear of being trapped by a judgment, conviction or ongoing pattern of communication is equally frustrating. Being trapped evokes frustration and distress. Experiences of being stuck, imprisoned or trapped (even if it's just in an argument or a traffic jam) really do seem to threaten our self-security—the affirmation of our free existence in relationship and life. 'Please don't oppress me!' is your silent (if not literal) cry.

A salmon will die rather than give up and swim back downriver. You keep swimming upriver in your life, too. You search for resolution and you keep persisting. This defiance is natural because it is better to fight against a raging river than to die in a still pond. It is virtuous because it represents physical courage. Some people get into relationships without courage. They never swim upstream. So they bail out of the relationship easily.

The anxiety about our mortality and our ultimate fate comes into view in the second half of life. As the obstacles of stress and preoccupation begin to fall away, as we begin to be concerned about pensions, healthcare and retirement, we get a clearer view of the horizon. It gradually becomes the permanent horizon within which the anxiety about being trapped in a fatalistic situation is at work in marriage. 'Oh I am too old for this,' we say as we struggle with everyday stress. 'At my stage in life I should not have to cope with the irritations of the trivial. I am too old to be fighting with someone over something that is not important in the context of the horizon that lies ahead of me.' Our anxiety and distress about our fate emphasises the lack of certainty of love, its unpredictability (an affair), its purposelessness (the death of a child) and its vulnerability (everyday fights) to whim (moods) and the accidental (stressors).

Our dread of nothingness stands behind our awareness that every moment of time vanishes completely. I bet you, like me, watch old video tapes or DVDs of the children when they were small and you are shocked at how time passes and how all that was so real then has vanished. It is so disconcerting and challenging to experience that urgency that comes from realising that a little bit of you dies every day! And from that, you strive to give birth to something new. 'He not busy being born is busy dying,' wrote Bob Dylan. 'Ah, but I was so much older then/I'm younger than that now,' he sang in another haunting song.

Every day in every way, we pass away. We notice the decay of our body. We get alarmed at a strange symptom or illness. We are deflated by the loss of sexual drive and romance. Each day we are haunted by the homelessness of our own existence. We can even feel displaced in our own beds or sitting in our cars. 'I want to go home,' your heart cries 'but where can I find it?'

Intimate family life exposes your insecurities. You have the ability to suppress and repress your anxiety in the outside world. You suppress this anxiety at work, with friends or when engaged in activities. But you need to get home in order to be yourself and let the real truth of your nature find expression. For this reason, the family home is the place where love is most intense and violence most prevalent.

You will admit to the fact that sometimes you can't wait to get home in order to 'unwind' or 'let go of stress' because the strain of having to bind up your natural anxieties can get too much at times. You are in danger of revealing your vulnerable, anxious self in public; socially, this is not encouraged. To lose your temper at your boss or to shed tears at the deli counter is not how we are supposed to be. We prefer to go home and vent our irritations on our spouse or seek comfort in their arms. We bring home our humanity. We bring home our essential vulnerability. Relationships not only expose you to fate and death, they become the place where you inhabit these things. To take it a step further, it is a place that exposes you to yourself.

Our fear of fate is what evokes feelings of being trapped in a marriage or relationship. It is very common for couples in distress to use these kinds of metaphors to describe their relationship: I feel 'trapped', 'imprisoned', 'smothered', 'stuck' or 'helpless'. This feeling of 'not knowing what to do' is expressed every hour in my clinic. Some of this can be understood in terms of fate. It is that desperate feeling that fate has placed us in a situation from which we cannot escape, from which there are no exit doors. It is that desperate feeling that change is beyond our control, that no matter what we try to do we end up in the same place. It is that vague sense that fate is working against us. It is that faint acceptance that fate has a part to play in our everyday life.

For most of us, the feeling of being trapped and helpless is more terrifying than having to face any overwhelming obstacle. The latter allows us to engage with life. The former, being trapped and helpless, awakens our most essential and deepest fears of nothingness.

Chapter 16
Doubt

Doubt is the distress you feel about whether there is some meaning and purpose to your life. I don't mean doubt about whether you made the right decision here or there, but doubt about whether you are living the life that is right for you. I mean doubt about whether there is real meaning, value and purpose to your life; whether you are doing what you are supposed to be doing with your life. The feeling that you might be 'wasting your life' in some way is actually a very common one and it is an indication of the degree to which we are subconsciously sensitive to how life is not a dress rehearsal.

At times, you will certainly have felt a kind of displacement, an unsettling emptiness or a panic about whether there has been meaning to your stress and striving. As you trudge through the grocery store some wet Wednesday afternoon, worried about whether you are going to be on time to pick up the children from school, you will ask yourself: 'Why am I doing all this? Is there not a better way? Am I missing something? Do I count? Does anyone think about what I might need?' Your heart asks these questions from time to time. They can haunt you late at night or when you are walking somewhere on your own. This is the anxiety of doubt and emptiness, when you doubt the meaning of your life. You might wonder on occasion: 'Would it matter very much to anyone if I was not here at all?' To that extent, you can feel invisible.

Another variant of this is when you feel *lost*. It is like that feeling you have when you go into another room to get something and, when you get there, you forget what it was you were looking for. It is like having that same feeling about your life as a whole! You forget your purpose in life and in love. You go through the motions and in your moments of doubt you ask yourself: 'Why did I get married at all? Who is this stranger sleeping next to me every night? Why did I bother having children that seem to just use me?' You feel that maybe you have been living in a trance. You feel that you are lost and sleepwalking through the scenes of your life.

It is indeed a disquieting and disconcerting feeling; but it is one that that we *all* have. These feelings are known to everyone. They are universal because they relate to existence itself. Existence has thrown you into your life and into a role that, at times, you doubt.

The experience of emotional doubt is the dread of having wasted one's life, the dread of not having had a purpose. You feel this acutely when things in your life begin to fall apart; which, at some point, they must.

Ultimately, when you lose meaning, you lose the focus of life. You lose an ultimate concern. This ultimate concern does not have to be lofty or inaccessible. For many, their purpose in life is to be liked or loved by others. For some, their focus may be to find someone to mind, protect or control them. However, the danger of these ultimate concerns is that one's fate, esteem and contentment lie in the hands of others.

It is better that your esteem lie in your own hands, rather than in another's. It is better again that your esteem lie in the hands of the *beyond*, rather than in your own hands. By that I mean you need to lean on something larger than yourself and to inhabit the non-judgment of the eternal.

The loss of faith in one's own virtue is most terrifying. It is so frightening to feel that you have been swimming up the wrong river, that your inner guide, your inner self, has been lost. It is a terrifying experience to find that what you trusted most—your inner guide—appears to have led you astray. It feels as if your inner compass has failed.

There is nothing wrong with you if you have these feelings: they are part of our human condition. It is hard to love your emotional and existential homelessness; but it does not end just there. This vague sense of doubt or homelessness prompts us towards meaning, towards finding a home, towards love.

How do we find relief and resolution to this haunting doubt that plays like background music behind our life? As I have discussed elsewhere, we can find some relief by control, compulsions, activity and motivation. We can find relief by, for example, countering our self-doubt by elevating ourselves to being 'number one'. We may also find relief by surrendering ourselves to someone else who can tell us what to do; and it is many of you who will have handed over the agency of your own life to a partner, job, guru, church or ideology. In many ways, it can spare you of anxiety.

The alternative is to affirm your self-doubt. Instead of seeing it as weakness, you can appreciate it as part of the mystery of life. With a disposition of humility, you can ease your anxiety. You can find solace in life when you meet fellow pilgrims who, because they know what it is to be lost and homeless, know the value of searching and growing in life. If you are not lost, you never know the longing that drives the human heart forward! If you do not let yourself feel what it is to be spiritually homeless, you are unable to feel compassion for those who do. Because of our innate and deeply human doubt about life, we often feel homeless behind the walls of certainty.

You can find consolation and an emotional home in the words of the poet, the song of the musician or the vulnerability of your lover.

When I reside in the homeless shelter of my own heart, I enter a doorway to a spiritual (more than literal) purpose. It is by way of this spiritual purpose—to inhabit my homelessness in the universe—that I affirm myself. I do not affirm myself by way of thought but by way of courage and acceptance. Have you ever felt touched by a nameless person who catches your eye? They seem to say to you: 'I, too, am searching. I salute your courage.'

Doubt is actually the condition of all spiritual life. It is existentially real and not humanly weak. You can try to escape some of this doubt through a fundamentally religious attitude or through other forms of personal fundamentalism. You can use religion to protect yourself and when doubt raises its head, can slam it down with righteousness and dogma in your urge to justify yourself.

In our youth, we dwell on intellectual and religious questions. The answers to these questions attempt to purge doubt from the human heart: 'Who made the universe?' 'What is evil?' 'How could God become man?' However, as we grow older, we get answers to questions that were *never really asked*. We get these answers when we are broken with bereavement. We get them when we were chosen by love. We get them when we understand the mystery of life that ebbs and flows like a tide through us. We get them when our life becomes both universal and solitary. We get them when we see love flow through every ordinary, human act.

But these answers cannot be spoken literally, so we express them through art, poetry or music. Our unspoken answers move beyond the questions. Our doubt sits with the answers. We dwell in the twilight between mind and spirit. We dance in this beautiful space that Wordsworth described:

The Moon doth with delight
Look round her when the heavens are bare…

Chapter 17
Openness

The loneliness of love
is not reclusive or depressive,
but a sympathy,
an empathy with a life of
grief and pain,
where flowers bloom
even still.

Other than becoming more self-serving, narcissistic and grasping, what is one to do in life? Greed is everywhere. Domestic abuse and violence is endemic. Our sometimes desolate conditions do impel humanity towards violence, abuse, projection, discrimination, racism, genocide and so many evils committed by humanity down the ages. But there are, as we know, many other ways. Humanity has another history. Relationships have other ways of being. It begins with an optimistic acceptance of life's conditions and an openness to the anxiety they cause. The flood of anxiety that follows from such a realisation is not the end for us: all spirituality begins at this point. The soul's search always begins at the point of abject poverty of spirit. The longing and impulse to love, show gratitude, walk with humility and know courage begins at this point of apparent desolation. Our hope and spirituality begin at this moment, at this burning point.

In Christian terms, this point is at the foot of the cross. In Buddhist terms, it is the surrender of one's ego. In therapeutic terms, it is the acknowledgment of one's helplessness. In personal terms, it is *letting go*.

You do not need to believe in God or another supreme being to understand why we humans invented gods. Agnostics or atheists can spend as much time in wonder and awe of life. They can have a real appreciation of the privilege of being present on this planet and an appreciation that, as sentient beings, we are only in our babyhood. Spirituality does not need to include words like 'creation' or 'theological'. Humanists and atheists are as spiritual as any others. We are sentient animals and this knowledge brings us all to the point of passion, desolation and hope.

Spiritual longing is inherent in human nature. Only by opening one's heart to the mystery of life does one resist reductionism and truly get a sense of immortality. Only then do we come to terms with death. To achieve this, we have to look beyond the consolation of others and the status provided by things in the world. Our ultimate concerns are more theological than they are biological because we find our ultimate meanings in the symbolic world. This is not just my conclusion but that of many great philosophers and psychologists such as Carl Jung, Ernest Becker, Otto Rank, Joseph Campbell, Norman O. Brown and others. Equally, it is the concluding point of all world religions. It is a truth too compelling to ignore and one that the psychotherapies have yet to come to terms with.

Spirituality that does not arise from a fearless encounter with our very condition is cowardly and a superficial avoidance of what we are. To arrive at this point of both anxious suffering and acceptance is the very air in which the soul and spirit can breathe. This profound *awareness of who we are* is a better teacher than any social prescriptions about life because they can be lied about, twisted and tamed by perception, culture and defences.

In other words, the true heroic validation of your life lies beyond the horizon of sex, intimacy, the other or the private religion of your reduced and obsessive life. It comes from the majesty of creation and the passionate integrity of life itself that pulsates through you. As we have shown earlier, when you seek conclusive security in your relationship or ritualised life, you are pulled downward in a search for meaning in your everyday preoccupations. What happens is that you end up feeling empty and inferior because you realise that you have developed a dependence on status or approval given to you by others in order to feel good about yourself. You realise that your emotional centre of gravity lies outside yourself and you can thus never stand on your own two feet.

In order to transform and transcend yourself, you must break down that which you need in order to live. You must venture out of your comfort zone. Like King Lear, you must stand naked in the storms of life. This means standing courageously at the centre of your existential circle and showing yourself to your beloved, while somehow holding onto yourself. Many of us romanticise freedom and liberation while, at the same time, we prefer the comforts and familiarity of the prison of our everyday self. Like many prisoners, you are comfortable in your limited and protected routines, with safety and security. The idea of probation into the world of freedom actually terrifies you!

The self must be broken in order to become a self. Something must give way; a native hardness must break down and flow like liquid.

Chapter 18
Perspective

Skylark
sings all day,
and day not long enough.

Basho

Paradoxically, love flourishes when we do not try to achieve a form of controlled triumph or success through the relationship. In other words, love is more in tune with passionate vulnerability when its purpose has nothing to do with any kind of victory or justification. Good emerges when you avoid the temptation to use your partner to meet your hunger for status. Good emerges when you are kind.

You may think that your partner disappoints you, angers you, shames you, belittles you or ignores you. However, all these experiences are not a consequence of them, but a consequence of *life flowing through the two of you*. Those who expose us to our mortal impotence do nothing more than reveal the nature of life. Your partner reveals earthly mortality, imperfection and decay. In this, they are as imperfect and beautiful as anything in creation. Your partner can never prove your significance in the universe. That can only come from the deep well within—or the vast expanse beyond.

One of the most humbling things about marriage is that your partner sees you in all your ordinary, animal vulnerability. For many, this is terrifying; but in truth it is redemptive. How liberating it ultimately becomes when your agenda is not to perpetuate your righteousness but to emancipate the other! When you consider the significance of compassion, emancipation and acceptance you see that they are also religious impulses in response to the overwhelming and beautiful facts of *life*.

You must not try to achieve a controlled perfection in your relationship. You must not make it into a testimonial to your life importance. Rather, it must always be a symbol of the wonderful, tragic, fragile, vulnerable and wounded beauty of life. Love thrives at the centre of the cruciform, at the tension point between helplessness and control, between vulnerability and security, between inadequacy and competence, between humility and arrogance. It is at this point that love sparks into being. It needs this inherent contradiction between the birthing and dying of life. The ancient Celtic cross captured this symbolically: where the horizontal and vertical worlds connect, there is a circle that unites them.

Because the condition of human life and our place in the universe are of such immense mystery to the human being, we need symbols and symbolic communication to give expression to what is inaccessible to reason or language. Music, symbols, signs, art, religious icons and all forms of human gesture and communication are symbolic representations of an inner and outer reality that lie beyond and beneath the currencies of everyday life. We are people who communicate through and respond to symbols. Language itself is symbolic communication. Music, literature and art are popular and inspirational ways that we awaken our subconscious intuitions and symbolic channels of human expression.

THE ARCHETYPAL IMAGE OF THE CROSS

Take your national flag and consider what it means and evokes in you. It symbolises so much more than geographical boundaries. People have died for your flag. All over the world, people stand before their flags at sporting, political and social events; and they can be moved to tears because of what it means to the human psyche. Symbols are, in many ways, reminders to us that we are more than our everyday lives: we are part of something bigger than ourselves. When we experience that connection to something larger than ourselves, we are moved by deeper emotions than we are typically aware of.

For that reason I will refer to the symbol of the cross. I will not use it as a Christian symbol but as a universal one. It is an archetypal symbol and universal image that symbolises both the horizontal and the vertical dimensions to life—a symbol that Carl Jung said we would lose at our peril.

The Horizontal Dimension

The horizontal line of the cross is symbolic of our anxious life and everyday preoccupations. These are the things that cause us stress, worry or anxiety; and the responsibilities we attend to on a daily basis. The horizontal dimension serves to distract us from a vertical life of depth and transcendence. We live on the shallow horizontal level most of the time, as we are distracted with the preoccupations of everyday life and the securing of our status, safety and significance. The horizontal line might be represented like this:

STRESS   ATTENTION   ANXIETY

The Vertical Dimension

The vertical axis symbolises physical and spiritual existence. At the top of the vertical dimension is the spirit and at the base is what we would call soul. The spirit refers to all those transcendent experiences that enable us to rise above our horizontal condition and bring a lightness of heart, joy and hope. The soul refers to the deeper experiences of grief, loss and suffering. At the level of soul, we are aware of our mortality and the soil and earth from which we have emerged.

SPIRIT

SOUL

The vertical dimension to life is where we embrace suffering and hope; mortality and transcendence; death and birth; joy and grief. On this dimension, we are attuned to the beauty and fragility of life. On this dimension, we see our horizontal stresses and worries for what they are—preoccupations and distractions from the essentials of life. When we bring the horizontal and vertical dimensions together, we get the image of a cross as a simple symbol of human existence.

Now, if we seek to integrate the horizontal with the vertical, then we can introduce a circle at the centre of this image. This circle symbolises the integration of horizontal and vertical living. Our symbol then takes on the wonderful symbol of the Celtic cross.

The Celtic cross symbol can be seen as a symbol for this book. I use it not in a Christian or religious way but as a universal symbol of an *integrated life*. It is a symbol of where we must locate ourselves if we are to relate to those we love with the respect and sensitivity necessary to sustain love. We must live within the circle, at the burning point of life, where our horizontal preoccupations and irritations intersect with our soulful and spiritual existence. At the burning point, ordinary life is lived in the context of an extraordinary existence. At this point, love has a different meaning. This is because one is open to the light-heartedness of spirit and the grief of soul, while remaining grounded in the immediate present.

Our life purpose is one of *integrity* and *integration*. We can rise above our stress and distress to experience joy and hope. We can inhabit our stressful life with the heart and imagination of the vertical. We are rooted in the soil while we look to the sky. We are ordinary people who are guests in an extraordinary life where we are moved by the joy and grief that attends all living things. At the burning point of life, we know the happiness and the lightness of heart that come to those who embrace the passionate ordeal of living.

Within this circle, love is awakened to its essential place and purpose. When it lingers at the edges of a horizontal life it focuses itself on getting what one wants and justifying itself. Thus, it gets stranded in the shallow waters of everyday stress.

*

We confuse the two dimensions of life: the horizontal and the vertical. We must bring the vertical world to bear on our horizontal relationships, not the horizontal world to bear on the vertical relatedness.

We can find release from our everyday preoccupations through vertical awareness. When it happens, the heart is lifted above the terrors of life and one is in touch with one's vulnerability and, thus, one's courage. In counselling and psychotherapy, this is often what happens for couples: they find a space within which they open up to the bigger picture of their lives and can step back from the agitation and distress of what appear to be fatal problems only to find that their injuries are superficial.

You can spend your life trying to prove your significance to yourself and your beloved—or you can operate on the assumption that your significance is a given. If you do not need to prove yourself, and do not need others to confirm that proof, then you do not use your partner for this hidden purpose.

LOVE AS OUR STRIVING FOR SIGNIFICANCE AND VICTORY

You are stimulated to believe in your heroic destiny by the sight of another face; it shows the miracle of creation shining out of humanity. Research shows how newborn babies are fascinated by the wonder of a human face. In domestic love, we see the same thing. The lover does not need to reflect your power, control and worth, but rather your mortal and vulnerable beauty. Ultimately, we love out of the humble acceptance of our human limitation and our heroic aspiration to face this unflinchingly.

One of the disappointments I have in life is seeing people's delight in proving other people wrong! People delight in catching other people making mistakes. This momentary victory over someone else is the genesis of conflict. It is the urge to purify the self in some way. But the real challenge is to catch people being right, to catch people doing things that are good! This is the attitude of grace.

In working with divorcing couples, I find that there are heroic examples of people who refrain from vengeance and victory when the opportunities are rife. When they identify their persecutor not as *evil* or bad but as *flawed* and wounded, their heroic options open up for them. The positive motives and forces that come to assist us in these times are a kind of providence that comes to sustain the hero who chooses to walk the path of courage, without concern for profit or loss.

We must not use our partner in the pursuit of a cause that serves to give us a sense of righteous justification aimed at alleviating our existential weakness. Just as we know that the seeds of evil can take root in the kitchen of everyday life, so too do the seeds of heroism and virtue.

The family is the host within which *good* first takes root and it can grow down through the generations and blossom in the lives of grandchildren long after the grandparents have departed. Powerful and primitive virtues get released in the most private and intimate of settings. They trickle, like blessed waters, down the mountainside of a family tree to bless those who are its descendents. The invisible heroes of family life are those who are attuned to these kinds of eternal truths, knowing in some unspoken way that their sacrifices of today release a future generation from the emotional prison of tomorrow.

Chapter 19
Sorrow

DWELLING AT THE TEAR-POINT

When I work intensely with couples, I often engage them at what I call their 'tear-point'. Your tear-point is that point when tears of recognition come readily to your eyes. I do not mean tears of hurt or self-pity but tears evoked by the sudden awareness of the profound meaning of something. Genuine tears come to us particularly at the burning point of life, at the meeting point of our horizontal and vertical life, at the centre of the symbolic mandala of the Celtic cross. When we open our hearts to the vertical life, while remaining rooted in the present, we feel the unavoidable grief and blissful joy that attends our life. In those moments, our everyday life is infused with the pathos and vitality of mortal love.

Your tears reveal the sorrow of knowing that your joy cannot last. Tears come to your eyes when you experience an intense love for someone along with a grief that recognises that it cannot last forever. Tears are shed when you experience love and joy in some exquisite moment: watching your little child succeed at something, holding a newborn or expressing heartfelt gratitude to someone. The grief is in that subconscious and sometimes unspeakable awareness that every beautiful thing comes to pass and that you cannot capture and hold forever the love you feel.

So when I work with couples who are struggling, there is inevitably a moment in the early sessions when tears well up in the eyes of both partners. These moments will be at different points but I will always hold that moment, dwell on it with each person and gently call forth the meaning of those tears. I might say: 'I notice when you talk about what has happened, tears come to your eyes. I want to know what those tears mean and what they are saying.' And people usually try to brush them away as some form of over-reaction or weakness but I rarely let them do so. When a person is held at their tear-point and their emotion is named, honoured and called forth, the person moves into the vertical dimension. Despite their best efforts to remain objective and logical, their tears open the gateway to both their grief and their hope. Herein I find their truest passion, their longing, and what is deeply meaningful to them. Most often it relates to the loss of a dream or a hope that they had for themselves and their marriage, which opens up the unspoken grief that has lain hidden behind their anger or irritation. It also opens up their heart's desire and what their hopes have been. When these hopes are honoured, they awaken a voice that may not have been allowed to speak for some time—very often a lifetime.

A man's tear-point is particularly revealing in couple sessions, as it often reveals the hidden helplessness of the controlling husband. It is many a wife who has said to me even after an initial session that they have never before heard their husbands say the things said in session. This is very simply because of the man's fear of 'going vertical', of staying and dwelling at the centre, at the burning point of their own lives. We all need someone else to encourage us into this space. And we go willingly, because we know this is where our truest desires and fears dwell.

As long as one's tears are not those of self-pity or anger, as long as they are evoked by an awareness of one's grief and joy in life (one's dreams and longings), then they are a window of wonder to the compelling inner world of love and courage.

So, as you watch your little daughter
leave your side and skip her way to the school doors,
tears come to your eyes
as your love for her wells up,
and you realise that despite this love
you cannot protect her from all the sufferings of life
that await her

nor have you the gift to sprinkle her
with the joys that she deserves.
Your heart breaks with such love
and, as her little body goes through the doors
with confident innocence,
your tears melt into a gladness
at the courage of her little life.

Chapter 20
Humility

Those who want the fewest things
are nearest to the gods.

Socrates

Spiritual poverty is a condition of selflessness in which things are seen without reference to profit or loss, even profit or loss of some remote, spiritual kind. Thomas Carlyle put it this way:

My brother, the brave man has to give his Life away. Give it, I advise thee;—thou dost not expect to sell thy Life in an adequate manner?
...
Give it, like a royal heart; let the price be Nothing: thou hast then, in a certain sense, got All for it! The heroic man—and is not every man, God be thanked, a potential hero?—has to do so, in all times and circumstances.

To live fully is also to feel lost at times. The person who accepts this has already begun to find themselves. It is ironic that we often discover our true purpose when we have been bereaved. People who have been through such loss know the meaning of life. They live closest to its true essentials.

When you allow yourself to experience that in some ways you are a castaway, you know what it is to be lost. You know what compassion is. And you know the longing that is love. You are drawn to intimacy. In that movement towards the other, in that holding onto the other, you appreciate vulnerable life and experience the origin of compassion.

However, if you are not aware that you are in some ways shipwrecked, you never experience your vulnerability. You do not experience humility or gratitude. You cling to your raft, your beloved, not with appreciation or tenderness, but with entitlement and righteousness.

If you deny that you are adrift on the great sea of life, you never experience the terror of abandonment or the relief of rescue. Nor do you experience the deep gratitude and appreciation for the saving hand of the other. You remain numb, denying that your wish to reach out comes from a passionate exposure to your isolation and the gift of the other's love.

The arrogant person loves out of a sort of pity or entitlement. This love is really a love of power—a control over a dependent other. The arrogant have lost touch with their need and their terror: a set of emotions that they do not let surface until life forces their hand through tragedy, breakdown, illness or death. When you do lose touch with that feeling of being deserted, you are drawn towards the use of power and control as tactics to deal with life. And in doing so, you drift away from love. You close off your anxiety.

When one becomes truly lost, when one feels deserted and adrift, when one encounters the desolation in life, what rises up is a cry of the heart, a reaching towards something beyond oneself. From a full encounter with this experience, from a brave acceptance of the fate of life, one does not reach towards the other to eliminate or avoid this vulnerability:

> One offers it as an integral part of oneself.
> One does not seek to cling to the other as a refuge from one's desolation,
> rather one offers one's hand to the other
> as a revelation of one's vulnerable heart.
> One does not exaggerate love to secure favour,
> nor does one diminish its vulnerability to find security.
> The courageous lover gives no more and no less than
> the cry of the castaway
> and the joy of the saved.

If you can do this, you place yourself right at the centre of the *mystery* and hand yourself over to what you might call the *divine*. This impulse is, at its truest, an impulse of humility. We can see here that those who approach saintliness are really void of arrogance and righteousness for these very reasons: their attitude to life is to surrender to a life of humble service.

In the context of relationships, it is only when the self can relate to the powers of the soul or the spirit of creation—rather than to the alleged powers of the self—will it be capable of compassionate love. In the world of the divine, in the actions of virtue, it knows the song of a joyful heart. The self then knows that:

> *Love is love of the universe*
> *and your partner*
> *embodies the eternal.*
> *They are complete in themselves.*

The dominant professions that impact directly on marriage (especially through separation and divorce) are law, psychology and social policy. However, none of these worldviews comes close to understanding the issues and forces that shape the character of intimate relationships.

However, literature, philosophy and many psychological thinkers (Carl Jung, Ernest Becker, Otto Rank, Martin Buber, Friedrich Nietzsche, James Joyce and Søren Kierkegaard) have all come to the same conclusion about humanity. It is this: we are beings that search for both the meaning of our lives and an experience of being alive. Although we accept, up to a point, that we do not know what it is all about, our hunger for knowledge ensures that we continue to evolve not just as biological entities but as psychological ones. At the furthest reaches of understanding, psychology and science have to give way to human imagination. This is because they cannot tell us what to do with our inevitable suffering nor provide us with the passion of being fully alive.

We must incorporate a view of life that absorbs the mystery *as well as* the solution. It is an imaginative transcendence of our condition. The solution to marital breakdown and divorce has also to include the imaginative, ethical and aspirational. For example, in court reports that I write for couples caught in family law disputes, I always try to encourage spouses to rise above their horizontal pessimism and to access vertical virtue as it is all that can sustain them. Arrogance and righteousness bully the noble virtues of humility and generosity.

Chapter 21
Sacrament

O you are not lying in the wet clay,
For it is a harvest evening now and we
Are piling up the ricks against the moonlight
And you smile up at us—eternally.

Patrick Kavanagh

The essential experience of any mystical tradition is the notion of identity behind the surface of everyday life, behind the surface display of duality. Behind everyday life, the one radiance shines through all things. When we focus on everyday things and take this radiance of life for granted, we lose touch with our humanity and the virtue of gratitude. The radiance is that death and life work in accordance with each other because they are two aspects of the same thing: the act of becoming.

All religions and mythologies place death alongside birth at the centre of life. It is a basic theme: that which is born dies; that which dies is born. You have to have death in order to have life. There is a deep psychological association between conception and death.

The notion that a divine radiance shines through all human activity is not a new one and certainly not just a Christian one. The awareness that the gods make themselves present in people and relationships is not new either and was central to most Aboriginal mythologies about natural, animal and human life.

The notion that marriage is a sacrament—a place or context where holy life makes itself present and available—is an ancient human awareness. At the deepest psychological levels, the intimate relationship is the primal human situation.

It is around the heart of the family that people learn how to be in the world. They learn: how to find meaning and dignity; how to behave; how to show respect and reverence; how to experience life; and how to live and die. In mythological and spiritual traditions across the globe, regardless of religion or culture, we find that the bonding of man and woman, and parent and child, is sacred and holy. It is a great shame that in this day and age our language of community and family life at a political level is reduced to the language of law and economics.

In the ancient religions, all of life was sacred and there was a divine purpose attached to intimate relationships. I frequently meet engaged couples who want to be married with a church ceremony for reasons that they are not aware of. They claim it is because of family or tradition, but it is often because they intuitively want to place their marriage within something bigger and more meaningful than just themselves. At a deeper level, they are conscious of the enormity of what they are facing; and they use the church as their setting to show this.

It is a great loss to society that we do not have mythologies that interpret the divinity in intimate relationships for us. It is left to the economists, lawyers, accountants and celebrities to define for us what is relevant and meaningful.

People cannot find their heroism in everyday life as they did in traditional societies, through working, worshiping and raising children. In other cultures and in other times, these things were ascribed noble and heroic meaning. In modern and post-modern relationships, there is a gradual erosion of such significance. This is the price we have paid for the eclipse of the sacred. When we dethroned the ideas of 'God' and 'soul', we were thrown back on our own resources—on ourselves and those around us. Intimate relationships and family life are not a substitute for absolute meaning.

Intimate relationships, and the blessing of parenthood, can bestow a great responsibility. In assuming this responsibility, you connect with history and place yourself in a larger meaning. When this happens, your view of yourself can change. Just as you will have occasions when you visit some wonderful place—maybe in wandering into a magnificent cathedral, lying under the stars on a clear night, walking alone by the ocean's edge, holding your sleeping child in your arms, making love with your partner or experiencing some enlightenment— there are these times when the universe breaks in on you and you experience yourself as part of something ancient, something so much greater than yourself.

In these moments, the deity is revealed to you.

This is the ultimate revelation of intimacy. Unless we bring attitudes of reverence, and can open our hearts to experience something through our partners that is much larger than their personality, marriage in everyday society slips away in importance to become just another legal and economic entity that enables the management and care of children. It is actually, potentially, so much greater than this. How that is achieved is a most difficult ordeal because there are fewer and fewer inspirations in everyday life to enable couples and families along this arduous path. But the ancient religions, the ancient mythologies and the poetic heart point us in the right direction.

*

Modern life is a long way from the daily reminders of where we have come from. When we are divorced from nature—the skies, forests, mountains and seas—we do not encounter the daily reminders of the forces, powers and magical possibilities of life, of which we are a part.

When you take time in the countryside or by the ocean, you find that the power of nature echoes in your heart. You remember how you are just an intimate part of the wondrous mysteries of the landscape and created life. Just as nature is an awesome artistic creation that leaves you in awe, so too is the human face. So too the face of your beloved can awaken awe. The mystery of all of life is revealed through those closest to you. It is what allows me to say that:

When I look at the ocean
and gaze out into the great loneliness,
I miss you all the more.

The divine makes itself present in those bonded to you. Just as often as you experience your partner as an irritating obstacle in your life, you can also experience them as a sacred revelation.

We find it hard not to obsess about our partner's imperfections and we find it hard not to criticise them for these. This is inevitable. These forces are part of the ordeal of relationship. These forces will take over the psyche unless they are balanced with a compassion and sensitivity that transcends the everyday.

Now the cynic in you may ask: 'So what? What is the usefulness and relevance of these things? All the airy-fairy talk of myths and spirituality is, at the end of the day, irrelevant to the everyday lives of couples.' I think not. Spiritual symbols and myths lie in the background of everyday life. We need something to lean on when we are tired, fatigued or traumatised. We need to be supported at certain key times in life. This may be death, national recession, war, trauma, severe depression, despair or worry about those we love. It is at these times that our character emerges. It is at these times the deepest truths about who we are become apparent.

In intimate relationships, extraordinary things happen between people. The bonds and chains of love can tear through the pretence of everyday roles to reveal the raw emotions of life. Yet beneath everything there is a gentle vulnerability from which the fountain of love flows.

The transcendent moment awakens the couple to their inner connectedness and creates the conditions for empathy. This transcendent realisation is what makes a lover willing to die for the other; it is what makes a parent willing to give their life for their child. This is not recklessness; it is simply the breakthrough of a deeper reality.

My wife Jean is in love with our baby in a way that is as passionate and romantic as any love. Some of her friends scoff at her sentiment and sheer adoration, recommending a more cynical stance. 'Oh that will wear off!' they say. But it must not; and it only wears off when life tries to restructure itself. My older daughter is in her teens and struggling with all that entails. When I stand back, I see that she is going with the flow of life and in my heart she is still the same wonderful infant that I have cradled and loved. I know, at the deepest levels, that I would die for her.

In intimate relationships, in marriage, the hero is one who gives their life to a realisation of that truth. When you are in tune with the truth, you give over your very life. We see this happening every day, all the time: people being kind, gentle and considerate. Our media and popular culture shine lights on crime and awful tragedies and brutalities—but for every awful crime there are a thousand acts of generosity that go unrecognised and without applause. This is the sacrifice of love.

History and time flow through relationships like a river. A couple meet, fall in love, have children, rear them, etc. As soon as you have history, you also have loss. Time means suffering because what you had then is no more; and what you have now is only passing. The intimate relationship, at the level of time, has to be a dying to itself.

If you remain at the hub of the wheel of life, you will not be going up and down all the time: you will be at your centre. There is a still point at the centre of the rotating wheel. There is a still point at the centre of the turning world.

Chapter 22
Symbol

Look thy last on all things lovely,
Every hour.

Walter de la Mare

Y ou have no alternative but to live a symbolic life. You must live
a life within which everything you do has a special meaning,
value and purpose known only to you. In fact every person
you know is living out their particular life in a way that symbolises
something that is meaningful to them but entirely invisible to you. It
is only when you ask someone 'Why are you doing that?' that you are
introduced to the symbolic meaning of what they do and the narrative
within which it is set. This is the glorious and wonderful thing about
people. We live through symbolic action. Everything we say and do
for and *to* our partner is symbolic of the nameless and wordless that
flows between us.

We also live a symbolic life because it is not possible to live the
many other lives that are possible for us. We can only travel one path.
Every life is tinged with regret because we are not able to do everything
we have wished. We regret that we did not have many lives to live so
that all the possibilities could have been explored. This is our ache in
the face of the abundance of life. To pluck one apple from the orchard
is to not taste a thousand more.

But remember this: all of humanity is present on this earth. Be
reassured that there are many people on earth who are living out the
other choices *you* never made. Your unlived life is being lived. We are

all connected. We are all living parallel but connected lives. If you never climbed the Himalayas, then be joyful that someone else is doing it for you—in the breadth of life. It has been achieved.

Your obligation is to live your life not just for yourself *but for humanity*. You might have to ask someone out on a date, travel to Africa or repair your relationship with your ex. Whatever it is you must do, do it for humanity. Do it for the person in the hospice right now, who remembers with regret that they *did not* ask someone out on a date, travel to Africa or repair their relationship with their ex. Humanity needs you to do it as much as you need you to do it. And in just the same way, the person in the hospice right now must live their own death with a passion and honesty that brings redemption and forgiveness to *you*. For you, they will not berate themselves with regret but will find a disposition of gratitude. Grateful acceptance is an attitude of mind that says:

> *Never refuse to give anything...*
> *Never refuse to take anything...*
> *Whatever it is, take it,*
> *for it is all God offers.*

R. H. Blyth

So the discipline is to connect your natural passion (even if it is a quiet and gentle one) into symbolic action that inspires you and keeps your destiny alive. Kiss the girl. Write the book. Visit the country. Paint the walls. Meet your brother. Be kind. Make love. Let go.

Whatever it is, find the act that your heart recognises as your poem, your work of art, your gesture to the universe, your song, your symbolic act that represents all the many things that you would long to do or be. It may be small, but its meaning can be huge. Herein lies your destiny: to manage your small garden; brush away the dust from your footpath; work those late night hours; pick the weeds from your life with an attention that sustains the love in your life. Through the tedium, you can live in accordance with your deepest purpose. You can live with purpose—with whatever is available to you. So choose to suffer with simple joy. You can sing, despite yourself. You can dance, in spite of the world.

Do not die without being able to say this: 'I could not do everything, to my regret. But what I did do was done as a toast to all the possibilities within me, to what I am and could have been. I did it as a celebration of humanity because I was obliged to do so. And so, it has been wonderful.'

And this is the creative and artistic disposition. It comes from imagination. Life should be both sacrifice and celebration. This is the truth. Allowing oneself to live the imaginative life is extraordinary in its implications. What will be the creative and symbolic works in your life? A DIY chore, a job, a relationship, a virtue, a task, a journey? Whatever it is and however small it is, do it with a song in your heart. Allow the background music of life itself to sustain you in your fatigue. You do it for humanity.

If our minds are focused on the *spiritual qualities* of the other person, then we will find goodness. If it is on the *personal qualities* of the other person, then we will find disappointment. Marriage is not a love affair. It is the place where one experiences all of the awe, terror, wonder, anxiety and ultimate majesty of one's created life. At times, when you encounter the deathly in life, you see the beauty of your beloved with a passion you forgot you had.

Spiritual symbols and myths are in the background of everyday life. When we go through a death, a national recession, a war, a trauma, a depression, a despair or a great worry about those we love, character emerges and the deepest truths about who we are can become apparent.

Chapter 23
Transcendence

Sometimes, when your heart least expects it,
and when it least desires it,
life opens itself to you,
and you remember who you are.

If you want a full explanation for the forces and powers at work in intimate relationships, you are never quite satisfied by the reductive explanations of popular psychology or agony-aunt advice. You are never fulfilled by the explanations that are given for: the passion of romantic love; the loyalty of aging love; the intensity of family life; the pleasure of having a home; the origin of domestic violence; or the grief of broken relationships. As I have argued, when you reduce love, sex and violence down to smaller elements in order to explain them, you can miss something fundamental about human nature.

In our efforts to control our lives and manage problems, we have a compulsion to examine and blame what is closest to us—our intimate partners. We have the potential to become obsessed and overwrought by our relationship. However, we also have the potential to transcend it and to experience something different within it. We have the potential to make an intimate relationship a prison within which we seek to control another—or an open landscape within which we find freedom. Relationships can be the gateway to a more tolerant love and a courageous freedom.

The ability of humans to rise above the circumstances of their lives is an astonishing and awesome faculty. If you are to understand love, you must appreciate this special and unique ability that all humans have—including you. Some might call this 'transcendence', others 'heroism' and others 'imagination'. Let me call it 'rising above'.

In everyday life, and in relationships, you will be familiar with those occasional existential shocks you get when you are suddenly made aware of your own mortality, vulnerability or good fortune. These are moments when you briefly see into the life of things and experience a sense of gratitude for life.

Most of the experiences or moments in life that have affected you in this way have been in intimate relationships. You remember your first kiss, your first break-up and your early romances as if they happened yesterday. You have been shaped by relationships. You are affected by those relationships that ended when you were rejected or when you had to reject someone. The experiences in your life that have moved you, changed you for the better or allowed you to see yourself for the first time have been in relationships to your partner or children. There are these moments, these experiences when you have been opened up to something profound within you.

In being able to 'rise above' ourselves we are aware that we are not just victims of our relationship. We are aware of having a distinctive freedom in how we 'sink into' that relationship. We are aware that there are limits to what we know about our beloved. We are aware of the inexhaustible possibilities and of how much more there is to know!

Often, transcendent experiences happen during times of crisis. These are times when we are taken out of habitual, everyday life. In the crisis of an intimate relationship, transcendent issues rise to the surface. Questions, which have percolated beneath the security of the everyday, now boil over. At these points, couples find they are called to account for their actions. They are called to that silent and infinite reality in which they exist—a reality that is not subject to them.

The experience of the sacred in another person has a luminous quality. This is *not* because the sacred is located only in the other person; but because the sacred *in all of life* shines through them. You recognise in them something that you know resides in *you*. You are connected to the background music of life. I do not mean this in a sentimental way. I mean to point to the deep, physical and substantial movement that resonates within you.

Heightened experience occurs when something is revealed to you about how your relationship to your beloved is connected to the ground of your existence. You experience a connection with the other person that is beyond the horizontal concerns of everyday life. When this happens, you are *being* with the other and experiencing their movement as synchronised with your own. There is a radiance that shines forth from the other and is evoked in you. Think of your early bonding experiences with your infant children. Think of the early experiences of falling in love with your partner. You can still access those feelings, if you look at your partner in the right way.

Awe is another emotion you can experience. It is not about admiring some beautiful quality in the other person. It is more about experiencing something sublime in them; and something sublime between the two of you. That which is sublime has more than beauty—it has a quality that evokes awe. The expansive universe is sublime, rather than just beautiful. There is a bigness and majesty to nature that evokes our sense of smallness and inspires us to bow in respect. It feels like both awe and fear. When you diminish your own ego, you move into the sublime. When you encounter the brutality of life, as well as the sheer majesty of life, you touch the sublime.

People who live through a crisis often awaken this awareness within themselves. The person in the midst of a great personal trial often experiences something that is sublime. This is because they forget themselves as they are invested in the passion of fighting for their life. A good friend of mine once made a wise-crack I will never forget. He said: 'I found the cure for depression—get cancer!' The same man had been diagnosed with lymphoma months earlier. His comment reminded me that there is both a peaceful and wrathful aspect of the world.

Evolution and the history of the universe show us that we are living in the midst of the eternal. We experience this 'eternal' in moments of sublime openness. The mystery of life is beyond our understanding. We can't quite get our head around it all and that, in a strange way, is both unnerving and awe-inspiring.

There is an exercise I do with couples where I invite one partner to imagine seeing the other partner as if for the first time—without letting their partner know. This can evoke something new, as it captures some of the essential dimensions of breakthroughs or epiphanies. We take for granted our understanding of the people in our lives. We rarely reflect on how extraordinary it is that two unique individuals can dialogue and live with each other and achieve a measure of genuine and empathic understanding.

These breakthroughs are revealing not just of our relationships, but of the horizon within which our relationships exist. These shifts in awareness focus us on how we are together in the world. This is moving our attention from 'me and you' together, to 'us' together, to 'us in the world together'. This is where there is fullness of participation in life and where freedom and infinity is found. In being together in the world, the eternal potentiality is experienced for brief moments. This is very often the consequence of intimate sex between partners. Sex prompts the participants to experience themselves outside the orbit of the everyday and to touch into the sublime, to connect with something between them that is different from everything else. For many couples, this sexual connection saves them. For others, it reassures them. For most, it is an unspoken connection with the oceanic in life. Sex can be deeply reassuring.

These 'moments of surprise' awaken fundamental questions about our relationships—and about what it means to know another in an intimate way. When we are awakened to the sublime, everyday illusions about the other begin to break up and we see ourselves as part of something far bigger than our daily concerns, worries and agendas.

When you 'rise above', you recognise the personhood of the other. You witness the other as a knowing *and* a feeling subject. You also value, appreciate and love the other in a way that has nothing to do with profit or loss. By comparison, you may previously have been a complacent spectator or observer of the other as someone already known to you. But, through your epiphany, the light shines through and you see your partner as if for the first time.

There is a wonderful song by Jackson Browne called 'Fountain of Sorrow'. In it, he describes finding an old photograph that he once took of his lover. He had caught his lover by surprise and, even though his lover laughed and smiled for the camera, there was 'just a trace of sorrow' in their eyes that was forever captured in that photograph. He says to his lover that there were other photographs that were apparently more flattering—'But they didn't show your spirit quite as true'. This 'rising above' the obvious has allowed him to really see his lover.

The possibility of sudden realisations is ever present, as are the factors that stand in their way. Illness, suffering and death have a way of startling us into awareness. We should not overlook those moments of recognition that come with subtle shifts in our everyday circumstance.

To love another human being requires a concrete engagement with them as an embodied subject with a particular point of view, set of concerns and history. To be moved and affected by the situation of the other is an embodied experience, an experience of one's whole being. Thus in 'rising above' or 'sinking into' the relationship, we do not move beyond the relationship. We move more deeply into it. In these moments, we do not turn away from our precarious existence: we fully participate in life. Rather than drifting away from the other, we become immersed in them.

The moments of surprise refer to: the mystery; a deeper sense of who the other really is; the silent and infinite reality that encircles both. Transcendence evokes the meaning in our lives and sustains us. These moments can be deeply personal and poetic experiences that affirm our common humanity.

In relationships, we are often caught in the sparkling meaning of the seemingly insignificant moment: light dancing across our partner's face; a moment of silence; watching our partner sleep; the vulnerability of our partner's tears. These events barely register if we become hardened to experience. But they are vital in reminding us of who we are. This is when we see into the life of things.

We passed in silence, and the lake
We left without a name.

Frederick George Scott

Chapter 24
Eternity

It probably seems strange to suggest that love or relationships have anything to do with the eternal. In everyday conversation or thought, it hardly crosses your mind. It rarely pops up in conversation around the table or at the pub. Or does it? I want to urge you to consider that it is a conversation that lies just beneath the level of words. It is a constant, dreamlike awareness you have that you can never quite call into consciousness.

However, on close examination you realise that your day is peppered with references and allusions to your relationship with the eternal. In fact, the more you think about it you see that it crops up in phrases, humour, greetings, gestures and sayings everywhere. But, like anything that evokes our awareness to mortality, it is taboo and best left in the shadows.

On any given day, you may greet a dozen people with: 'Hello, how are you today?' On the same day, you may say to a dozen people: 'Goodbye and take care.' If you allow yourself to dwell on the purpose and meaning of greetings, you will realise that they are our everyday acknowledgment of our precarious mortality and vulnerability. They are humanity's way of recognising that you have, in some way, survived another day. Greetings and salutations are our way to honour and appreciate that fact.

Saying goodbye to someone is felt to be necessary because there is a subconscious desire to give the other person good wishes to help them on their way. 'Goodbye' comes from an original greeting that asked that the gods be with you as you go about your life. Most rituals of greetings between people involve light-hearted allusions to the taboo of mortality. Responses to the greeting 'How are you?' include sayings like 'I'm hanging in there.'

'How are you?' is only necessary and honourable because of one's inherent vulnerability. To check the status of another's physical or emotional health is an allusion to the fact that it is always of concern. This, of course, does not need to be spelled out. The welcome and display of interest of another person is a tipping of one's hat towards the eternal. So, when I speak of the eternal here, it is not an abstract notion. It is the elephant in the room of everyday life. It is the sea in which we all swim.

Your courage to be able to tolerate the anxieties of life and to risk your emotional death in the service of a virtue is a character strength that is greater than the ego. The courage to face one's psychological death is a courage that transcends the anxieties of the body. At times, you can experience a courage that overcomes all your fears. At times, you can tap into the eternal. It is being able to say that if death came to me now I would not have any fear and I would co-operate with the eternal. We have a religious impulse to connect with *being* itself and the eternal existence within; and to transcend our small life. As Shakespeare put it:

> If I must die,
> I will encounter darkness as a bride,
> And hug it in mine arms.

The spiritual element of life can be denied or trivialised—but it is always present. Spiritual life means escaping from the confines of one's individual mortality and placing one's life in the context of a broader meaning of existence itself. The power of the infinite is the source of our courage to love and to be someone.

Every day, your relationship with life must be expressed in symbols. It is not evident in any literal way. It is symbolised in the tenderness of your parenting, in the empathy for your partner. It is present when you lift them up while you are weak yourself. It is in the hundreds of little kindnesses you offer in support of love. It is in the courage to be open, to confess and to admit.

The vocation of being a parent is a deeply spiritual and symbolic way of inhabiting one's imperfect life and being connected with the eternal. In a wordless way, you genuflect towards mortality, all the while being inspired by the eternal. The love and sacrifice of parenting symbolises all of this. This symbolic living gives your life a spiritual character.

Passionate love draws its power from the eternal in life itself. A parent, for example, transcends self-sacrifice because such love represents a self-surrender in a higher form. Parents often say that they do not sacrifice themselves. They feel they have no choice but to willingly surrender to love. It is an affirmation of the eternal self. Although courage is still essential, you lose that defensive 'profit or loss' mentality. The 'what's in it for me' question disappears.

When you are in touch with the eternal, your individual self is diluted. Fate is much less of a threat because when you are in flow your individual concerns are in the background. You will gladly step in front of a car to save your child. Your individual fate is less a concern to you when you are plugged in to physical love. Self-doubt is also swallowed up in this spiritual courage. When you are immersed in life itself, the doubt does not enter. Guilt and condemnation fall away because of the immediate fulfilment of the present. At these times we feel:

The sorrow of
remembering sparkling moments
and weightless days...

The courage to take the death that is implied in mortality upon oneself is a way of life that is accepted by large sections of humanity. Our everyday striving for some kind of peace and perfection includes the ability to tolerate helplessness. This is a paradox of life. Spirituality is an unavoidable element of one's relationship to life. It is not a 'special case' situation. Our identity with *being* itself cannot be erased. Self-affirmation affirms *life* itself, which is above death.

For all parents, the experience of vitality in bonding with their child in the face of their own decay, and the experience of the absolute purposefulness of this vitality, represents courage, hope and faith.

Courage, hope and faith are the essence of life. This kind of acceptance of one's place in the universe as being purposeful represents a faith in the divine. Joy in the face of a fate we do not control and a self-doubt we cannot escape, is the courage to live. The integrity of love is one that sits well with helplessness, self-doubt and anxiety. It persists in spite of all of these things.

Life is both an endless joy and a terminal illness. Your terminal condition and the anxiety that comes with it belong to life itself. So when you speak of being blessed by life, it is against the background of this sort of 'non blessedness', if you will. The infinite in life—which is around us in an infinite universe and behind us in an infinite history—applauds the sacrifice of the finite. The infinite universe applauds the finite nature of your life—and *all* life. It is a wonderful and extraordinary paradox. *The infinite honours the finite.* The infinite kneels before the finite. *No* is taken into *yes.* The *symbolic* nature of this discussion reveals our only way to talk about it. We realise that through all this mortal flesh and dress the 'bright shoots of everlastingness' can spring.

Chapter 25
Grace

*Loneliness is that state of spiritual poverty in
which, needing nothing, we possess all.*

R. H. Blyth

We quietly reject ourselves. We live with shame, inadequacy,
self-accusation and self-rejection—always finding reasons
why we are unworthy. The first existential truth is that this
response to life is appropriate: of course you feel unworthy. Against
the background of creation, the universe, a passionate life over which
you have only limited control, and an existence that you never choose,
of course you feel small and inadequate. But here is the rub: that is
all right. The universe loves your littleness and emptiness. It needs
your littleness. The world and others survive and thrive because of
your littleness. Despite the wonder of your littleness, you sometimes
hide it and strive for control, power and perfection. In a hundred little
ways, you measure your status and significance. You monitor your
self-image so that the world will think better of you.

With these persistent attacks on yourself, in rejecting those aspects
of who you are, you are rejecting your body and soul. You are rejecting
the cornerstone of your heroic life and transformation. The parts of
you that you want to reject are the very parts of you which you must
bring on your heroic journey. This, in truth, is the most dramatic of
realisations. Your vulnerability, mortality, fear and powerlessness—all
the qualities that mark your apparent insignificance—are the very
qualities that become your heroic virtues.

We are a mass of contradictions. We are a mixed blessing. In Christian thinking, original sin is the original shame, the original sense of being inadequate, of not being enough. It is a relief if I can see how I am mixed—that there is something beautiful *and* something tragic within me. Our faith is the belief that between this light and dark we can find freedom.

However, when we strive to escape these conditions, when we seek our immortality and false divinity, we do so through self-rejection or adoration. In seeking relief from our tragic beauty, we seek relief in the horizontal rather than the vertical. The truth is that who we are can only be found in accepting our conditions and fate. Our assessments of each other are often judgmental and critical but the universe, creation, 'the beyond', God (whatever you wish to call it) is always gracious. We are loved and significant in our unworthiness.

In your life you always want to be better, to be more confident, to be more worthy, to not feel ashamed, to be more attractive, to lose that bit of weight, to get applause. You know your weakness in this and that it is all the striving of your ego. However, when you choose the path of the soul, you discover beneath the layers of your 'self' that who you are, in all your brokenness, is beautiful.

In your anxiety you forget this. How your soul, heart and mind can breathe with the same rhythm as God's breath, flowing through you. When with nature, you remember this. What you must do then is ask yourself what Einstein called the most important question: 'Is this world a friendly place?' If you can believe that the answer to this is *yes*, then you know that your task in life and relationships is 'to let go of the fear that goes by the name "self-image"'.

What are those things that you cling to as if they are essential to your life? What are the things that, when you are faced with death, might turn out to be without value?

Spirituality requires an understanding of grace. Grace is that acute awareness of being gifted by life, of being held by life. It is that intuition that there is nothing you need to do to prove yourself anymore. There is nothing you have to do to make yourself better or more important or more powerful. There is absolutely nothing you can do to be more significant or worthy than you are. On the day of your birth, you were ascribed one unit of worth. Nothing you do can make that bigger or smaller. This is grace. If you sink into the innate powerlessness, then the mystery awakens in your soul. And you relax into it.

In marriage, every time we are hurt we feel a little bit lower in status and importance. This can trigger a response of blame or self-accusation. We often prefer to do this than to tolerate the anxiety of not knowing our status level. A large part of us does not want grace: we want a reward–punishment system so that we know where we stand. It is so hard to extricate ourselves from an ancient sacrificial system that used the diminishment and abuse of others as a means of resolving our inner conflicts. But the heroic lover stands in the space between victory and defeat, between knowing and not knowing, and tolerates the anxiety of life while inhabiting its glory.

The sins of humanity are simple—they are greed and violence. The teachings of the great spiritual thinkers have been equally simple. They tell us to love the conditions and path of life and to show compassion for those who travel with you.

When you love the conditions of life, you know that the universe loves with you. You discover that in all your inadequacies you are gifted. Compassion flows naturally from you now because you know these things. You have no ability to communicate to another that they are special unless you can know it for yourself.

You must fall back and relax into the beauty and wonder of being a part of a life that is bigger than you. Call it God, the Great Loving Universe or whatever you wish; but someone is breathing through you.

The burden of modern life is that you must keep explaining your own life, justifying your own life, making yourself special, improving your own life, and making yourself significant when you know you are not.

Grace, however, is remembering who and what you are. It is remembering that you are loved. You have nothing to prove when you are touched in this way. An angel places a hand on your shoulder. The river of life holds you up.

THE METAPHOR OF GOD

Your lover who walks
along the distant shore
works a miracle of grace
in your heart.

Your existence, the fact that you have been blessed with a unique life that allows you to sit and read this, is astonishing. You and your life exist for just a short time. There is a way you can look at this life you have and experience a divine acceptance that life has created you and given you the privilege of this sublime existence for just a little while. You can, when you look at things this way, feel worthy, honoured and utterly accepted by the eternal that has created you. To experience this worthiness and blessedness is to know grace. It is not self-justification or arrogance. It has humility. It has the humility to not have oneself at the centre of one's life; but to draw, with gratitude and humility, from the source of life. I call this 'the divine'.

The divine naturally accepts us and we must accept this honour; and honour this acceptance. We can experience gratitude for universal acceptance. In a strange way, this also involves being willing to accept a kind of universal forgiveness. Whatever you think about yourself and your obsessive guilt and worries, life forgives you. Life loves you.

The metaphor of a loving God condenses so much of the mystery and essential solutions to life. God is the best and most apt metaphor that I have to symbolise the great unfathomable of life. We do not need to believe in a literal God to appreciate what the metaphor means. You can believe in a metaphorical and symbolic God that is compelling. God expresses in a poetic way the vitality, sacredness, blessedness and mystery of life. There is some courage involved in living through the poetic metaphor of God.

Self-affirmation is the inner, quiet confidence in oneself. It places oneself outside the orbit of guilt, inadequacy and personal failings and within the embrace of something larger than such obsessive self-critique. The power of the healing and anointing for the dying is above religion when someone sees it as a necessary enactment of what life offers. I placed my hands on my father's head as he died. I did this on behalf of *life* and I blessed him as he had wished. In the midst of this, we both touched the garments of heaven. As humans, we cannot be forgiven by a thought or will, but by another *person* who personifies life itself. You need certain courage to experience gratitude for God's acceptance of you.

Gratitude for life and the recognition of one's acceptance, sacredness and inherent goodness is beyond words. It's not achieved through talking but through open-heartedness as stimulated by poetry, music, family, nature and birth. The ultimate source of healing comes through accepting the conditions of life given by God. This acceptance by God becomes a real source of courage which allows you and me to inhabit and tolerate our anxiety.

No spouse can make you overcome the threat of death which is experienced in your own private self-rejection. Spiritual self-confidence relies on God and not the other person or your clever self. The courage to be confident in your own skin comes from unconditional life—the acceptance of God. You direct the vessel of your life but you are driven by the winds of fate and guided by the stars. You do so much less than you think. Confident courage accepts helplessness and inadequacy. This is the meaning of providence.

> *Amazing grace! How sweet the sound*
> *That saved a wretch like me.*
> *I was once was lost, but now I'm found,*
> *Was blind but now I see.*

Life doesn't have to show kindness to us; it just does. We don't have the resources to meet life's challenges or conditions; but grace meets our need. Grace is the fundamental principle of our relationship with life. We are inadequate, wounded, powerless, anxious and thoroughly broken. Yet, we love life and life blesses us in some wonderful ways. Grace is a sense of gratitude that life has blessed you with life itself.

It is *grace* that provides your justification, not power, control or righteousness. It is life placing on you a right or a worthiness that satisfies something deep within you. When you remember this you know you are not deformed or wretched. You remember you are a holy, beloved, well-pleasing child of life.

Grace is free because it originates in life. It begins and ends with life. Grace doesn't wait for some sign from us; it doesn't need our okay. We understand grace better when we are talking more about our *purpose* in life than about daily living. All too often we revert to performance as our measuring stick for who we are and the security of our 'salvation'.

But when you understand life's grace, when you grasp its implications, you understand that it isn't about you at all. It isn't about what you do or don't do. It is all about what *life* has done and is doing. And that means that if we understand grace, we'll understand there is no time to be wasted on fear and guilt. Your *love* is the overflow of life's grace.

Yes, we must walk in a manner worthy of life; we must serve; we must show compassion; we must do good things. But we don't work in order to *earn* life's blessing; we work as a *response* to life's blessing. Even those works are empowered by grace. We must understand it is not *our* strength that empowers our labour, it is life's strength. Life's grace provides the fuel for our work, enabling our growth in co-operation and humility.

Chapter 26
Sensuality

O unworn world enrapture me, encapture me in a web
Of fabulous grass and eternal voices by a beech,
Feed the gaping need of my senses ...
Patrick Kavanagh

The headlines in today's paper refer to: the endemic child sexual abuse within the Catholic church; the starvation of millions in Somalia; the sadistic abuse of children by their own mother; the collapse of economies because of the greed of people in power; the corruption in media organisations; the implosion of Iraq; the murderous rampage of a killer in Norway; and the siege of Libya. The economic crisis of the new century illustrates the victory of evil in so many areas of human life.

The prevalence of domestic abuse, violence, sexual assault and the perversion of paedophilia in or near the family brings this despair closer to home. When it comes to marriage and intimate life, we see the proliferation of perverse pornography over the sensual and erotic. We find spouses being slaves to power and control, rather than humility and tenderness. We see the victory of greed over generosity. The wounding of children in the midst of adult righteousness in divorce proceedings is common. You have enough evidence to concede, therefore, that the end of humanity is close at hand.

We need to let go of our fond illusion that we have a privileged or providential status in life, in marriage or the universe. It is obvious to see that the malignant death instinct is a built-in guarantee that the human enterprise will cancel itself out unless humanity breaks free of its denial, self-destruction and repression.

The end of the road for humanity is the repression of mortality and its vulnerabilities. This results in control, abuse, violence and evil.

If you choose to ignore mortality, it will have its own way in the end—and at a price. If you choose to ignore the human body, its vulnerability and its passionate exuberance, you will suffer. Death is a positive force. Hunter Beaumont has said that death makes everything possible. If it is repressed, it turns into abuse. If it is accepted, it turns into compassion.

The question you are faced with every day is whether you can tolerate your emotional and physical vulnerability. Can you achieve the resurrection of your vulnerable and passionate body in its full natural exuberance and playful joy? We need a sensuous life. We must delight in the full life of the mortal body, which we fear. To resurrect your body is a return to your original state of bliss before you created the dualities and conflicts of your nature. Surely your happiness in intimate relationships is seen in playfulness rather than constriction; in erotic exuberance rather than sulking control; in healthy narcissism rather than painful self-doubt.

There must be no unlived lives in the relationship. Life is affirmed in a body that is willing to die! This is the most extraordinary achievement in life: to inhabit your own mortality with grace. This brings great peace if it is coupled with self-affirmation.

Vulnerability and our terror of death require a deep respect. Optimism and love sink into triviality if the labour of love and life is diminished. Courage, integrity and self-responsibility are not easy.

Deep within all of us is the intuition that playful love must be our destiny. We long for such a harmonious way of being. When we are emotional people, without a lust for power, we are sensual.

Wordsworth considered that his revelation was expressed in the forms and symbols of everyday life. For him, paradise was possible in any 'peculiar nook of the earth'. Gerard Manley Hopkins displayed a deep awareness of nature in his poetry. In 'God's Grandeur' he reminds us that our neglect of nature is actually a neglect of our spirit. Rainer Maria Rilke suggested that the qualities of love must be taken from God and returned to nature, creation, love and death.

The body is a spiritual fact. It is through the ordinary physical world that we find bliss, love and grace. The real structure of life is sensuous self-enjoyment. It is the energy of desire and not the inertness of facts. We need a soft sensuality rather than an aggressive dominance towards reality—or towards each other.

Chapter 27
Freedom

Freedom is a fundamental need of the human person in both domestic and social life. Its social and cultural aspects have often been discussed. It is not often that the notion of freedom in family life is considered.

True love gives freedom to the beloved. It is often neglected but it is absolutely essential to loving relationships. When you give this kind of love, what you are saying to your partner is this: 'I want you to be free to be yourself, whoever you need to be. In our relationship I do not want you to feel controlled or pressurised to be other than true to who you are. Therefore, my love for you is not contingent on your compliance with my expectations. Rather, my hope is that you will be free. This means that you are free to move away from me emotionally, to follow your big and small dreams, and to be confident that I support you.' To receive this kind of love in a relationship is deeply affirming. To know that expressing your freedom (of thought or deed) will not result in rejection is reflective of courageous love.

The opposite of freedom is control. Control can create that feeling of being imprisoned by your partner. Control of another person takes many forms. It can be active control like dominating, threatening or bullying. It can also be passive control like manipulation, mind-games and subtle forms of blackmail.

The promotion of freedom within a relationship is an unusual and often neglected responsibility. We tend to forget about our need to feel free; and also our obligation to promote the freedom of those close to us. The attainment of freedom is such an essential human need and right. Each one of us strives for this—in both domestic and social life.

It is difficult for many couples to envisage what freedom in a relationship looks like because it seems, at face value, to be opposed to what a relationship should be about. On the surface, one imagines that committing to an intimate relationship requires a loss of freedom. Many jokes about married life emphasise this very point and many people in difficult relationships talk about feeling trapped or imprisoned. However, for these very reasons, we begin to realise that emotional freedom is essential in mature and respectful human relationships.

Freedom is a basic human need. It is difficult to achieve because life is so full of obligations, confinements, limitations, commitments, responsibilities and rules. It is easy to feel trapped and unfree. When relationships deteriorate, issues of freedom rise to the surface in dramatic ways. Teenagers fight for freedom in the face of what they imagine to be rigid imprisonment. Spouses long for freedom from relationships that leave them feeling smothered. Battles for control and freedom form the character of everyday family life.

In our social, cultural and political life, freedom is considered to be a basic human right. This right to self-determination, expression and movement is considered inalienable and an essential condition of human growth and flourishing. The right to be free to control one's own life is central. What I want to emphasise here is that it is as essential to committed relationships as it is to all other facets of human life. The right to be free of another's oppression is a domestic striving as much as a social one. We find many infringements of freedom in the family home: abuse, control, violence and emotional terrorism.

FAMILY DEMOCRACY

In family life there are coups, revolutions and fights for independence. In the family home, we find dictators, mutinies, civil wars and revolutions. At its worst, it can be family imprisonments, emergency rules, punishments and autocracies. In lots of ways, family life mirrors larger socio-political life.

A six-year-old who freely decides that they should be allowed to eat a bag of crisps before dinner can cause a full-scale battle over freedom. Even a six-year-old will innocently claim their right to be free to eat what they want. Right in the kitchen before dinner, parents can get involved in an inquest about human rights and responsibilities!

It would be interesting if families drew up their own *constitution* with laid out principles and beliefs regarding responsibilities, obligations, freedoms, rights and democracy. What might your family constitution look like? What freedoms, rights and responsibilities would each person in your family be entitled to? As a 'citizen' of the family, what would be the basic responsibilities for each family member?

The ideal family is one that has clear hierarchical lines and boundaries within which democratic principles and ideals are gradually promoted as children learn to assume the essential responsibilities of living in a family. The establishment of democratic principles within the context of parental rights and responsibilities is certainly not easy. But it is well worth the struggle.

Often, I suggest to parents that 'freedom attained is proportional to responsibilities carried'. Teaching children that small freedoms are gained through assuming basic responsibilities is surely the art of good parenting.

*

When you peel back the layers of family conflicts, you will find that most struggles of family and intimate life are struggles related to freedom. All power struggles and attempts to control another person are about freedom. Here are some examples from everyday life that are, at their core, struggles about freedom. No matter how trivial these examples might seem, they are all about the struggle for freedom:

- Your partner prevents you from doing something.
- Your teenage daughter wants to stay out later than she should.
- Your three-year-old child wants to walk down the street without holding your hand.
- Your ageing father refuses to go to the hospital.
- You pressurise your spouse to be the kind of person you want them to be.
- Your husband intimidates you into being a certain way.
- You ground your child for bad behaviour.

- Your teenager uses foul language in the house.
- Your husband wants to go away for a weekend with the lads.
- You long to take a break from being a stay-at-home mother.
- Your partner interrupts you whenever you speak.
- You feel you are trapped.
- You place expectations and obligations on those close to you.

WHAT FREEDOM LOOKS LIKE

Freedom is the opposite of enforced conformity or emotional imprisonment. When freedom is present in a relationship, you see partners wanting to set the other partner free to be whoever they want to be. You see partners encouraging the other's independence. You hear them responding positively to the other's free expression of ideas about the relationship. When personal freedom is endorsed, the relationship seems to flourish. Each partner seems fearless of the other's separateness and difference.

The freedom to have one's own independent thoughts and views can be the source of extreme difficulties and distress in relationships. People get into terrible fights over each other's points of view. Sometimes you can feel that, if your partner has a different point of view from you, that is a threat to the security of your relationship and trust. The freedom to have and express alternative views is not easy to tolerate at times because freedom has also to be balanced with responsibility to the other and to the relationship. That is why we speak about *freedom within limits* rather than freedom without boundaries, irresponsible freedom or self-indulgence.

When your partner can emancipate you from control, with empathy and respect, it vitalises the relationship. This happens in the small currency of everyday life. Signs that your human freedom is being recognised and honoured in a relationship include:

- Your partner is interested in your ideas.
- Your partner allows you the freedom to be yourself.
- Your partner freely lets you come and go without hassle.
- Your partner encourages your separate identity.
- Your partner accepts you as you are.
- Your partner does not try to control you or possess you.
- Your partner does not monitor your every move.
- Your partner is not preoccupied with changing you.

It is amazing how often I hear metaphors of freedom and control being expressed by couples in distressed relationships. The following statements are all too common:

- I feel trapped.
- This feels like a prison.
- We need to break free.
- I need to escape.
- He is a control freak.
- I can't get him to do what I want.
- He has never let me be free, really.
- She treats me like a child.
- I am accountable to him for everything.
- She expects me to ask for permission to do anything.
- I don't want her to leave.
- He cannot want out; when I married, it was for life.
- If I don't do what he says, I will have hell to pay.
- It is easier to just give in.
- I feel under pressure from him all the time.
- She threatens me with things.
- I have to get her to be responsible.
- I will not give up drink just because she says.
- He is free to go but he can't come back.
- I had to take out a barring order.
- She keeps bossing me.
- He needs me to agree with him.
- She gets defensive if I say something she does not like.

PATHOLOGICAL VERSIONS

When one's need for freedom becomes over-extended, many destructive traits come to the surface. The main ones involve an *over-reaction to feeling controlled.* You encounter a narcissistic sense of entitlement to one's freedom regardless of the effect on one's partner.

This can be expressed in many ways:

- I'll go where I please and hang out with whom I please.
- I am not answerable to you.
- If you have a problem with my drinking, that's your problem—not mine.

- I had an affair, I apologised, and that's the end of it.
- Don't you dare try to tell me what to do!
- It's my money and I can spend it if I feel the need to.

Alternatively we see a *controlling* sense of entitlement to diminish the other person's freedom. This is done through pressure, coercion or abuse.

- I don't want you hanging out with those people.
- Your family cannot set foot in this house again.
- I expect certain things to be done when I get home.
- If you end this marriage, I will make your life hell.

The list can go on. You will appreciate that even in these everyday incidents, couples are struggling with their need for freedom. Each person wishes to have their freedom recognised and honoured.

Many men talk about the need for freedom in negative or indirect ways. It is referred to in terms of feeling confined or restricted. Many men who enter into relationships do so with a wholehearted commitment. They willingly sacrifice their sense of freedom only to discover in later years that they are afflicted with a kind of depression at a 'lost life'. They will speak of feeling tied down and trapped but unable now to find the energy for any escape or conversion. Rather, it is converted into a contrary negativism, which results in their being critical of their spouses and on occasion developing a self-pitying cynicism about their life.

All of these kinds of issues are struggles to find a balance between freedom and captivity, between emancipation and control. We all struggle for freedom and resist confinement. We accept *influence* but hate being *controlled*. We hate to feel emotionally imprisoned or trapped. We want to be free to be ourselves and, despite our sense of responsibility, resist the effect of having to inhibit ourselves too much.

Chapter 28
Encouragement

En-couragement means *giving courage*. Encouragement counters natural fear, guilt or self-doubt. We give encouragement because we appreciate the fears of life.

Encouragement is when you support your partner's efforts in doing what they need and want to do. When you encourage your partner, they feel your support, good will and guidance. This, as the word suggests, gives courage. This can be shown in small and big ways. When your partner is struggling or finding things difficult, you are there to give them a 'push start' and are cheering them on.

It also involves affirmation. You affirm your partner's efforts. You refrain from fault-finding and criticism. You say: 'Don't worry. You are doing your best and I believe in you, no matter what.'

Encouragement touches the heart of the recipient. In the act of encouragement, there is a hidden genuflection towards the ordeal of life. Whether you are a parent giving encouragement to a child, a wife giving encouragement to a husband, or an adult giving encouragement to an ageing parent, you are giving a precious gift. Encouragement is literally 'to give courage'. And courage is, according to ancient philosophers, the most noble of all the virtues.

The opposite of encouragement is personal criticism. When you are encouraged, you are given the support and energy to keep going. When you get personal criticism and are put-down, it drains your energy and makes you want to give up on the relationship. It is such a sad fact that many of us are far better at giving criticism than encouragement! We think that pointing out a person's flaws is better for them than encouraging their strengths. More often than not, our criticism is really a selfish act of trying to get some compliance from the other. Encouragement is generous. It does not ask for anything in return. It is *for* the other person.

When someone encourages you, you blossom. It feels right because encouragement does not judge you or evaluate you. It wants you to be true to yourself. To the degree that you are encouraged, someone wants your dreams to be fulfilled—no matter how small. When you encourage someone, you applaud their small efforts, you appreciate their little successes, and you help them move towards their goals.

Encouragement received during times of distress is like a balm. Words or deeds that say 'hang in there' are worth so much more than praise during your times of success.

If you are a parent, you will know that your child's success in life depends in large part on encouragement. Whether your child is trying to tie a shoelace, complete a sum, colour a picture or finish a project, encouragement helps them to persist. It sometimes touches the soul because it recognises the lonely isolation of solitary effort.

Something as little as an encouraging word, a caress or simply saying 'it's ok' can mean a great deal in the language of intimacy. Nonverbal signs that someone is for you, on your side, behind you, holding you up or there to lean on can be deeply reassuring. You will even notice that the compliment of a complete stranger can have an endearing effect.

There are few things as deeply affirming as the encouragement of your friend, spouse or parent when self-doubt comes to haunt you. When you are climbing the incline of everyday life, when you seem to wade in a river of stress, you sometimes need only a small bit of encouragement to ensure that you make it across to the riverbank of your goals. Someone says: 'You are my hero, you know that?' And this is to your heart what a little water is to a wilting flower.

Encouragement says: 'If you make a mistake, that's okay. We all say things we don't mean, do things we don't like, or feel like giving up when things don't work out for us. It's okay to feel that now. Tomorrow is another day and you can try again. Failure is not falling down; it's when you refuse to get up. I am here to help you up.'

What encouragement means for a child or adult is that fears can be overcome. Encouragement tells you important things. You will be held if you fall. Anxiety is normal. You are not a failure. Someone believes in you. You can lean on someone. Someone sees how hard you have been trying. You are not being judged. You are not alone.

> *Courage is fear turned inside out—*
> *The sword of faith that will slay self-doubt,*
> *Your striving and effort is what I love and admire,*
> *Therein is your success, your passion and fire;*
> *So rise to your feet and you shall see*
> *I will cheer you onward towards the best you can be.*

Encouragement validates even the smallest of dreams. It orients you to being more than you are. It imagines possibility, growth and expansion. It recognises that life asks something heroic of you: to overcome the small adversities of everyday life, be it a bad mood or things just not going your way. Encouragement simply says: 'I believe in you.'

When your partner praises or compliments you, you enjoy it but it does not acknowledge you like encouragement does. If they criticise you, you may reject them. If they ignore you or hurt you, you will find it hard to forgive. However, if they encourage you, it feels right. It feels different because it is without evaluation. It is a gift that your heart responds to. It passes on a certain courage.

For this reason, encouragement is related to your dreams, your longing, your reaching forward, your seeking more. To the degree that you are encouraged, your dreams are made real. This happens even in the smallest of ways. When your partner says or does anything that reminds you to *trust yourself,* it is extraordinary. It is profound when they say: 'Trust yourself. Trust your assessment of what you need to do. You have more wisdom than you think.'

This is what encouragement sounds like:

- I believe in you.
- I love and trust what you want to do and be.
- You can do it.
- If you try, it's okay if you fail.
- You're great.
- You can do it.

- I am behind you.
- I am there for you.
- I believe in you.
- It is okay not to get it right.
- Go for it!
- I want you to do this—for you.
- Don't worry about me.
- Don't feel guilty—you have to do what's right.
- Go on, it's okay. I really want to hear what you feel…

Discouragement can be very destructive. It involves being put down. It happens when you are diminished. It takes away your courage. It creates a lot of fear and doubt in your mind. It makes you feel bad about yourself and it takes away your hope.

Encouragement does the opposite! It is a powerful and creative force. It gives you courage, hope and positivity.

When a child is encouraged, it teaches them many things. This is what they hear:

- Fears can be overcome.
- You will be held if you fall.
- Fear is normal.
- You are greater than fear.
- Someone believes in you.
- We all need to lean on someone.
- Someone sees into you.
- Someone sees how you have been trying.
- Your invisible efforts are actually visible.
- Someone you love does not judge you.
- Failure is not the end of the world.
- What may seem easy to others does not have to be easy for you.
- You can feel good about your efforts.
- You are not judged by your fears or insecurities.
- You can lean on someone and into something.
- You are not alone.
- Life requires courage.

Courage is the defining virtue and en-couragement the greatest gift. When an adult is encouraged, this is what they hear:

- You will be assisted in being true to yourself.
- You can't do it in isolation—that's natural and it's ok.
- Your dreams are valid.
- You can be oriented into being more than you are now.
- You have so many possibilities.
- You can grow and expand.
- You have something heroic in you.
- You do not have to fear any guile, resentment or jealousy from me.

Encouragement is such a precious gift in life. We need to feel encouragement in the face of tragedy and trauma. We also need encouragement to stand in the presence of wonder and beauty.

Chapter 29
Approval

A ctive love, as distinct from reactive or passive love, is the stuff of great literature, music and film. It is everything that is noble about humanity. It is the expression of the desire in all of life. Active love is the active expression of affection, appreciation, care and desire.

At the level of human existence, the need for affection and active love is physical. To the newborn child, the physical bond and relationship between the mother and child is as essential to the child's development as food. The active provision of warmth, touch, holding, soothing and loving to a small baby is not sentiment or affection— it is the currency of bonding. Right through to old age, the need to receive active physical touch, emotional warmth and genuine affection means the world. You see this in the bond between grandparents and grandchildren.

The currency of affection and active love is an essential means through which we experience recognition, validation, legitimacy and justification. Affection is a living proof that we matter, that we belong, that we are in some way redeemed.

The need for approval is one of the most powerful psychological pre-occupations that affects us. Equally so, our dread of disapproval is a powerful force. One would be inclined to think that concern about approval is quite an immature attribute and hardly the most important concern in our lives. However, it would be wrong to say so.

Loath though we are to admit it, the approval or disapproval of others is a psychological obsession that shapes our development. In many ways, one's entire personality is shaped around the need for approval and the fear of not getting it.

Active love communicates approval and acceptance of the other person. This emotional approval is so essential to us because, right through our psychological formation, it has been the currency through which we measure and experience our self-esteem and self-worth. We like to think that the mature personality is someone who does not rely on the approval of others for a sense of self-worth. However, it is too late to create such a being! Our maturity has developed as a consequence of the kind of approval we have accrued throughout our lives. Much of our psychological development centres on how we gain and secure the approval of others; and how we avoid disapproval.

Approval is the recognition and validation that we got from parents or other caring figures as we grew through childhood. When we grow up in an environment where we get little approval, we tend to withdraw into ourselves. Instead of building our life around the approval we have secured, we build our life around avoiding the disapproval that we expect. When people get enough approval, their concern recedes somewhat into the background of adult life. However, it is never far from the surface.

In fact, many people who appear very 'together' and self-confident are what we call *active-independents*. They have actively developed their independence from others in order to keep disapproval at arm's length. Many such people avoid close relationships and are terrified of being dependent on another because of their deeply held dread of disapproval or rejection. Many highly successful people are driven by an obsessive preoccupation with a fear of failure and its associated disapproval. The drive to succeed is often born out of the experience of harsh rejection.

There is also another type of person: the *passive-dependent*. This person behaves in the opposite way to the *active-independent*. The passive-dependent is very needy of the approval of others and has found, through childhood, that the best way to secure this is to accommodate to others and to secure approval by tending to submit or be agreeable. In itself, this is not such a bad trait: people who are accommodating are good company and well liked. However, their inner emotional life can be flooded with anxiety and the need to check for the approval of others at every possible turn. In fact, the fear of disapproval can be so strong in such people that they will even choose death, imprisonment or emotional self-destruction rather than face the disapproval of others. The reflex to avoid disapproval can be a motive that determines a person's destiny. Notice how your self-esteem fluctuates around approval.

People stay in destructive relationships, jobs, families and vocations rather than face the *imagined* annihilation of disapproval. People sometimes stay in bad relationships, jobs, families, vocations or situations because the felt dread of rejection and disapproval is so viscerally powerful that they cannot come close to mustering the strength to face it. The tsunami of guilt and self-loathing that would follow such a bold step is anticipated as being of such a magnitude as to almost cause psychological death. Believe me, I do not exaggerate. People will rather *die psychologically* than face the disapproval that might ensue if they chose freedom over captivity. My heart has broken so many times on witnessing the self-surrender of a person to their abusive partner. The legacy of emotional loyalty to one's family is a great burden indeed.

For some couples, the emotional electricity that sustains the relationship is one partner's addiction to the approval of the other. One couple I met recently displayed this. The woman had such a naïve fear of her husband. Her vulnerable dependency on his approval felt to her as if it were love. In addition, his distance and independence from her—and his confidence in her weak inability to disapprove of him—felt to him like it was love.

It is so hard to untangle the emotional threads of love to find its true colours! Fear is often camouflaged as love. Attachment to someone who gives you approval can feel like love. What is even more disturbing, being emotionally attached to someone *whose disapproval you fear*, can also feel like love. Tragically, some people only know abusive attachments. These attachments have the intensity of love but the character of violence.

Our need for approval is a constant, never-ending psychological preoccupation. In every moment of every day we scan our world to compute our emotional safety through the currency of approval. It is so automatic, and so much part of our inner emotional life, that it is impossible to distinguish it from the moment-to-moment rush of sensations, thoughts, feelings and intentions that are the stuff of life.

Chapter 30
Tolerance

No matter how much we have in common with the one we love, each of us remains a unique human being. And no matter how much we love each other, the differences between us will eventually lead to conflict. At times, we will feel hurt, ignored, resentful or angry. Our arguments often make the problems worse. Something's got to give—and we usually nominate our partner as the one that has to give it.

Sound familiar? If so, you are not alone. Trying to get your partner to change when strife seems to be pulling your relationship apart is human nature. It is easy to understand your own point of view. It is much harder to see where the one you love is coming from. It seems obvious to you that your relationship would improve dramatically if only they would see things your way and make a few little alterations in behaviour.

As you undoubtedly know, trying to change another person—even a person motivated by love and loyalty towards you—is a tall order. Eliciting change from your partner without demonstrating acceptance of their unique position is difficult and often impossible.

Most of you probably think that most of your problems can be solved with communication skills and problem-solving. We usually believe that with these efforts positive change will ensue. Most couples I meet state that *communication* is their core problem. However, we know from research and experience that, despite our best efforts, many problems do not go away. This is because they are *personality* centred rather than *situation* centred. In other words, the problem is related to the personality of the other and not specific, acute situations. They are what John Gottman described as 'perpetual issues'. In his research, he showed that they constitute about two-thirds of all relationship conflicts.

In dealing with these problems, it is more helpful to be focused on *acceptance* than on change. Every person in an intimate relationship has to discover ways of accepting the normal incompatibilities in that relationship. If you can find a position of acceptance of another person's vulnerabilities and inadequacies, then many needs for change simply evaporate.

There is a film called *Blue Sky*, in which Tommy Lee Jones and Jessica Lange play a married couple called Hank and Carly. There are some emotionally volatile scenes in the film. In one, Hank, Carly and their two daughters enter the dilapidated house that is to be their new home. Upset at the move and the condition of the house, Carly has a major emotional outburst and tears down the curtains, knocks furniture around and then jumps in the car and scorches off. Hank chases her, rescues her and brings her back home. The next morning, as Carly sleeps, the daughters are still upset about the incident. Hank tries to comfort them and explain the situation. He assures them of his and their mother's love for them. He uses the metaphor of water to explain their mother. Just as water can be liquid or steam or ice, so their mother has many shifting properties. He tells them: 'I made a decision a long time ago just to love her basic properties.'

Hank's explanation beautifully illustrates what we mean by acceptance. He clearly experiences pain from his wife's emotional outbursts; but he is able to tolerate that pain, recover from it and accept it. He sees her specific behaviour in the large context of her whole life, in the context of her shifting properties. He sees her behaviour in the context of their life together. In dealing with her outbursts, he never seems weak or submissive, but strong and loving.

To accept someone is to tolerate unpleasant behaviour sometimes. You can tolerate it if you understand the deeper meaning of that behaviour. Acceptance does not mean being submissive, which comes from a position of weakness. Submission means enduring something when you feel you have no alternative. We must not accept abuse or degradation, but we must find noble ways to accept the human imperfections of those we love.

Chapter 31
Desire

It is wise to conclude that the essence of being human is not in thinking but in *desiring*. Our experience and expression of desire for someone else, for a goal, for a dream or for life itself defines us more than what we think about things. If I am to know you I want to know what you desire, what you want and what you long for.

If you are in an intimate relationship, it is worth reflecting on the concept of desire. By desire I mean a general *wanting to be with another person*. 'Wanting' is a good word to describe the desire that sustains relationships. When people in a relationship *want* to be with each other it makes everything possible. It usually implies that they want to work at their relationship. In general, mutual wanting or mutual desire can carry a relationship a long way. Desire is usually used in reference to sexual desire but it is so much more than that. Sexual desire is one element of wanting a person.

The first thing I notice when I meet couples for the first time is the interest they have in each other. It is the desire they have to know one another. It is hard to disguise and it is hard to fake. It is a simple and uncomplicated expression of how much a person wants to be with the other. It is usually evident in body language such as eye contact, tone of voice, courtesy, attentiveness and simply looking at the other person when they are talking. Through body language, one notices all the little cues that illustrate desire. You know a lot about a couple just by how they *are* together, the courtesies they show and the interest they have in the little things about their partner.

Looking at someone when they are talking is a simple courtesy that reveals a lot about a person's interest in the other. It is simply the desire to know what the other is thinking or feeling. It is the desire to value what the other is experiencing. In a good relationship, partners will say things like: 'That's very interesting', 'Tell me more about that!' or 'Go on, I want to know what you think'. Couples who have become bored with each other never say things like this because they think they have the other person pigeon-holed.

Interest in another person comes from the desire to understand them and be involved with them. It is the energy that sustains relationships. When it is gone, the relationship dies. In intimate relationships there are four elements to this desire:

- Sexual element
- Friendship element
- Selfish element
- Caring element

In other words, you can want your partner because of: a sexual bond, a friendship, your own benefit or a caring bond.

The sexual element to desire is a wanting to be close to the other person physically and the desire, willingness and openness to physical, sexual intimacy. Sexual desire also includes physical affection and warmth. It includes physical closeness and the desire to touch, be touched, hold hands, sit together or just be together in silence. It can be as simple as just enjoying a long car drive together or holding hands while strolling around on holidays. Sexual desire can sustain a relationship for a period of time but is insufficient by itself. When the sexual element is present, you and your partner can say things like:

- I want to be physically close to you.
- I want you to be open to my sexual advances.
- I approach you tenderly in sexual ways.
- I enjoy the physical affection you show me.
- I value our sexual relationship.
- I do not just want sex—I want *you*.

The friendship and fondness element of desire is the wanting to be together because you enjoy the person's company. You like what they have to say and what they want to do. You ask for their advice and you take it seriously. Your partner is one of your best friends and you like and admire them—for even the simplest of things. You admire them not because they are a great person or have achieved so much in life but you admire their virtue. You admire their courage, humility and their ability to deal with adversity. When the friendship element is present, you and your partner can say things like:

- I enjoy your company.
- I am interested in what you have to say.
- I know your ideas and values.
- I take you seriously.
- I have fun with you.
- I am fond of you and I admire you for who you are.

The selfish element to desire includes the wanting to be with another person because of *what they give you* and what you get out of the relationship. You may feel safe and secure when you are with them and that alone may make you want to be with them. They may make you feel attractive or important. They will probably make you feel like you *are someone*. These experiences are central to a relationship but they are never sufficient in themselves. When the desire of getting from the relationship is present, you and your partner can say things like:

- I am a better person because of you.
- I feel safe and secure in our relationship.
- I have more confidence because of you.
- I feel attractive and wanted by you.
- I like being around you.
- I know that our relationship is good for me.

The caring and compassionate element to desire is the desire to make someone happy. It means *wanting the best* for the other person. You care because you want the other person to be well. It includes the desire to see them being the best person they can be. It is noble because it is the opposite to the selfish element of desire. It is that willingness to be the wind beneath another person's wings. When the caring element is present, you and your partner can say things like:

- I want you to be happy.
- I want the best for you.
- I know that you want the best for me.
- I feel supported by you.
- I feel cared for in our relationship.
- I know I can depend on you when I feel weak.

All of these different elements come together to create that *wanting to be with someone else.* It is the basis of couples falling in love, getting married and continuing to share a life together. The uncomplicated and innocent desire to be with someone is what keeps relationships going. Without it, relationships wither and die or else stagnate without change. The desire to be close to the *particular* other is what makes that other person feel loved.

Many relationship problems are caused by a discrepancy in each partner's level of desire. When couples have difficulties it is often because one person's desire has faded. This discrepancy is obvious with distressed couples where one (or both) can begin to have mixed feelings about the other. It is often problematic when someone wants the security of relationship in *general* but does not want the *particular* person they are with.

Chapter 32
Protection

There are many ways in which you seek to ensure your partner's emotional safety and protection. It is a form of love that includes minding, caring, protecting, respecting and securing. There are many ways to provide this safety and protection. For example, commitment is a form of safety-provision. It is saying: 'I am committed to you and I do so to provide you with the security you need to be involved with me.' It includes the willingness to take and carry responsibility within and for the relationship. Many people experience neglect in their relationship in the face of their partner's lack of responsibility. With emotional protection and safety, partners feel safe and conclude that their partner is not a source of threat or danger to them. If the provision of safety and protection was all that was given it would, of course, be a one-dimensional and limited form of love. However, couples and parents know that it is an essential ingredient to creating a safe place for love to survive and thrive.

Old-fashioned values suggested that the way a man showed love for his wife and family was to work hard in the outside world. This was a way for a man to provide for the security and safety of his family and it was considered to be the essential component of the love relationship. The self-sacrifice of the man in doing this was often as much as was expected. Thankfully, modern relationships have expanded the notion of 'protection' to mean so much more.

Safety is critical to secure attachment between parents and their infant children. It is a core condition for secure bonding. Emotional and physical safety is therefore critical to psychological development. With safety, a child or adult has the security to explore and develop. It dampens anxiety, so that energy can then be focused on more industrious things. Positive emotions come from safety: peace, contentment, curiosity and happiness. An obligation of love is, therefore, to protect your partner from the world—and from yourself.

Danger is the enemy of love. If your partner becomes emotionally dangerous or threatening to you, you feel unsafe. Most couples find themselves feeling unsafe at some point in their relationships with regards to some issue. Danger can also come from emotional fears within the self—the fears of revealing oneself, being shamed or being humiliated.

Danger can also come from a partner's emotional disposition and attitudes. In more extreme forms, it comes from abuse, aggression and intimidation. In working with victims of domestic violence and family abuse, the word that is central to all therapeutic intervention is *safety*.

Loving relationships have to permit each spouse to occasionally slip into the role of a loving, caring parent who watches out for the other, minds the other and cares for the other. These are displays of interest in and concerns for the other's wellbeing and life.

Protecting someone you care about has heroic connotations and the great image of the hero is one who serves *and protects*. Protection sometimes involves a forgetting of oneself in order to look after the other. You see this in the way parents, grandparents and children do lots of little things to make their loved ones feel safe, protected and minded.

Safety is central to existence. The forces of mortality and life itself let us know that danger surrounds us everywhere. Therefore, acts of protection and safety are of enormous significance: they symbolise being shielded from death. Life itself is inherently dangerous, tragic, accidental and unpredictable. Our bodies are charged with the alert anxiety of this fact all the time, whether we are aware of this or not.

We react to all signs of danger. We jump when we get a fright. We get defensive in relationships when we feel threatened. This is why protection from life is so welcomed by people of all ages: children, adults and older people.

When this protection is *not* felt in a relationship, people can say things like:

- I am afraid to say what I feel.
- I am walking on egg shells around her.
- I never know what he is going to do.
- I have to defend myself against his assaults.
- He is on guard all the time.
- She is always defensive.
- He does not care for me or about me.
- She takes me for granted and lets me to my own devices.
- I feel like a stranger in my own home.
- I feel desperately exposed.
- He never stands up for me in public.
- She lets the children abuse me.
- I feel defenceless and terrified.
- I am so afraid all the time.

When protection *is* felt in a relationship, people can say things like:

- I feel so reassured.
- His care for me at this time means the world to me.
- She minds me—and I feel safe.
- I would walk into anything with him by my side.
- She is the wind beneath my wings.
- He held my hand as the tears came to my eyes.
- She reassured me that it was okay.
- He listened intently to my distress.

Protection does not have to be displayed in large and lofty ways. We can show our protection for our partners in small acts and kind words every day. Try saying and doing some of these things for your partner:

- Don't worry about that; we'll sort that out.
- You take it easy for the day; you have had such a hard week.
- No, stay put; I'll bring the coffee in to you.
- I'll pick up those few groceries on the way home; don't worry about it.

Chapter 33
Influence

Influence refers to your desire and willingness to influence your partner *in a positive way*. When you are influencing your partner, they feel that you want them to do well. You share your ideas, suggestions and encouragement in a way that makes them feel that you can be relied upon as a guide, support and source of feedback.

When you are influencing your partner, you are being helpful in that you are confident about telling them what to do or how to solve a particular problem. You give advice in a way that does not seek to control them but lets them know *you are there for them*. It is the opposite of indifference, where you don't really care what they do or how they do it.

If influence becomes heavy-handed it becomes critical and controlling. If it is done with a gentle touch, your partner welcomes your input and guidance. You offer the good influence of a caring friend.

John Gottman has reported that there are huge differences between men and women when it comes to accepting influence. His research shows that women accept influence at a very high rate, while only about 35 per cent of men readily accept influence from their wives. This is also the case for small boys and girls. Preschool girls are likely to accept influence equally from little boys and little girls. If a child says 'Let's do *this*', a little girl is likely to go along. This is not the case with little boys: they are more likely to say *yes* when it is another boy but *no* when it is a girl. Some researchers suggest that the reason girls and boys stop playing with each other when they get to about seven years old is because girls eventually get fed up of playing with boys who do not want to be influenced! This is also what goes wrong in many adult relationships and why many women eventually want out of their marriages.

Accepting influence is not a high-level skill, according to Gottman. It goes something like this:

Wife: *Will you be able to paint the garden shed this weekend?*
Husband: *I don't think so because I have to prepare that presentation for the staff meeting on Monday.*
Wife: *Well, you promised you'd get it done because this is our last weekend before school starts and you won't have another chance ...*

If the husband is *rejecting influence*, he will say something like: 'Look, there is no way I can do it. I have to prepare for that meeting and it's my priority. It's no big deal to paint the shed, anyway.' He just returns the serve of her request.

If the husband is *accepting influence*, he will say something as simple and uncomplicated as: 'Ok, if I must. I guess I could get up early on Saturday and have it done by ten—that way I'll be able to prepare for my Monday meeting, too.'

Accepting influence is not a difficult thing to do but it does require an openness to being influenced by the other person. You must feel that such influence is no infringement of freedom. The problem is solved with the giving and accepting of influence.

Gottman talks about 'no fault discussion' as part of therapy for couples. These are conversations that couples have to have that are not geared towards finding fault or blame but only on finding *solutions*. Most couples in conflict spend a lot of time arguing about whose fault something is. What you have to do is forget about fault and let go of past resentments. To have a 'no fault discussion', you are not allowed to try to figure out the cause of the problem or the level of blame each should take for the problem. You are only allowed to focus on future solutions. Try it. I bet you will find that many of your arguments serve no other function than just trying to attribute blame.

The person who is married to a partner who does not accept influence ends up saying things like: 'No matter what I do I cannot get through to them. I feel they do not listen or care. I feel they shut me out. I feel my needs are not important enough to them. They just do not take me seriously.'

Respect is less of an emotional and more of a *principled* stance. With respect, your partner knows that you have real regard for their feelings, ideas and motives. When you show respect, you do so from a belief in your partner's entitlement to your cherishing them as a person. Respect is shown in the courtesies of everyday life: allowing your partner to be different; valuing their opinions even if they differ from your own; and relating to them as an equal person. You do not talk down, ridicule or vent your anger on them. You do not act superior in any way. Respect really comes from a deep sense that the other person is unique and deserving of particular care.

Thinking that you respect your partner is very different from *showing* it. 'Ah sure, they know I love them' is not good enough if you treat your partner with disrespect or belittle them.

THE ART OF ACCEPTING INFLUENCE

I have realised from my extensive work with abusive and violent men that they have real difficulty accepting influence from their wives. This has been confirmed by Gottman's research. Abusive men are typically averse to influence. They find it very difficult to say things like:

- I understand what you are trying to say.
- I appreciate what you are saying because I never thought of that before.
- I realise that I was wrong.
- I never thought of the problem the way you are describing it. That's very helpful.
- I realise now that you are right: maybe my drinking has become intolerable.

To be honest, most people struggle with accepting influence because of a form of paranoia that believes that any attempt to influence is an attempt to control or diminish them. Men in particular tend to be vigilant for these signs and overreact to influence because they misinterpret it as control.

But true, well-meaning and honest influence can be a really positive part of a healthy relationship.

Chapter 34
Responsiveness

We have seen the many ways how you can *actively* show and display responsible love. It is not reactive, prompted or forced but comes willingly from the person. The other vitally important way that you show love is in how you *respond* to your partner. It is a responsive or reactive love. How you react to your partner's expressions of love towards you is a vital element of love. Let me explain.

Responsive love is different from active love. It is how you react, receive and honour the love that is shown to you. Love is measured not only in how you actively show love to the other person but in how you receive that same person. Some people, for example, are good at showing love but awkward about receiving it. Others are weak at showing love but bask in receiving it. So it is important to evaluate whether you are better giving or receiving and whether you are more active or responsive.

You must be able to act *and* react. Responding is as important as acting but it is often neglected. Many men, for example, will measure their love by what they provide for their family; and they neglect their responsibilities to *react* positively to their family's needs. To show love does not mean that you are just good to your partner; it also means that you respond well to them. For this reason, many people in relationships say that they know that their partner loves them but that there is something missing. The piece that is missing is often how their partner responds to them. They appreciate the commitment and effort but they do not see joy and pleasure in being with them.

For example, a husband may be very active in how he shows love. He may be traditional in being responsible, protective, thoughtful and encouraging towards his wife. However, he may not *respond* to her so well. In response to *her* approaches, he may remain closed, grumpy and non-communicative. He might not self-disclose or be very open. When she criticises him, he may get defensive: 'What more do you want? I work hard, I don't drink and I do my best to provide for everyone.' His answer reveals what is missing: his receptiveness to her.

Similarly, a woman may be good at showing love but may be weaker in responding. She may be a very active wife and mother and show a lot of love through being very responsible, caring and thoughtful. However, her need for control may override her ability to submit or accept her husband's influence, particularly around domestic issues. She may mind him like he is one of the children—but he will notice that she does not respond to him with friendliness.

There are two gateways through which you show love. One is through your active approaches and displays of love, interest and respect. The other is through your responsiveness to your partner's approaches to you.

These are the *active* ways that you show love and regard:

- Giving freedom
- Giving encouragement
- Showing affection
- Taking responsibility
- Protecting and caring

These are the *responsive* ways of love:

- Being independent, not clingy
- Being honest, not closed
- Being positive, not defensive
- Being trusting, not doubtful
- Being flexible, not being stubborn

The ingredients of response love depend upon friendliness and co-operation. In reading about the responsive ways of love (below), consider how well you do this in your own relationship.

Being independent, not clingy

It is important in a healthy relationship that your partner senses that you are independent and are not needy, clingy or overly submissive. It is important that your partner sees that you can come and go. It is important that you are able to do your own thing separately from your partner. It is vital that you have a clear sense of who you are, outside of your partner. Displaying one's separate identity—in a friendly way—is an act of love that is often neglected.

Being honest, not closed

Disclosing and revealing what you feel is another way of responding positively to your partner. It is not enough to show love, be loyal or do the right things. You must also reveal your feelings. You respond to your partner by trying to be honest, sharing your self-doubt and revealing your inner life. You try to share the secret life of your thoughts, feelings, worries, anxieties and dreams. Being silent, withdrawn and secretive is not good enough—no matter how loyal and devoted you may be.

Being positive, not defensive

It is important to be positive to your partner's approaches and efforts. In this way, you are an open person who accepts what your partner gives to you with a generous heart. Even the clumsy and awkward displays of care or affection are appreciated by you. They are received by you and responded to in a genuinely positive way. Openness means having an open door through which the other person can enter without fear of rejection of criticism. It is the ultimate way you can receive love. You do not criticise efforts but appreciate the gestures. In these ways you are relaxed and playful; and you show signs of delight in being in your partner's company.

Being trusting, not doubtful

We can be responsive by showing trust. Trust assumes that you rely on, believe and accept whatever your partner offers. You show trust by accepting and respecting what they have to say; and by assuming that their intentions and motives are good. Trust is risky, of course, but it is deeply meaningful to know that someone trusts you deeply. It means that you can see behind their mistakes, errors and human foibles to the person within. When you respond to your beloved with trust, you show a form of love that is reactive more than active and is thus responsive love. You comfortably count on them. You accept their help and care-giving. When you trust your partner, you willingly accept their ideas and go along with reasonable suggestions. When you show trust, you are comfortable learning from your partner. You comfortably take their advice and guidance. You can depend on them. Comfortable trust is a lovely thing to witness between partners—or between parents and children. We can make clear our trust by saying simple things like: 'You know, that is a really good idea. I really like your suggestion.'

Being flexible, not stubborn

We can engage in responsiveness by accepting our partner's influence. This can be a tricky one at times, but it means that you are influenced by their suggestions, advice, requests or instructions. In a relationship where people do not accept influence from each other, there are constant arguments about who has the right to tell the other person what to do. However, when couples accept influence, little bits of advice or instructions are taken in good faith.

If you are open to influence, when your partner suggests that you buy some item in this week's shopping you can cheerfully say: 'No problem.' If you are *not* open to influence, you will query their right or motive in asking you. You might say: 'What's your problem? Is there something wrong with the way I shop now?' You know the scene!

Receiving love is a separate art from giving it. When you are open to influence, you care about what your partner wants or needs. You can be flexible because you value the *relationship* more than you value *being right*. You can be independent and have your own mind while being flexible.

Chapter 35
Faith

My late father was a beautiful man. He had a gentle heart and a great intellect. He was a lover of art, literature and science. He could quote all the great poets at will and could engage in heady discussions on advanced mathematics. He was also an artist and I witnessed him painting hundreds of watercolour paintings of the Irish landscape, a landscape with which he had a passionate relationship. He would often stop the car when driving to urge us as children to appreciate some unexpected glory in the sky or across the valleys and mountains. He loved light; and on summer evenings he would head off with his brushes and stretched watercolour paper under his arm to find some shaft of evening light that would delight his eye. He was a scientist and worked his life as a meteorologist; but he thought and wrote a lot about the interface between science and art.

He was also a man of great faith and, above all else, he would genuflect before his God. He would urge me as a young man 'not to lose the faith'. The faith was an old Irish reference to religion and God and was the one constant for so many Irish people through war and famine. It became for many families the standing stone that remained through great suffering. At one time in Irish life, it was common to say to people on parting: 'Don't lose the faith.' In truth, it was an encouragement to persist and not allow life's adversities defeat you. In fact it was an urge towards the heroic.

My father inherited this faith. I have not sustained the belief in orthodox religion that he had but I observed the profound meaning and effect that faith had in his life, and in the life of his marriage to my Mom. My dear mother shares the same convictions and now in her bereavement walks through life with a grace and character that inspires much of this book. Faith sustained and inspired both of my parents and I witnessed through them how faith can inspire love in a very concrete way.

I understand my father's faith as that quality in us as people that enables us to have a reference point for how to live that lies *outside* and beyond us. This faith is a faculty of human imagination and human heroism that allows us to imagine a source of life that calls us forward towards a better future. I am happy to call this 'faith' as a reference to an intuition that is grounded not in reason or argument but in imagination, sensation and connection to life. It might even be considered our source of hope—that intuitive conviction that things can and will get better. Faith is a belief in possibility and resolution.

The rationalist would argue that this 'faith' is all imagined and that it is therefore irrational and deluded. However, our imagination is in fact our greatest human faculty and, more than reason, has inspired humanity down the ages. It is our redeeming quality. The ability we have to draw on sources within our imagination is what has enabled us to evolve. Imagination comes before action.

Faith, in this broad sense, also seems to foster humility. When you are able to acknowledge your own limitation, and defer to an imagined (and thus real) source outside yourself, you are less likely to be self-justifying and righteous. Although some people can use this process to justify fundamentalist or dogmatic views of the world, it can be used to strive towards a life of virtue and loving-kindness. Faith can sustain the magical in life. It can foster gratitude. It can encourage someone to see beyond their partner's weaknesses and inadequacies to the greater narrative within which they are both set.

What does all this mean for couples? It means that, to the degree that they appreciate that their life is not just about meeting their *own* needs and relieving their *own* anxiety, their problems or distress can be eased. They can defer, in a real way, to a bigger truth that can explain their agitation. It is an awareness and appreciation of how they are also participating in a much larger narrative that includes them, their children, their parents, their siblings and their grandchildren. They can be inspired to put their own problems in a larger context and find imaginative and creative ways of dealing with them. Unlike a lot of what psychotherapy may do, faith can foster a lightness of heart. It can help people carry their burdens lightly and develop a sense of humour about their existential predicament. It is endearing to witness older couples. Often, these partners are able to tease each other about their annoying traits with a sense of humour and acceptance that is in contrast to the grave complaining and whinging of their younger counterparts!

Faith does not just prompt tolerance. It can be the reference point and the source of courage for people seeking to escape an abusive or toxic relationship. Again, for someone to get free of an abusive relationship takes courage and persistence and that person often needs to draw on a source and inspiration that lies outside of them. This source is not literal. It is, as I said, imagined. But, to the degree that it is imagined, it is psychologically real. It is so real as to enable: a victim of abuse to survive the abuse; a victim of war to stay alive; a victim of tragedy to cling to the very source of life.

I hope that you can somehow identify the times in your life when you have drawn the water of courage from a spring within yourself that is connected to a source outside yourself. You will surely realise that, even as an adult, your inner life follows the paths you followed as a child. Your inner imagination about who you are and what your purpose may be is a world of imagination and feelings. As you lie in bed as an adult, you think and dream in the same way you did as a little boy or girl. Your adult thoughts and worries tumble into the unchanged, rich, inner imagination and landscape that you knew as a child. You draw on this feeling. You go to this well and draw from a source that is not of your literal world. You draw from something so much bigger. You go to the well that is filled from the spring that is connected to a great underground river, knowing that the water in the river has fallen from the sky that arcs above all of life.

The gateway to this source may be opened in you when you go to certain places in the world. This could be the ocean, the mountains or some special place in the natural world that reminds you of your deepest identity and your connection with life. It may be a window that is opened when you meet certain people who bring out the best in you and put your problems in a broader context. It may be a secret doorway in your heart that swings open when you have time alone and can appreciate and reacquaint yourself with who you are. All these kinds of activities illustrate how important it is to remember who you are in the narrative of life. You must always remember that you are so much more than someone's spouse, parent, partner or colleague.

'Faith' was a word my father used in a religious sense but I understand it in the *imaginative* sense. How profound and character-building is this realisation that your life is fulfilling a purpose in which you participate but do not direct. Faith is being able to love this unknown potential in your partner and inviting them into a disposition of gratitude.

It has been illustrated throughout this book that love really is sustained by imagination. *Your life is how you imagine it to be. Your beloved is how you imagine them to be.* An irritating trait can be imagined as an intentional disregard for your feelings or as a humorous sign of your shared ordinariness. You can tease your partner affectionately about their bad habits or you can berate them righteously.

Think about the life partners of some friends of yours. I bet there are very few of them you would want to be married to. There may be some of them who make you wonder how your friend even copes with them! May I remind you that they might also think the same of you and your spouse? Now, you might begin to wonder how people can manage being in relationships at all...

Remember: love is a commitment inspired by imagination as much as objective reality. You can see in your beloved things and qualities that are not objectively observable because you superimpose, by way of your imagination, qualities that come from deep within you. By way of your imagination, you animate the other to life. It is the gift that you give *and* receive. You see in the other what is not visible to the world. It is this that makes them feel loved. It is this that makes you feel honoured by them.

Conclusion

This book was really a love story. It longed to be a poem in praise of love. I hope I showed that the path to love, and the courage to stay in love, involves waking to your vulnerability. To awaken to your vulnerability is to access your ever-present mortality and helplessness in the throes of intimate and domestic life; and in the face of the awesome mystery of existence.

When the veil between the essentials of life and our everyday obsessions is lifted, we are filled with the ache of life. The ache of life is this: we are in love with a life that must pass. The world, and our life, is the lover that must depart. Life, in this way, is inherently romantic.

We hope that if we can understand the nature of human attachment, and learn the things that good lovers do, then maybe we can copy love. If we do, then maybe we can control it and make it happen. We find ourselves suggesting that love is a skill that can be learned. This 'how-to' approach to relationships has much merit and is necessary in many ways—but it needs *heart*. It is without passion if the motive to learn how to love is in order to control it. The motive for love must be simple *desire*.

One can see that couples in turmoil, separation and divorce are driven by: the frustration of love; the grief at the loss of love; or the anger at unrequited love. But the drive still comes from the energy of love, even if that energy has become entangled. Much of the anger and negativity is caused by a love that is unable to recognise itself as such. The conflicts of marital and family life are often caused by *a love that has turned away from itself.* If one refuses to become cynical about relationships, one sees that love is at the centre of the creative enterprise of all life.

As most philosophers have remarked, self-awareness or consciousness is a mixed blessing. It awakens us to the mystery, miracle and wonder of life; but it also awakens us to our mortal fate. The basic contradiction that human love has to face is the conflict between life and death. In terror, delusion or false idealism, we want life but not death. We want joy without suffering; security without risk; love without vulnerability; life without helplessness. But to choose life and not death is actually to reject *life* itself and to reject *ourselves*. It is to live in a world of illusion that fosters a gradual neuroticism and retreat from life by using the strategies of self-control and other-control.

The unpalatable truth is that we cannot evade the broken and mortal symptoms of our partner: their imperfections; their impatience; their moodiness; their difference; their selfishness; their irritability; and their incompetence. And we cannot just want their life-affirming qualities: their beauty; their tenderness; their laughter; their love; their kindness; their compassion; their uniqueness; their reliability; their sexuality; and their affection. The brokenness in life enables us—actually *forces* us—to love with humility and passion.

If we are to love life, to love our partner as they really are and to love ourselves, we are then obliged to love the total reality. We must accept not only the idea of death but all those acts which anticipate and reveal it. I cannot repeat it often enough: when we reject the imperfections of our beloved we are, in reality, running from the presence of death and bereavement in all of life. We are avoiding the truth.

In intimacy, every sacrifice, every kindness, every effort and every gesture of love you make is an acknowledgment of the transience of life and the inherent loss involved in living. To deplete oneself for another is a kind of death. And yet, the ultimate existential, religious, human, courageous and mystical response to life … is love.

Love only thrives at the centre of the cruciform, at the tension point between: helplessness and control; vulnerability and security; inadequacy and competence; humility and arrogance. It is at this point that love sparks into being. It needs this inherent contradiction between the birthing and dying of life.

In this way, love is a transcendent function. It is the impulse that rises above the physical anxiety and mortality of death. Love is conceived in the conflict of these opposites. And yet, once it happens, it lifts the heart above the terrors and anxieties of life! In those moments, we are touched with the infinite and the sublime. Once the soul connects with the infinite, the concerns of the personal ego dissipate. The mysteries and the deeper meaning of life are not analysed—they are *experienced*. In the surrender to love, we have the experience of being alive; and in such experience, our hearts lift above the conflict of life. We can touch the eternal.

Listening to the rains beat against the window on a windswept night, with the warmth of your lover at your side, reveals for a moment the wonder of living. In times of trauma and distress, we forget ourselves while supporting those we love. In those moments, the divine appears. In those epiphanies, the beautiful and the mysterious are revealed. We rise above and beyond the anxiety of life.

Your love is not just a way of doing. It is an intuitive, sensitive way of being. It is what emerges when you fully inhabit your existence. It is an act of surrender based on the sensitivity to a freedom, an infinity and a mystery. This mystery is beyond the turmoil of life and death; beyond the inner war with oneself; beyond the anxieties of everyday life. It is at the still point of your psyche where, in prayer and meditation, in dance and exuberance, you can experience pure *being*.

The surrender of oneself despite the tension and terror of life is a gateway to freedom. We can surrender ourselves in action, prayer, meditation and art. In these arenas, one touches the deep presence of life. It does not matter whether we call it God, spirit, the universe or the fragile beauty of all creation. From the ground of our being, from the deepest presence of life, emerges the soft intuition and the brave action of love. It is here that prayer, poetry, meditation and gratitude are born. In the poetic moment, in the humility of prayer, we can affirm that all that moves through our hearts can be known by the name of love. Somewhere in each of our hearts is this intuitive knowledge of the truth of these things.

Deep in each of our hearts the music of love plays. In different hearts we hear the music of love being broken and betrayed; being healed and liberated.

I work with paedophiles and abusers; with anti-socials and addicts; with hateful, controlling people and masochists. In every sadistic mind can be heard the echoes of a broken and betrayed heart.

The batterer who was abused as a child has been taught to betray himself. When the tender footsteps of longing arise in his heart, he stands up to defeat them because somewhere in his history those were the footsteps of a father who, instead of soothing him to sleep, beat upon his door like a monster. This awful terror of love has taken a foothold in his heart.

We must never, not for a moment, surrender to such psychic terrorisms. We must face them with bravery and work to free the hostage that is love.

LIFE AGAINST DEATH

The ancient truths tell us that life itself includes that which is dark and deathly, but death does not prevail against life. Life embraces itself *and* that which is opposed to it. Death belongs to life, as darkness belongs to light. We could not think about life, or light, without their negatives. Life is only necessary because of death. In fact, the concept of life has little meaning without it.

Without death, there would be no sense of the wonder and beauty of life. There would be no sense of awe or meaning. In a poetic sense, you can say that death gives life its integrity and purpose. Death is made a scapegoat for all that is bad but, in truth, it makes possible all that is good. Death sacrifices itself for life. Like a strong parent, it forces life to grow up. Death gives God a purpose; without it, God is idle.

All of this would just be philosophical talk if we did not experience it on a daily basis through the flesh and blood of relationships and the ordeals of living. It is in the context of relationships that we discover these truths. Love includes hate (with a small 'h') but it *does not* win out against love. It is through cynicism, belittlement, dismissiveness, rejection, put-downs, silent treatments, deceit, secrecy, and a thousand invisible ways that we turn away from love. We turn away from love when we ignore, control, monitor, suspect, trivialise, objectify and degrade. It is in all the ways we diminish our partner and elevate ourselves. Yet love embraces itself *and* these things that are opposed to it. Hate belongs to love, as darkness belongs to light. We could not even think of love without reference to its negative.

The meaning of love derives from the existence of non-love. The possibility of abandonment drives love out into the clearing—it forces love to express itself with purpose. The possibility of abandonment and rejection drives you out of isolation into love. Without having known the cold wind of abandonment, your desire is lifeless. Your divine *yes* cannot happen without a courageous admission of the *no* that exists within you. The courage lies in your ability to inhabit the potential that exists within you to reject and punish the other. In knowing your darker potential, you make love honest. You release it from sentiment. You find the courage to love.